Measured Home Performance
A Guide to Best Practices for Home Energy Retrofits in California
Version 2.0

A Report To The
California Energy Commission
Public Interest Energy Research Program
(PIER)

December 2012

Contract Number: 500-08-051
Gas Technology Institute

SPONSORED BY THE CALIFORNIA ENERGY COMMISSION

- Melissa Jones, Executive Director
- Golam Kibrya, Project Manager
- Contract Number: 500-08-051

Measured Home Performance: A Guide to Best Practices for Home Energy Retrofits in California was developed in task 4.1 of the Radiant HVAC Systems for California Homes project (contract number 500-08-051. Task 4 is managed and conducted by Chitwood Energy Management under subcontract to the Gas Technology Institute (GTI). Information from this project contributes to PIER's Buildings End-Use Energy Efficiency Program.

PRIMARY AUTHOR

Rick Chitwood
Chitwood Energy Management
508 Sarah Bell St.
Mt. Shasta, CA 96067
530-926-3539
Rick@ChitwoodEnergy.com

CO-AUTHOR

Lew Harriman
Mason-Grant Consulting
57 South St.
Portsmouth, NH 03801
603-431-0635
LewHarriman@MasonGrant.com

GAS TECHNOLOGY INSTITUTE PROJECT MANAGEMENT

Neil Leslie, P.E.
Director, Residential and Commercial Technologies

Larry Brand
R&D Manager

DISCLAIMER

This report was prepared as the result of work sponsored by the California Energy Commission. It does not necessarily represent the views of the Energy Commission, its employees or the State of California. The Energy Commission, the State of California, its employees, contractors and subcontractors make no warrant, express or implied, and assume no legal liability for the information in this report; nor does any party represent that the uses of this information will not infringe upon privately owned rights.

PIER PROGRAM

The California Energy Commission Public Interest Energy Research (PIER) Program supports public interest energy research and development that will help improve the quality of life in California by bringing environmentally safe, affordable, and reliable energy services and products to the marketplace.

The PIER Program conducts public interest research, development, and demonstration (RD&D) projects to benefit California.

The PIER Program strives to conduct the most promising public interest energy research by partnering with RD&D entities, including individuals, businesses, utilities, and public or private research institutions.

PIER funding is focused on the following RD&D program areas:
- Buildings End-Use Energy Efficiency
- Energy Innovations Small Grants
- Energy-Related Environmental Research
- Energy Systems Integration
- Environmentally Preferred Advanced Generation
- Industrial/Agricultural/Water End-Use Energy Efficiency
- Renewable Energy Technologies
- Transportation

For more information about the PIER Program, please visit the Energy Commission's website at www.energy.ca.gov/research/ or contact the Energy Commission at 916-654-4878.

ABSTRACT

This report describes best practices which have provided homeowners with measured energy savings after retrofits of typical single family houses in California. The measures outlined in this report are aimed principally at significant energy reductions (40 to 60% of annual heating and cooling costs). But they also provide measured improvements in occupant comfort.

Best practices are not simple to execute. Large energy reductions and comfort improvements generally require redesign and reinstallation of the home's HVAC system along with extensive air sealing and insulation. Major appliances, water heaters, lighting, pool pumps and other baseline electrical loads are also components of an effective retrofit.

Home energy retrofits demand a clear understanding of building science with respect to heat and air movement, as well as the design principles and installation measurement & verification procedures of residential HVAC systems. But overriding all the necessary complexity, success has ultimately been achieved by following a few simple (but absolutely essential) principles. Chief among these principles are: integrated and simultaneous redesign and reinstallation of the home's principal energy features; in-process measurements of relevant installation quality by the installing technicians themselves; and adherence to guidelines for safe retrofit and operation of combustion appliances after air sealing of the building.

This report will be useful to interested and energy-aware homeowners, as well as to it's principal audience: the field technicians and project managers working for home performance contracting firms engaged in residential energy retrofits.

KEYWORDS

California Energy Commission, residential, energy reduction, energy savings, retrofit, consumer savings, best practices, home performance, performance contracting

CITATION

Please use the following citation for this report:

Chitwood, Rick and Harriman, Lew. 2012. **Measured Home Performance: A Guide to Best Practices for Home Energy Retrofits in California** Version 2.0 Prepared for the California Energy Commission.

ISBN 978-1-58222-994-2

COPYRIGHT

The copyright for this report is held by the Gas Technology Institute. Note that other individuals and organizations have in some cases allowed the use of their photographs, or information developed by themselves or their organizations which appears in tables or graphics contained in this report. Copyrights for these images and information are held by the providers of same, which are noted where such images, tables or graphics appear.

Version 1.0 © 2010 Gas Technology Institute, DesPlaines, IL

Version 1.1 © 2011 Gas Technology Institute, DesPlaines, IL

Version 1.2 © 2011 Gas Technology Institute, DesPlaines, IL

Version 2.0 © 2012 Gas Technology Institute, DesPlaines, IL

AUTHORS' NOTES

This report is based on years of field experience with successful Home Performance Contracting in California. The Best Practices—those which really deliver major reductions in annual energy consumption—have been achieved using everyday equipment and materials.

One big difference between what is described here and common practice is that long-standing good design and installation methods are really used, rather than assumed to be used.

Another big improvement over conventional practice is that all the energy features of the home are designed and installed to work as an integrated whole by a single organization, rather than in pieces by separate organizations with different and sometimes conflicting goals and motivations.

But in the final analysis, the really profound advances described by these Best Practices come from the *measurements* made in the field, during installation, by the technicians who are doing the work. Giving these workers the necessary high-tech tools, the training, the trust and responsibility along with positive motivation based on measured success is what really makes the difference between typical results and excellent results.

Installation technicians are the ultimate decision-makers in the success or failure of integrated design and installation. There are major benefits in terms of economics, energy, occupant comfort and technical workforce development that come from treating installation as the advanced technology that it really is. We dedicate this report to these workers, and to their capable and far-sighted employers.

Rick Chitwood & Lew Harriman
December 2012

ACKNOWLEDGEMENTS

The information in the report is based on a wide variety of advice, support material and time generously donated by our project partners, and also by the capable Performance Contractors of California. Not all of these capable professionals take the same approach to Performance Contracting as what we describe here. The market for such services is very dynamic, and there are many business models—all based on measurements of installed success—which have proven successful for saving energy and providing a sustainable economic model for the contractor. So it's safe to say that not every one of our contributors is likely to agree with every statement made in this Guide. Also, if there are errors or omissions in this report, our partners and contributors are in no way responsible. We are deeply grateful for their wise advice, and for their many contributions.

Principal Contributor
Steve Easley, S.C. Easley Associates, Danville

Steve is the author of Chapter 10 (Tips & Traps for Replacing Windows) and of the swimming pool section of Chapter 5. We are grateful for his deep knowledge of these subjects and for his down-to-earth and engaging writing style, which all add great value to this book.

Co-funding Partner & Technical Advisor
Jim Larsen, Cardinal Glass, Eden Prarie, MN

Cardinal Glass made possible the addition of Chapter 10 to this book, for which the Project Partners are very grateful. Without Chapter 10 this book would be less complete and useful to the ratepayers and Performance Contractors of California.

Special Thanks
Special thanks to Dave Jackson, Bryan Cope and Kim Hein of Redding Electric Utility, along with Mike MacFarland of EnergyDocs.net. EnergyDocs guided and monitored the Measured Home Performance retrofits described in Chapter 12. That work was performed under a program developed and managed by Redding Electric. Thanks to Redding Electric for creating that program and for sharing the pre- and post-project measured energy data.

Utility Partners
A. Y. Ahmed, Sempra, San Diego
Bruce Baccei, SMUD, Sacramento
Paul Delaney, SCE, Los Angeles
K.C. Spivey, PG&E, San Francisco

Performance Contractor Advisors and Contributors
Arthur Beeken, Hybrid Home Performance, Healdsburg
Andrew Durben, Home Performance Matters, Claremont
Mark Fischer, Green Home Solutions by Grupe, Stockton
Matt Golden, Recurve, San Francisco
Gavin Healy & Dan Perunko, BalancePoint, Nevada City
Bob Knight, Ph.D, California Building Performance Contractors Association, Oakland
Craig Lawson, Pinnacle Homes, Santa Rosa
Mike MacFarland, EnergyDocs, Redding
Bob Wiseman, Canoga Park Heating & Air Conditioning

Research Project Partners and Advisors
Doug Beaman, Douglas Beaman Associates, Modesto
Carl Bergstrom, Magus Consulting, San Diego
Steve Easley, S.C. Easley Associates, Danville
Donna Carter, J-U Carter, San Clemente
Pamela Rasada, California Research Bureau
Craig Savage, Building Media, Santa Barbara
Larry Weingarten, L. Weingarten, Santa Cruz
Mark Modera, Ph.D, Dick Bourne, Ph.D, Will Allen, D.Phil and Blake Ringeisen, Western Cooling Efficiency Center, Davis

Industry Partners and Technical Advisors
Clarke Berdan II, Ph.D. Owens Corning
Greg Maxfield, UTD
Rob Penrod, P.E. Beutler Corporation
Paul Shipp, Ph.D. USG Corporation
Teresa Weston, Ph.D. E. I. Dupont Corporation

1. Introduction 8
The Purpose Of This Guide 9
How This Guide Came To Be 9

2. Measured Home Performance .. 10
Measured Home Performance 11
   Self-funding projects 11
   Beyond the self-funding project 12
   Measured home performance contracting is different 12
   Why Measured HPC projects have such robust results 13
   How much an HPC project can be expected to save 14
   The sweet spot for HPC projects 15
   What Home Performance Contracting is NOT, and why 15
Homeowners' Frequently Asked Questions 17

3. Typical Projects & Time Lines ...26
Typical Project Components 27
   1. Pre-visit preparation 27
   2. Visit 1 - Test-In 28
   3. Develop proposal 28
   4. Presentation & adjustment - Visit 2 29
   5. Final proposal 29
   6. Acceptance & job plan 29
   7. Do the work 31
   7a. Remove equipment & remediate deficiencies 31
   7b. Attic and crawl space cleaning & sealing 31
   7c. Correct wiring deficiencies and replace lighting 33
   7d. Install new HVAC system & water heater 33
   7e. Replace appliances and install insulation 37

4. Pre-visit Preparation 38
Pre-visit Preparation 39
   Phone interview : Understand client needs, wants, motivations and expectations 39
   Quantify the opportunity - Utility bill disaggregation........... 40
   Gather & document the real estate facts 42
Tips & Traps for Pre-visit Preparation 43
   Don't forget the husband, or brother-in-law, or daughter. . 43
   Use the client's words (whenever possible) 43
   Understand the neighborhood potential 43
   Understand local incentives 43

5. Test-in Site Visit 44
Test-in Site Visit 45
Site inspection while driving up to the home 45
Occupant interview 46
   Basic principles for the occupant interview 46
   Info which is only available from the occupant 47
Whole house inspection tour 48
Natural Draft Combustion Appliance Tests 50
Whole-house air leakage test with the blower door .. 60
Duct Leakage Testing 63
HVAC System Assessment 64
HVAC comfort & energy consumption 64
   Installed AC capacity 65
   Installed heating capacity 65
   Total system air flow measured at the return grill 65
   Evaporator superheat[3] 67
   Systems with TXV's 68
   Systems with fixed refrigerant metering devices 68
   Condenser subcooling[5] 69
   Significance of AC equipment measurements 70
   Room-by room supply air flow measurements 70
Floor Plan Sketches & Data for Load Calculations 71
Lighting & Appliance Inventory 73
Swimming Pool Pumps, Sweeps & Lighting 74

6. Tips & Traps for Proposals 78
Part I - Client's Concerns, Needs & Wants 79
Part II - Measurements and Observations 80
Part III - Project Scope, Costs and Benefits 82
    Safety first, last and always 82
    Combustion appliance safety measures 82
    Replacement of knob-and-tube wiring in the attic 82
    Correction of wiring deficiencies 82
    Replacement or safe modification of can lights 83
    Beware of equipment replacement 83
    When the project must be "phased for budget reasons" .. 83
    Window replacement and renewable energy systems 84

7. Proposal Adjustment 86
Presenting & Adjusting Your Proposal 87
Connect Customer Concerns to Test-in Results 87
Relevant and Supportable Project Scope 88
    Supportable project scope 89
    Responsible Budget Responsiveness 89
    Big budget reductions without big consequences 89
    Smaller budget reductions 89
    Improving rather than replacing the HVAC system 90
    Budget reductions which ruin the project 91

8. Tips & Traps For HVAC 94
Tips and Traps for HVAC Design & Renovation 95
Better HVAC Design Goals and Assumptions 95
Calculate Loads After Assuming Correct Installation of Energy Features 95
    Total cooling load about 1 ton/1,000 ft2 96
    Total heating load under 20,000 Btu/h/1,000 ft2 96
    Duct leakage near zero 96
    Ducts with near-zero conductive losses 96
    Attic insulation that really performs 96
    Real-world walls and windows 96
    Air Distribution Design *Really* Based on Best Practices ... 97
    Duct runs can be mostly short and straight 97
    Supply ducts & grilles - The "Goldilocks principle" 98
    Fast-and-straight air delivery 98
    Locate grilles so they don't blow air onto occupants. 99
    Don't waste money running tiny ducts to small spaces ... 100
    Return ducts have to be "....juuust right" 100

Design That Supports Excellent Installation 101
    Room-by-room load calculations 101
    Constant year-round supply air flow rate 101
    Moderate supply air temperatures year-round 101
    Equipment Selection - Comfort without energy waste 101
    Combined hydronic air handler is an excellent choice 101
    Air-source heat pumps are another good choice 103
    500 cfm/ton... Use a larger evaporator coil 103
    Limit high-efficiency filters to special situations 103

9. Tips & Traps For Air Sealing 104
Sealing the Enclosure 105
Pre-sealing Preparation & Safety Issues 105
    Safely remove vermiculite insulation................................105
    Clear and clean the workspace...106
    Make sure exhaust ducts and vent stacks don't vent inside the attic 106
    Fix water leaks and moisture accumulation problems 106
    Test natural draft combustion appliances and fix them if necessary 106
Establishing the Ending Sealing Rate Target 107
Duplicating the Test-in Air Tightness 107
Locating & Fixing Typical Attic Air Leaks 108
    Kitchen and bathroom cabinet soffits.................................108
    Open stud bays 109
    Attic access hatches 109
    Duct chases and shafts...109
    Chimney penetrations...110
    Combustion exhaust stacks..111
    Plumbing & electrical penetrations 111
    Can lights 112
    Bathroom exhaust fans 113
    Ceiling gypsum board seams and wall top plates 113
Air Leaks From The Crawl Space 114
Progress Testing with the Blower Door 114
Finding Less-obvious Gaps, Cracks and Holes........... 114
    Thermal cameras 115

10. Tips & Traps For Windows 116
Tips & Traps for Replacing Windows 117
Here's the Deal With Windows....................................... 117
    Keep it real - Window replacement usually involves more than just the windows 118
Windows and Site Assessment....................................... 118
Window Retrofit Options... 119
    Full window replacement...119
    Inserting windows in existing frame..................................119
    Sash replacement 119
Energy Savings From Window Replacement............... 119
    Lowering AC loads keeps kilowatts in the cheap zone 119
    Incremental cost of excellent glazing is small 120
Energy Losses and Gains Through Windows.............. 120
    What's new about the new technologies 120
    High U-values bad, Low U-values good 120
    On balance, low solar heat gain is the best choice 121
Modern Window Technologies 122
    Low-E coatings 122
    Spectrally selective Low-E coatings..................................123
    Warm edge insulating glass spacer systems......................123
    Gas fills..123
    Triple and quad pane glazing..124
    Tinted glass 124
    Aftermarket applied films..124
Comfort and High Performance Windows 124
Window Condensation, a Real Pain in the Glass........ 125
The NFRC Label Is Your Friend..................................... 126
Energy Savings Comparisons... 127

11. Owner Education.................... 130
Suggestions which save energy 131
    ITurn off fans when people aren't in the room 131
    Save energy by turning stuff off when nobody cares 131
    Compact fluorescent bulbs save a great deal of energy.. 131
    Energy costs?... Tiered rates make every Watt matter 131
    Smart power strips can be great annual energy savers .. 132
    Replace HVAC filters every month 132
Items that don't save energy.. 132
    With an efficient system, setback is a bad idea 132
    Whole-house fans and attic fans don't reduce AC costs. 133
    Higher SEER and AFUE don't always save energy 133

12. Measured Results 136
Laws help, but results are better................................... 137
Redding Electric's MHP Program 137
    Measured results in Redding 138
    Persistent peak demand reductions 139
    Why it all must happen at once 140
    Importance of check numbers.. 141
    Importance of HVAC knowledge... 141
    Principal elements of HVAC redesign................................. 142
Summary... 143

Chapter 1

Introduction

Fig. 1.1 Golden opportunities
Handsome homes like this one look like models of modern construction technology. And they are. But that means they represent wonderful opportunities for saving 40 to 60% of the heating and cooling energy they currently consume. Home Performance Contracting can accomplish this reduction, provided the energy features of the home are redesigned and reinstalled as an integrated system, using the best practices outlined in this guide.

The Purpose Of This Guide

This guide will help both contractors and homeowners understand the key aspects of Measured Home Performance.

Measured Home Performance Contracting is different from other approaches to saving energy and making money in home improvements. The principal difference is the measured result of home performance contracting, as opposed to the hoped-for benefits of many other energy investments.

Intended Readership

This guide is not intended for the casual reader. Measured Home Performance is not simple to understand, it's not cheap, and it takes both time and great skill to execute. But as the famous football coach Vince Lombardi said to his team: "... we are going to relentlessly chase perfection, knowing full well we will not catch it, because nothing is perfect. But we are going to relentlessly chase it because by that pursuit we *will* catch excellence."

This material is been written principally for contractors and for contractor's crew members. But homeowners may also find chapters 2 and 3 useful. They provide an overview of MHPC, and they explains how typical projects are arranged and managed. Homeowners who are interested in home performance contracting are usually curious about the process. And they often have questions about why it's necessary to do so many things to the house at the same time. Chapters 2 and 3 explain why this is necessary. Both crew members and homeowners considering home performance projects will find that information useful.

What This Guide Does And Doesn't Do

For the contractor, the guide provides a brief, well-structured summary of best practices—the practices which have proven to provide both energy savings for homeowners and profits for contractors. For experienced contractors, this will not be a comprehensive guide. There are so many ways of approaching HPC, and so many types of buildings that a completely comprehensive guide would be impractical. Also, while the general principles outlined here are fundamental and not likely to change, the specifics of any one procedure will change over time with new technology and new business practices.

Therefore, this guide will summarize the principles and major components of HPC. Understanding these principles will give crews what they need to know to start delivering the benefits, while avoiding paths which seem to promise a simpler, less costly project—but which soon turn into blind alleys.

Finally, this guide is focused on retrofits. There are many best practices which make sense in new construction, but which are not practical after families are living their busy lives in the home. This guide speaks to what makes economic sense for retrofits.

How This Guide Came To Be

The information in this guide has been developed over 20 years by home performance contractors working in the State of California. These contractors have given freely of their commercial and technical experience. They have also donated training materials and photographs so that others may benefit from their hard-earned wisdom. We are especially grateful to these generous professionals.

The funding which allowed the collection and structuring of this material was provided principally by the California Energy Commission's Public Interest Energy Research program (PIER) under their research project no. 20892. The funding for the PIER program comes from you... the utility ratepayers of California.

Additional contributions of time, information and financial support were provided by the lead contractor for this research, the Gas Technology Institute (GTI) and the California Building Performance Contractor's Association (CBPCA).

Chapter 2

Measured Home Performance Contracting
What it is... what it's not... and why

Fig. 2.1 Measured Home Performance Contractors
Capable crews, equipped with the high-tech tools which show measured results during the project instead of afterwards. These people are the keys to successful improvements in comfort and energy consumption through home performance retrofits.

Measured Home Performance Contracting

Home Performance Contracting provides a homeowner with better comfort, better indoor air quality and a safer, more durable home which uses less energy. After an ideal home performance retrofit, the homeowner's monthly expenses are less—not more—than they were before the project, even after accounting for the added monthly cost of a loan which might be needed to fund it.

Self-funding projects

These are not small projects. To achieve monthly savings in heating and cooling costs large enough to make the project "self-funding," a home performance retrofit project will typically cost between $10,000 and $60,000.

It usually replaces the entire heating and cooling system, including new duct work. The new heating and cooling equipment will be less than half the size of the current equipment. The new air distribution system will be smaller, simpler and air-tight. The AC system refrigerant charge and the air flows will be measured and set.

The project will seal the complex construction assembly which separates the home from the attic, so that conditioned air cannot escape upwards into that attic. Then at the end of the project, the contractor will add insulation in the attic, burying the new sealed and insulated ducts so that heating or cooling capacity is no longer lost to the unconditioned attic.

Home performance projects also usually include replacing the home's water heater, pumps for well water or pool filtration and any lighting fixtures which penetrate a ceiling. Typical projects also upgrade the bathroom exhaust fans to near-silent units and provide a system which provides the home with filtered air for ventilation.

Those are the usual hardware components of a project. If this sounds like a big, complicated project—it is. But the most important difference between individual component replacements and a home performance retrofit is that all of the critical energy features are redesigned and reinstalled together, as an integrated system.

The resulting home energy system is not only carefully engineered, it's also measured in it's critical aspects as it is being installed—by the installers themselves. The installers' final "test-out" reports are an absolutely essential part of the project. These provide certainty that the building envelope and the HVAC components will work as a highly comfortable and energy-efficient system, in sharp contrast to the historically disappointing results of the traditional piecemeal approach to building houses. (See note 1)

Note 1- The value of an integrated approach
Imagine if cars were built and bought like most houses. Manufacturers would build each individual car outdoors, without weather protection, in the middle of a muddy field.

Each car would be slightly different in design and construction from all other cars. Cars would be designed under different laws, depending on where in the state or the country the muddy field was located. Each component would be bid and installed by separate subcontractors, with different work forces, working under their own supervisors and arriving on semi-dependable schedules. In the rush to complete the vehicle, sometimes the battery or steering wheel would not arrive on site in time, so the manufacturer would tell the owner to "just put it on the punch list" for eventual installation later, long after taking delivery.

Nobody would test the performance of any component except the car buyer, who would just check if "the upholstery looks nice and the seats feel good." Prospective car buyers would never drive the car before they bought it, and the manufacturer would never test the car before offering it for sale. The engine, transmission, braking, heating and AC systems for the car would each have been rated separately, by standards set by different regulators. Nor would the prospective owner ever ask about the car's mileage per gallon because no manufacturer would bother to measure how much fuel the car uses.

Given the way houses are built and bought, it's not surprising that we can improve them by an integrated approach to retrofit which relies on in-process feedback and measured performance validation for a superior result—similar to the way modern autos are really built.

The building as a whole—working as an integrated system—is what provides better comfort, combustion safety and high-quality indoor air at much less energy cost than what the home used before the project. Savings of 40 to 60% are typical, even after adding ventilation air the building never had before. Those savings are usually enough to make the project self-funding. In other words, after the project is complete, the homeowner's monthly expense is lower, even with the cost of a loan to finance the project. (See note 2)

Beyond the self-funding project

In addition to installing a self-funding solution for comfort and energy savings, the contractor can also provide a list of any moisture-related issues, electrical code issues or other problems which could affect the safety, durability or air quality in the home. The contractor might also provide options for replacing windows and doors, or adding solar panels or other renewable energy features if those items are on the homeowner's improvement agenda. Usually, the cost of such repairs or the cost of window replacement is not offset by enough energy savings to keep the entire project "self-funding."

On the other hand, the self-funding aspect of the basic project can make it very economical to do other home upgrades at the same time. And most home performance contractors are well-equipped to provide the same high-quality installation (backed by measured results) as the basic home performance retrofit. So it's a good time to consider adding those features, as long as one does not expect that there will still be enough energy savings to make the entire project cash flow-positive for the homeowner.

How measured home performance contracting is different

Homeowners and contractors who are not familiar with home performance contracting are sometimes confused by the expanding number of different approaches to home energy conservation. HPC is different in many respects, three of which are especially important to understand. With home performance contracting:

1. Installation quality is measured, not assumed. Measurements provide the feedback during installation which is so critical to finding and fixing the inevitable shortcomings. "Normal" shortcomings would double or triple energy consumption from equipment which (based on its laboratory testing) should perform so much better than it typically does in the real world.

2. The work is done as an integrated whole—as one project rather than in pieces over several years. None of the components by themselves will achieve significant energy savings while also providing comfort, safety and indoor air quality. In fact, field measurements have shown that when such projects are "done in pieces" or when expected results are based on manufacturer's energy efficiency ratings alone, energy consumption can actually increase. Also, there may be increased risk from combustion appliances and reductions in indoor air quality.

3. The selection of the project components, and the integration of those components, is based on measured success from thousands of homes—not on hopeful estimates based on limited laboratory testing and modeling.

NOTE 2: *Unless, of course, the homeowner decides to spend the energy savings achieved by the retrofit through major changes in energy use patterns. Expectations may change in a better house. After a home is greatly improved, occupants sometimes decide to invest the potential energy savings in more expensive temperatures than they ever expected before, when the house was drafty in winter, hot in the summer and poorly-insulated.*

Why Measured HPC projects have such robust results

The bad news is that, despite well-intentioned efforts of designers, builders and regulators over the last 10 years, home energy consumption is no better than in the past. In fact, the thermal performance of the building envelope and the energy consumption of the HVAC systems may even be getting worse in recent years. For example:

1. Measured values from over 10,000 "CheckMe" reports of residential HVAC installations show that 60% of the AC systems have either excessive or inadequate amounts of refrigerant. That problem, together with other measured shortcomings, wastes about 45% of installed cooling capacity in those thousands of homes (Proctor, 2005).

2. Measured values from 60 California homes taken by the Davis Energy Group in 2007 showed that 83% of systems failed to deliver the amount of supply air needed to meet the peak loads of the homes. Discomfort and energy waste come from such poorly designed and installed systems, because expensive conditioned air does not reach the occupied space. (Davis Energy, 2007)

3. Measured values taken in 2009 and 2010 from 80 homes completed in 2007 show that 80% of supply air grills deliver air far too slowly to mix the air in the space well enough to keep it comfortable. Thermal discomfort makes the homeowner tweak the thermostat, making the system run longer than would otherwise be necessary to heat and cool each space. Excess run-time costs money and wastes energy. (Wilcox and Chitwood, 2011)

4. Combining the results of field measurements from those three studies, it becomes apparent that only about 3.5% of that typical set of homes has the correct supply air flow, delivered at the correct velocity. Said another way, 96.5% of the homes tested have HVAC systems which don't work to even the most minimal standards of efficiency. A 96.5% failure rate is not something the HVAC industry can be proud of.

Fig. 2.2 Golden Opportunities
These photos show opportunities for energy savings in houses built under advanced energy codes between 2007 and 2009.

Dust tracks show unconditioned air infiltrating into the 1st floor from the crawl space, wasting energy and reducing indoor air quality.

Air flows up and out of the house through holes like this one, around the vent stack. These can be sealed up, and r-40 insulation added to save energy.

Without effective insulation, these ducts waste the HVAC equipment's capacity by heating and cooling the crawl space. Imagine the savings potential.

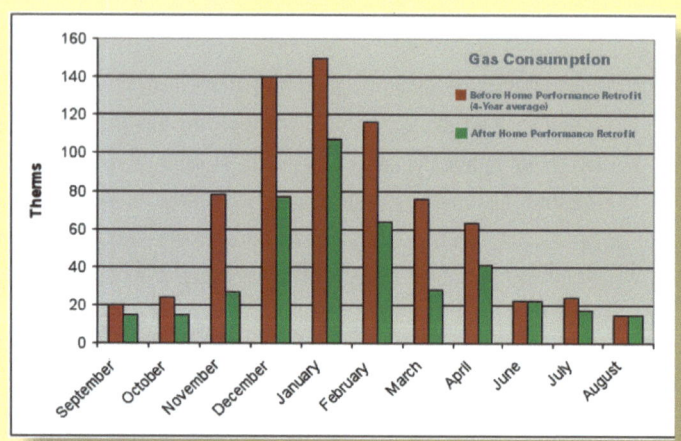
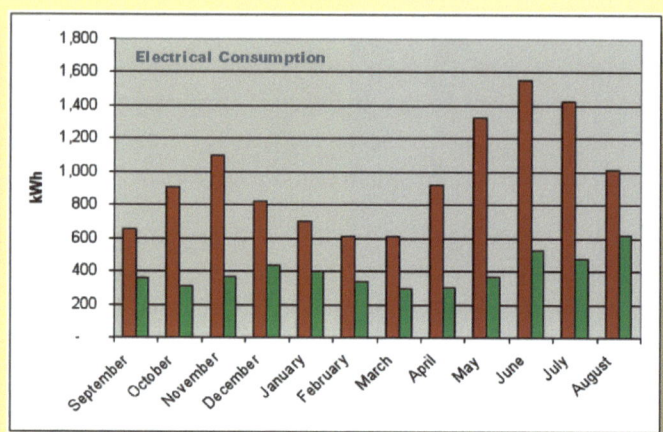

Fig. 2.3 HPC provides measurable results
The graphs show the results of a Home Performance Contracting project in a 2,832 ft² home in the Central Valley, near Sacramento.

HPC projects are different from other forms of energy reductions, because they rely on measured feedback to the crews, as they work.

The energy savings shown above are typical. And these savings were not just estimated—they were measured by the utility bills from the home.

5. The r-value of installed insulation is usually less than 50% of the material's lab-tested value because it is so poorly installed. It's usually compressed, or missing in big chunks, or lofted so it is not in contact with the buildings' air barrier. And often, there is so much extra structural lumber in the exterior wall that the insulation percentage of that wall is too low to be effective.

That's the bad news. The good news is that this situation allows homeowners and contractors an excellent opportunity for retrofits!

Home performance contracting increases the value of California homes and provides a reasonable profit for the contractor while saving monthly cash outlay for the homeowner. This is accomplished by removing, redesigning and reinstalling most of the energy-related components of the home.

How much an HPC project can be expected to save

When the house has air conditioning, typical savings after home performance contracting projects are between 40 and 60% of the pre-project HVAC energy consumption. But just like driving a high-mileage car, "your actual mileage will vary..." The dollar amount of savings will depend on how much energy the home used before the project. That's why the first step in evaluating a house for an HPC project is to obtain and review the monthly gas and electric bills for at least a full year, and preferably two.

The contractor's first task is calculating how much of the home's energy consumption has been for heating and cooling, compared to the electricity for the lights, pumps and appliances or other uses. This is called "utility bill disaggregation." The process helps the contractor and homeowner identify and rank the opportunities for saving energy. Nothing should happen until 12 months of heating and electrical bills have been collected so the contractor can complete these calculations.

The sweet spot for HPC projects

As of the writing of this guide (September 2010), in most parts of California there is relatively little opportunity for significant savings if the total annual heating and electrical utility bills are less than $0.80 per square foot per year. Those houses are already using so little energy that although more could probably be saved, it would cost so much to achieve the savings that the project may not be economically attractive for either the homeowner or the contractor, or both.

On the other hand, if the annual utility bills total over $1.50/ft2, there are usually excellent opportunities to reduce this consumption by as much as 50% or more through an HPC project.

Between those values of $0.80/ft2/yr and $1.50/ft2/yr, the potential for energy savings will depend on many factors. That's one of many reasons why the homeowner needs a well-qualified home performance contractor. Answering the question of how much energy a given house can save requires a thoughtful and comprehensive site survey including testing, an in-depth client interview, and then some engineering calculations. HPC may not be rocket science... but it definitely is science. When the owners' goal is energy savings, projects don't proceed without convincing numbers comparing current consumption to probable post-project energy consumption.

Some obvious cautions apply to any energy saving calculation. If the homeowner takes up electric arc welding as a home business after the retrofit, then the calculated electrical savings probably won't appear in the utility bills, even though the heating and cooling energy consumption may be less than half of what it was before the project. Likewise, if the home starts out with a furnace but no air conditioning, the homeowner is not going to save energy by installing a cooling system. And if the occupants change their thermostat set point preferences after the building is more comfortable, then the savings may not match the estimate.

But finally, HPC projects are rarely only about saving energy. History has shown that for most homeowners, the non-energy benefits of better comfort and less noise, coupled with increased home resale value, are usually just as important (and sometimes even more important) than annual energy savings.

What Home Performance Contracting is NOT, and why

Home performance contracting is about measured results, and about the comprehensive design and integrated installation of components and systems which work together to achieve those measured results. It's not about installing single features or single pieces of equipment in isolation.

So a warning is in order: if the homeowner's perceived needs only include insulation, or just window replacement, or just adding solar photovoltaic panels to the roof, or replacing the AC equipment with a "higher efficiency" model, a home performance contractor is probably not going to be the right company for the job. In those situations, the HP contractor may seem like an arrogant or ignorant sales-driven pain in the neck who's trying to get the homeowner to buy far more than what he or she wants.

There is a place for contractors who do one or two things and not others. That's the way of the world, and the way energy-related improvements have been handled traditionally; as single items, installed as money and mind-space allows. But for three important reasons— that's not Home Performance Contracting.

First, the history of energy-saving home improvements is littered with exciting hardware, good intentions and convincing marketing, but not so much in the way of measured savings. Home Performance Contracting is about measured results, not about exciting technology or general promises or estimates. Achieving significant reductions in measured energy consumption requires an integrated approach of reducing loads and increasing energy efficiency at the same time. Doing just one or the other won't save an exciting amount of energy compared to what it will cost.

Second, there is no way a Home Performance Contractor can compete on costs, when the homeowner does not appreciate the value of, and insist on, measured results. The traditional project delivery approach in home renovation is to ask for prices from several contractors who will both design and install the feature the homeowner has in mind. This has always seemed like a good idea, because it does indeed result in low prices. But problems arise when installation quality is assumed instead of measured. Home Performance Contractors simply don't work that way. They measure the installation quality and document it. The documentation cost is not the issue. The act of measuring the quality during the process is what makes the installation excellent, instead of ineffective. Competition may be a useful device to avoid overpaying for the service—provided that all potential bidders are required to measure the quality of the Home Performance retrofit as it proceeds, and also required to provide the homeowner with documentation of those measurements.

Third, the fact is that most of the energy-saving gizmos and "high-efficiency equipment" that have been sold to the public in recent years either don't work, or don't work as advertised, or they actually increase energy consumption instead of reducing it. But to be fair, many homeowners only need a simple solution to a single problem. For a leaking roof or a new refrigerator or a water heater which just burst and needs to be replaced in the next few hours, HP contracting is not the right choice.

The HPC approach sometimes seems less glamorous and uncomfortably complex compared to replacing your old AC equipment with a new unit with an impressive-sounding seasonal energy efficiency ratio. HPC is more complex, and for good reason. Saving significant amounts of energy demands modifications to many aspects of the building at the same time. So HPC projects are really the best way to go—whenever significant and measurable energy savings, improved comfort and assured safety are all important to the homeowner.

Fig. 2.4 In-process measurements provide essential feedback
*If there's a secret to the success of Home Performance Contracting, it's the **instant feedback to installation crews provided by in-process measurements of successful installation.***

The blower door, for example provides a continuous measurement of the air tightness of the building enclosure. So as crews work to find and seal the leaks, they know exactly how successful they are—or aren't. Measured results.... Can't beat'm.

Homeowners' Frequently Asked Questions

How can I figure out if Home Performance Contracting (HPC) might make sense for my house?

If your annual utility bills total less than about $0.80 per square foot of finished floor space per year, you're already using less energy than the typical home. To save more it will cost you quite a bit of money compared to the potential savings. On the other hand, if your annual bills total more than about $1.50 per square foot per year, there's definitely a potential for significant savings with an HPC retrofit. Between those values, "it depends," as they say. Your HPC contractor will help you figure out the economics.

But keep in mind that in addition to energy savings, HPC retrofits always improve comfort and reduce noise. These benefits may be just as important to you as energy savings, or perhaps more so.

How does HPC differ from other home energy programs?

The really critical differences are HPC's reliance on:

a. Measured results of the work, and

b. In-process instrument readings taken by the workers themselves, providing them the real-time feedback they need to achieve superior results.

Programs which measure results after the project is complete have not been as effective as HPC, because after completion it's too late to fix (at reasonable cost) the inevitable installation problems that happen when installation crews are "flying blind." 3rd-party testing before and after a retrofit project is not as effective as requiring the crews themselves to take responsibility for and to record and report the measured results.

HPC does not preclude 3rd-party testing. It can serve as a periodic audit of the effectiveness of a given contractor's crews and the integrity of their reported results. But by itself, 3rd-party testing has not been shown to ensure favorable results.

For example, since 2005 California's Title 24 energy regulations have required air conditioning contractors to measure and validate the refrigerant charge in all new construction AC systems, as they run under load, after the installation is complete. However, Title 24 has also allowed contractors to avoid this reporting requirement if they install AC systems which have thermostatic expansion valves (TX valves) instead of systems with other types of refrigerant distribution.

TX valves are certainly an improvement in technology. But the results of this exception, popular among many contractors, are nothing to be proud of. In a field study of 80 homes built under Title 24 between 2007 and 2009, less than 20% of the AC systems were measured as being properly charged. For that reason and others, losses in capacity (and therefore energy waste) from the 80 tested systems were between 30 and 60%. The average loss in capacity was 45%. All testing is good. But testing performed by the crews—as they work—is much better. That's the foundation of an HPC project.

Why does a home performance contractor have to inspect and test so many different aspects of the home?

Because the comfort, annual energy consumption, safety and indoor air quality of the home are all important. And each of those affects the others in complex ways that demand a clear understanding of:

a. What energy features are in the house,

b. Where they are located and

c. How they are interacting.

That clear understanding cannot be achieved by just looking at the bills, or by strolling around outside the home. Clear understanding demands measurements. It also requires peering into nooks and crannies that normal people don't have time to think about.

If safety, comfort and energy efficiency are not all addressed in a comprehensive way, bad things happen. Unexpected costs can arise after the fact. And occupant health can be compromised if the house is tightened without ensuring combustion safety and efficiency.

So as much as one would like to have a simpler fix for energy, safety and comfort, a house is just too complex for simple, quick solutions, when you need all three of those features.

Why do I have to replace my high-SEER cooling unit just because it's oversized? That unit's nearly new! Isn't it a good thing to have spare capacity?

You'd certainly think so. But unfortunately, oversized units create major problems for both comfort and energy cost.

SEER stands for "Seasonal Energy Efficiency Ratio." The rating number is based on tests under a carefully controlled set of conditions which do not reflect the realities of installation, nor the variability of daily operation. Equipment which has too much capacity is like a suit which is too big for it's owner. It doesn't fit right, so it's clumsy and does not perform well.

When cooling units are too big, they deliver intermittent blasts of large amounts of cold air. Then because they are so big, an oversized unit satisfies the thermostat quickly and turns off. As a result, for much of the day the occupants are either too warm or too cool. The larger the oversizing, the worse is the comfort. Also, the bigger the unit, the more energy it uses while creating that discomfort and the more noise it makes in the process.

To deliver energy efficiency and comfort in real homes (rather than in the carefully constrained SEER testing lab) the AC unit and all its system components must be sized and installed the way a fine tailor makes a suit—fitted perfectly to its purpose, and crafted with careful attention to the critical details which vary from house to house.

Figure 2.5 Oversized AC units and furnaces are like clothes that don't fit. They cost more and don't work properly.

Fig. 2.6 Duct design and installation affects energy consumption more than the SEER rating of the AC unit

Kinks like these reduce air flow. Low air flow reduces comfort, which makes the occupant turn down the thermostat, which means the home uses more energy than it should. The SEER rating of the unit does not reduce this waste, which is a result of poor system design and installation. That's why just replacing an old AC unit seldom achieves more than a fraction of the new unit's lab-tested efficiency.

Can't you just replace my old air conditioner with a modern high-efficiency unit? The difference in SEER ratings tells me a new unit should save about 30% of my cooling costs, for not nearly as much money as replacing the entire system.

The SEER is not as important as how the system is designed and installed. Temperature uniformity—the evenness of temperature throughout a space—is critical to comfort and therefore to energy consumption. If the temperature is comfortable in one part of the room but not in another, people in the second location will want to adjust the thermostat to deliver more cooling. That takes extra energy. The air distribution system is not changed when only the AC unit is replaced, and that's a problem.

The air distribution system must be included in most projects because of the critical importance of installation quality. For example, if duct connections leak air (as do most duct systems installed without measurements of leakage) then any increased efficiency of the new unit is wasted by that air leakage, and savings don't occur. Likewise, if parts of the duct system is "kinked" or makes hairpin turns, the system fan must work too hard as it forces air through the system and into the rooms. There's no reduction in fan energy use when a high efficiency unit is mated to a kinky duct system.

A third reason for disappointing results with unit replacement alone is duct design and return air flow. If the current duct system delivers air at too low a velocity, little mixing occurs as the air leaves the duct. The cold air just "falls out" of the diffuser and you end up with a pool of cold air at the floor and hot air at about eye level. So you turn down the thermostat to get more cooling. Also, if air is "dead-ended" because there is no return air path which allows air to get back to the system, the occupant of that room will not get an adequate amount of cooling air. That will make the occupant want to turn down the thermostat to improve comfort, using still more energy.

For all of these reasons, neither comfort nor energy savings happen automatically by simply replacing an old unit with a new unit which has a higher SEER rating. To achieve better comfort and energy savings at the same time, you need both a new, smaller AC unit, and a duct system which ensures nearly zero air or thermal leakage, and a return air system which allows air to flow smoothly through the rooms and back to the system.

Why can't air sealing, insulation and HVAC be done over a longer time, as money becomes available, instead of all at once?

Unfortunately, unless the air sealing, insulation and HVAC system are all installed at the same time, you're more likely to generate problems instead of improvements. For example, the foundation of energy savings is air tightness and effective insulation of both the building's enclosure and its HVAC system. But if you tighten the enclosure without making sure that combustion appliances can operate safely in a tight building, that's a health risk. And if insulation is added in the attic before it's sealed off from the floors below, mold can grow because humid air from indoors will rise up through cracks, gaps and holes and moisture will collect in that attic.

So to ensure favorable results and to avoid major problems, everything must be designed as a system and installed at the same time—not over months or years.

Why do I have to replace a perfectly good furnace with a 90+ efficiency rating just because it's larger than the load? Aren't you guys just running up the bill?

Oversized heating units generate the same discomfort and energy waste as do oversized cooling units. It's just that the symptoms of that failure are different. Instead of intermittent blasts of cold air, the furnace produces blasts of hot air.

When the furnace is too big, it runs for very short periods, satisfying the thermostat quickly. But unless everything else about the house and the duct system is well-fitted and air-tight, the house is too cold (or much too hot) in the spaces where the thermostat is not located. With short run-times, the system can't mix the air evenly throughout the home, to provide comfort in all spaces. So occupants without enough heating are complaining. They turn up the thermostat so the home

Fig. 2.7 Unexpected hazards in existing systems
This furnace vent stack terminates in the attic, just above the children's room. Products of combustion, among them deadly carbon monoxide gas, can drift down into the home.

This is an extreme example. But unexpected hazards are one reason that the entire project must be done at one time as a carefully considered whole, rather than just connecting new equipment to existing systems.

uses more energy than it should. The oversized unit and the poor duct system combine to produce an inefficient system, even though the lab-tested efficiency rating on the furnace was impressive.

So once again, like the man who gets sold a suit which is "the next size up," a home with an oversized heating system is less comfortable, not more so. And oversized equipment costs more to run, no matter how high its lab-tested combustion efficiency might be. All in all, comfort and heating costs are not controlled by combustion efficiency. The cost of comfort is controlled by how efficiently the total system can maintain temperature in the occupied spaces. And furnace efficiency is only a small part of that process.

Instead of all that redesign and reinstallation of the whole system, can't I just replace my crummy old furnace and AC unit with a ground-source heat pump and save energy?

It would be so pleasant if that were true. But it's not. Ground source heat pumps are a wonderful technology—provided that they can be correctly sized for both the heating and cooling loads, and provided that they are coupled to an equally efficient heating and cooling distribution system.

However, the problems begin with the idea of only replacing the existing equipment. Simple replacement of the units alone does not result in energy savings, for all the reasons discussed in answers to earlier questions in this FAQ list. One must also replace the distribution system and reduce heating & cooling loads to achieve savings.

Then there are issues of both operating and installed costs. Ground source heat pumps are not automatically more efficient, but they are definitely more expensive. As an example, consider two identical homes located in Redding. As measured over a year by researchers working for the US Department of Energy, the home with the ground source heat pump used more than twice the energy used by the other home, which had a conventional "hot water furnace" with air conditioning. (A hot water furnace is an air handler which has a conventional cooling coil, plus a hot water coil connected to the domestic hot water heater.) Also, the installed conventional equipment cost less than 50% of the installed cost of the system with the ground source heat pump (U.S. DOE, 2006).

This is not to say that ground source heat pumps cannot be made to work well. It's just that at present, they cost quite a bit to install. It's true that their electrical compressors pump heating and cooling from the ground. But that capability does not automatically—by itself—produce energy cost savings.

Can I get government or utility funding for an HPC project?

That's quite possible. Your performance contractor will be able to tell you which programs might apply to your situation.

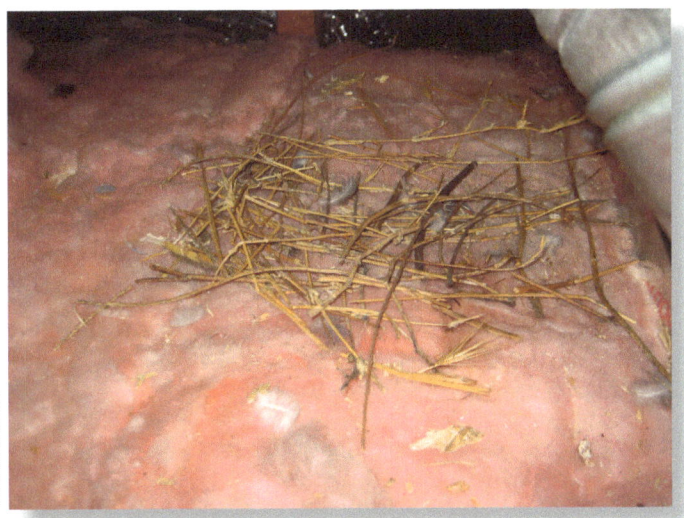

Fig. 2.8 How building tightness can improve indor air quality
By air sealing the home, pests are kept out, and air is no longer pulled into the breathing zone through the attic or crawl space.

My kids have athsma. Will HPC improve indoor air quality?

Definitely. When outdoor air is filtered through the HVAC system rather than dragged through the walls or crawl space, the quality of the ventilation air is much improved. It will have fewer particles, and it will carry fewer of the allergens which can trigger asthma attacks.

To be clear on this point, however, an HPC retrofit is not a cure for asthma, nor is it a guarantee that your loved ones won't develop asthma. But an HPC retrofit will improve indoor air quality.

My wife is sensitive to mold. Will HPC fix my mold problems?

If mold is a concern, HPC contractors are usually well-qualified to eliminate the cause of mold growth, which is always some form of excess moisture accumulation. The contractor may or may not be qualified to remove mold. Sometimes that requires a subcontractor. But HPC contractors will certainly be capable of making the repairs necessary to avoid a repeat problem.

Typical repairs include adding rain gutters, replacing windows with properly-flashed units, re-grading the earth which surrounds the house so water does not collect at the foundation or in the crawl space. If you want to know more about reducing mold risk and what it takes to accomplish that goal, consult the California Builder's Guide to Reducing Mold Risk, which is available in PDF format at no cost at http://masongrant.com/pdf_2008/California_Builders_Guide.pdf

Why can't I just seal the attic & duct work and add insulation to save energy? Why do I have to replace the entire HVAC system and the can lights that penetrate the attic? Aren't you inflating the project?

Sealing the building and duct work and adding insulation would certainly save some energy. The key things to keep in mind are the safety and comfort issues.

Safety first. It's OK to add insulation to the attic—but only after the assembly that separates the attic from the living space has been air sealed, and after the lighting which penetrates that attic has been made safe. You don't want moisture accumulating in the attic, and you don't want the lighting fixtures to overheat and start a fire in that attic. And it's OK to seal up the building, but after doing that, it's critical to also check the safe operation of combustion appliances and make any necessary changes to ensure safety. You don't want the water heater to "backdraft" (flames coming out of the unit and/or toxic carbon monoxide gas flooding backwards into the house). Provided you can also accommodate those safety measures in the budget, the performance contractor can certainly just air seal the attic and duct work and add insulation.

Next, comfort. After the loads are reduced by insulation and air sealing, then the existing AC and heating equipment is going to be really oversized. Some rooms will be way too hot and others way too cool. Resetting the air flows to the correct values probably won't be possible because the system and its duct work is still problematic and is simply much too big. The home probably won't be comfortable. (It's difficult to get bulldozer to drive like a sports car.)

Fig. 2.9 Modern air-tight, IC-rated can light
Old can lights must be replaced with air-tight units like this one, to avoid the waste of upward air leakage and to avoid creating a fire hazard after the fixture is buried under insulation.

For these reasons, air sealing and insulation are usually not proposed alone. By replacing the HVAC system with one which fits the new, reduced loads, comfort is assured and the total energy savings are more substantial—usually enough to actually lower your net monthly costs, even after paying the loan to fund the larger project.

Why do I have to mess with electrical system rework and lighting replacement before I put insulation in the attic?

It's a matter of safety, code compliance and resale value. Here's the safety issue. If either substandard wiring or old can lights are covered with insulation, they can overheat and start a fire. The additional insulation keeps the heat generated by the lights or poor wiring from being released into the attic air. On hot days, that heat under the insulation may be enough to ignite nearby combustible materials. Then there's the matter of code compliance. It's not OK to connect new equipment or new lighting fixtures to wiring which is defective or substandard. Ultimately, that's also a safety issue, in addition to a problem which will prevent resale of the house until corrected.

What if I don't want to fund a full home performance retrofit right away? Can't I do a project in stages?

Certainly. There's a lot that can be done with a small investment of money and mental energy before getting to the larger expenses. Here's a logical sequence for a "staged" program of energy reduction, beginning with small expenditures and building towards larger projects and bigger benefits, as your funds allow.

Stage 1- Light bulb replacement, smart power strips and education

About 60% of the energy used in most homes is "baseline" energy that has little to do with the HVAC system.

- Begin with replacing all your incandescent light bulbs with compact fluorescent bulbs. That small but significant change will make a noticeable dent in your monthly electrical bills. Compact fluorescent bulbs cost less than $2.00 each when bought in packages of five.

- Then add "smart power strips" to all your TV's and other entertainment appliances like game consoles, stereo gear, powered speakers, computers, computer screens and printers. A smart strip costs less than $50. One of it's outlets controls the others. For example, when you turn off the computer, the smart strip will turn off any other accessories plugged into the same power strip. The electrical loads from "sleeping" tv's, game consoles and computers are surprisingly high, and they are constant.

- Next, make sure that any ceiling fans or portable fans are turned off if nobody's actually in the rooms they serve. Fans circulate air to make people comfortable. But the electrical power drawn by the fan is released into the space as heat. If people are in the room, the breeze from the fan promotes comfort, so it's worth adding the heat load of the motor to the room. But if nobody's in the room to enjoy the breeze, the fan's just wasting energy and adding heat without providing any comfort benefit.

- The dishwasher may also be using more energy than necessary. The "heated drying" cycle is meant to dry dishes quickly, in cases of heavy use and multiple loads. But if the dishes are just going to sit in the dishwasher overnight anyway, use the "economizer" setting to turn off the supplemental heaters. This saves energy by letting the dishes dry at a slightly slower rate, without electrical power.

Finally, keep in mind the obvious but often-forgotten reminder to everybody in the home: turn off the lights whenever you don't need them to be on.

Stage 2 - Lighting fixture and appliance replacement

For the next stage, replace any can lights that penetrate the ceilings with air-tight fixtures rated for full insulation contact. New fixtures will allow the use of even more efficient pin-base compact fluorescent bulbs, and they are a necessary first step for any later insulation.

Also in stage 2, consider replacing appliances. Specifically, replace any older gas water heater with a high-efficiency, sealed combustion unit. This will save gas costs in the short run, and will simplify and reduce the cost of safety measures which will be necessary when the home is sealed up during a stage 3 project. Also note that the older, conventional natural draft hot water heaters don't usually last more than 7 to 10 years in any case. So chances are good that by replacing the unit now, you'll avoid the disruption of a broken water heater that has to be replaced on an emergency basis later. (See note 3)

The clothes washer and drier are also excellent candidates for replacement if they are not already modern models. Front-loading washers spin clothes at very high speeds to remove much more rinse water before the clothes go into the dryer. Removing water by spinning is far more energy-efficient than heating that same water to evaporate it in the drier. So you'll save major amounts of dryer energy when you wash the clothes with a front-loading washer.

Note 3: Keep in mind that when replacing the water heater, it's best to locate it close to the HVAC air handler for later synergies when the HVAC system is retrofitted. Also, it's important to fully insulate the hot water distribution piping. This reduces the waste of both energy and water. Insulated piping avoids the need, when showering, to run the warm water for several minutes to get rid of water which cools down in uninsulated piping.

Replacing the dryer itself is also a good idea, if it does not already have a clothing moisture sensor which terminates the drying based on moisture content rather than by an arbitrary (and usually excessive) time clock setting.

The hot water heater and washer-drier use energy in big amounts over short periods. But the long-term, low-draw appliances often use just as much energy over the long term. In particular, getting rid of any old freezers or second refrigerators is an excellent way to reduce energy at little or no cost.

Then consider replacing television sets which have either cathode ray tubes or plasma displays instead of LCD or LED flat panels. LCD displays typically use less than 30% of the energy of a plasma display or an old cathode-ray tube TV or computer screen. Also, if the refrigerator is more than 20 years old, chances are good that a new unit will use less than half of the power consumed by that older unit.

These appliance replacements (and getting rid of any plugged-in appliances not actually in use) is an excellent way to make modest reductions in energy consumption with relatively little expense. The next stage will take more time and money, but it will produce larger energy savings and also improve comfort.

Stage 3 - HVAC replacement, insulation and air sealing

The stage 3 project is where the comfort benefits begin (and where the biggest reduction in energy consumption is accomplished when the project is located in the warmer parts of the State). But keep in mind that, for all the reasons described earlier in this series of questions, all three of these must be done at the same time to achieve the benefits without creating problems. So the stage 3 project will be more expensive and take more time than appliance replacement. This Best Practices Guide is focused primarily on stage 3-type projects.

Stage 4 - Window replacement or renewable energy generation

The most expensive projects involve either window replacement or renewable energy systems like solar hot water heaters, or photovoltaic panels or wind turbines.

These projects will save energy, and window replacement with modern triple-glazed, low-e coated, insulated-frame units will certainly improve comfort. But at current energy costs and installation costs, these projects are not likely to save enough energy to provide an attractive return on investment. So if your budget is limited, you probably want to delay these projects until your finances allow for a low return on the relatively high installation costs of improvements.

Can an HPC contractor also install a solar hot water or solar PV or wind energy?

Certainly. A Home Performance Contracting project is an excellent time to add those features to the home. After the heating and cooling loads have been reduced, you won't need as large a solar heater or PV array. So you'll save money on that side of the project. Many performance contractors are also fully qualified to design and install those features. Like window replacement, the added costs of renewable energy generation are seldom paid back by energy cost savings in a short period. But as long as that's not a problem for your budget, by all means install renewable energy features at the same time.

Finally, if even solar's not in your current budget you might want to consider installing a pre-wiring package for future PV, or installing the pre-plumbing package that will make it easy to add solar hot water in the future. It's relatively cheap to get the solar prep accomplished now (when you already have that highly-qualified, highly-skilled crew on site) to make it much more economical to install panels later, when the time comes for a full solar energy installation.

Fig. 2.10 Measurements, measurements, measurements
Your Performance Contractor will be using many instruments to make certain the HVAC system is not only designed and installed correctly, but also tested and balanced so it performs the way it was designed. You won't be aware of the system. It will simply work. But you'll see the benefit of these careful in-process measurements in your monthly energy savings.

Chapter 3

Typical Project Components and Time Lines

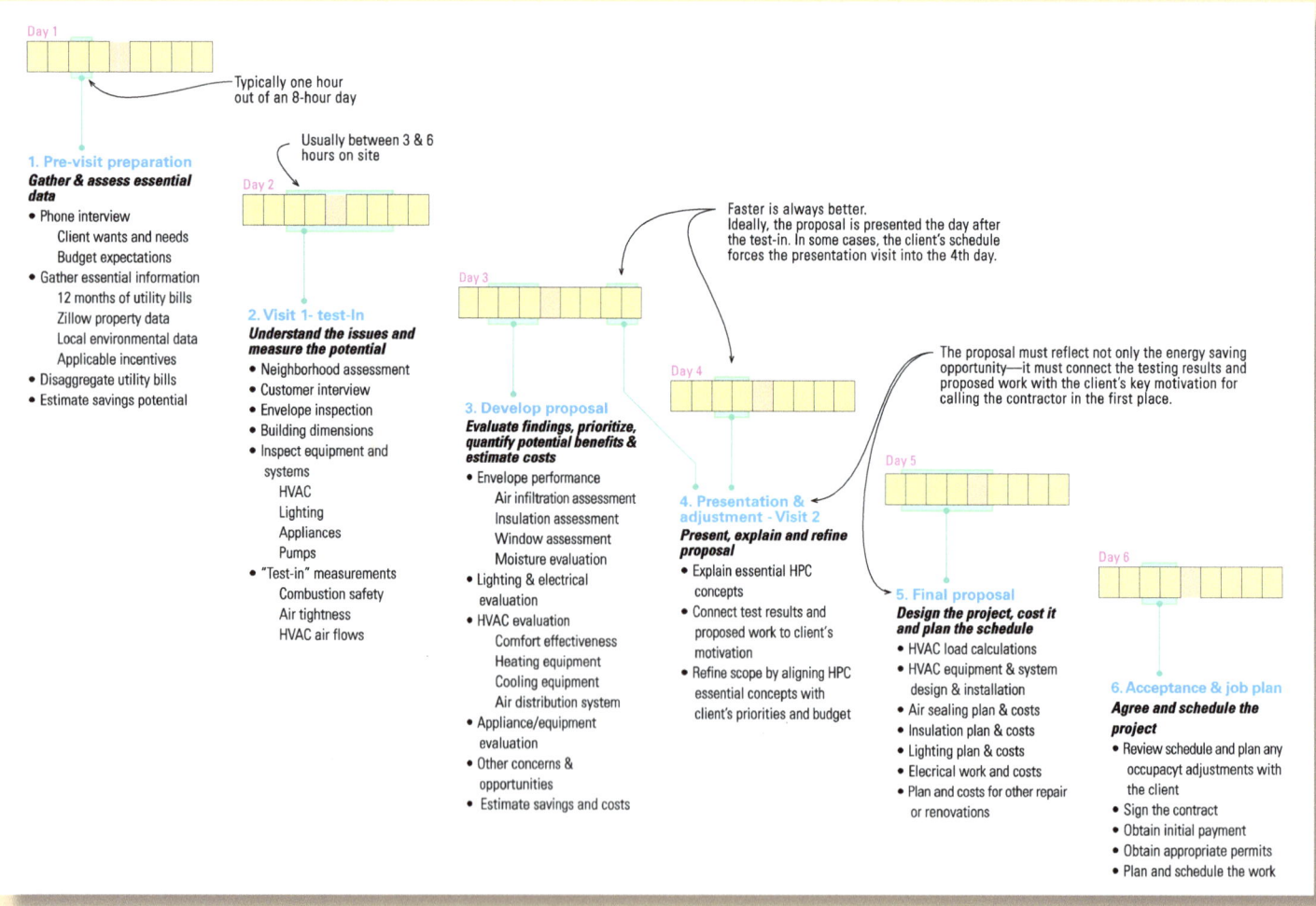

Fig. 3.1 Typical project development time line and tasks

Typical Project Components

The diagrams in figures 3.1 and 3.6 show the core components of an HPC project, along with a typical sequence and duration. The components described in this chapter and in the diagrams are typical. But every combination of home and homeowner is going to be a bit different. Some projects will have more than these components, and some will have fewer.

1. Pre-visit preparation

Before the homeowner can consider investing in a home performance contracting project, there's data to gather and assess. To start, the contractor will interview the homeowner over the phone to understand the client's basic motivations for enquiring about a home performance project. This interview will also collect information about the client's budget expectations and level of understanding about what HPC projects can achieve and what they cannot.

Fig. 3.2 Pre-visit preparation

Assuming that an HPC project has the potential to meet the homeowner's needs as understood by the contractor, the next step is to collect at least one complete year of monthly utility costs—both the heating and electric bills.

From those monthly bills, the contractor will be able to calculate the approximate amount of money spent during each season of the year on heating, cooling, hot water, lights and pumps. That information will give both the homeowner and contractor a preliminary indication of the savings potential from an HPC project, and exactly where the savings and comfort improvement opportunities can be found.

For example, if heating costs are higher than typical for the area, the contractor will look closely at how the hot air is distributed, and how much of it is really getting to each of the rooms in the house. Further, high heating costs often go hand-in-hand with uncomfortable temperatures during the cold months, because raising the thermostat setting is a logical response to cold air drafts entering the home through a leaky building enclosure. With high heating costs, the contractor will put inspecting for air leakage and air distribution effectiveness on his agenda for the site visit.

Assuming the project looks promising based on the building's annual energy consumption, the contractor will obtain the basic details which describe the home such as square footage, type of heating and cooling, whether there is a pool, spa, well, ancillary structure or crawl space, what other forms of energy conservation may have recently been installed, etc.

The contractor will also research any potential sources of support funding which may apply to buildings in the area. These include Federal and State subsidies for qualifying projects, and local government and utility provider incentives for energy conservation projects.

The next step is to visit the site.

Fig. 3.3 Visit 1 - Test-in

Fig. 3.4 Develop proposal

2. Visit 1 - Test-In

The first visit to the site will take three to six hours. This is not a casual visit. The contractor will interview the homeowner in considerable depth, and tour the home to gain a detailed understanding of all of the client's concerns and motivations for the project.

After a room-by room tour of the building with the homeowner, the contractor will inspect the crawl space and the attic, record nameplate data from the installed HVAC equipment & water heater and also inspect the lighting, wiring, electrical appliances, pumps and the main electrical service panel.

Then the crew will test and measure key aspects of the building's performance. This will include a blower door test of the air tightness of the enclosure and a combustion analyzer to measure the efficiency and safety of combustion appliances. Depending on the potential project, the contractor may also test other aspects of the home's performance, or take measurements and photographs to allow development of cost estimates for HVAC system rework or redesign, water heater replacement, remediation of electrical problems, etc.

Upon leaving the site after three to six hours of interviewing, inspecting and testing, the contractor will have the information needed to prepare a proposal which will save energy and meet the other needs of the homeowner.

3. Develop proposal

The contractor will return to the office and prepare a preliminary proposal. Ideally, this proposal will be completed quickly, so the contractor can return the following day to discuss costs and benefits in a second on-site visit with the homeowner. Speed is very useful and important. Otherwise some key details of the owner's needs (and their relationship to the test data) may be forgotten under the press of everyday concerns of family and professional life which govern the owners' available attention span for the project.

The preliminary proposal will typically include a work scope, and an estimate of potential savings and overall costs. To develop this proposal, the contractor will need to make some calculations and projections based on past experience in houses with similar characteristics. At this point the proposal will be general. Usually, the scope of the project will need to be adjusted in a meeting with the owner before it's wise to do a complete and complex project design.

Fig. 3.5 Visit 2 - Present & adjust proposal, explaining how the proposal meets the earlier-stated needs and wants of the client

4. Presentation & adjustment - Visit 2

At the second meeting, the contractor explains the proposal, roughly what it will cost, what it will save, what comfort benefits are expected and about how long it will take to complete. The contractor will also explain how and why the test and inspection results have suggested the scope recommended in the proposal. Along with the energy-related discussion, the contractor will explain how the client's non-energy needs and concerns are addressed by the proposal.

If a contractor cannot make clear why a given item in the proposal is necessary for either energy savings, or to correct deficiencies or to meet the needs expressed by the homeowner, it's an indication that the proposal will need adjustment. Also, as the details of the proposal are discussed at this meeting, the homeowner's priorities often become clearer, which prompts further adjustments to the proposal. And of course, new items may occur to either the homeowner or the contractor during the meeting, or between the 1st and 2nd meetings.

The usual result (and a very important result) is that the owner will make many decisions during this second meeting. But with Performance Contracting, these decisions will be based on a clear understanding of the test measurements, how these relate to the owner's needs and the costs of achieving the expected benefits.

The end goal of the 2nd meeting is to agree on a work scope and a rough budget for the project as a whole. The contractor's assumption is that, if the final proposal meets the revised scope and budget, the homeowner will be prepared to commit to firm a agreement and formal contract at an agreed cost.

5. Final proposal

After a general agreement obtained during the second site visit, the contractor prepares a final proposal with a firm cost, estimated annual savings, the specifics of what equipment and services will be provided and how long it will take to complete the project.

To prepare this final proposal, calculations will be needed, along with a preliminary project design which defines the costs for labor, equipment and materials.

6. Acceptance & job plan

Upon presentation of the final proposal, the homeowner accepts or adjusts the scope and costs, and signs the contract. At that point, the project is scheduled, the final design is completed and the material is ordered.

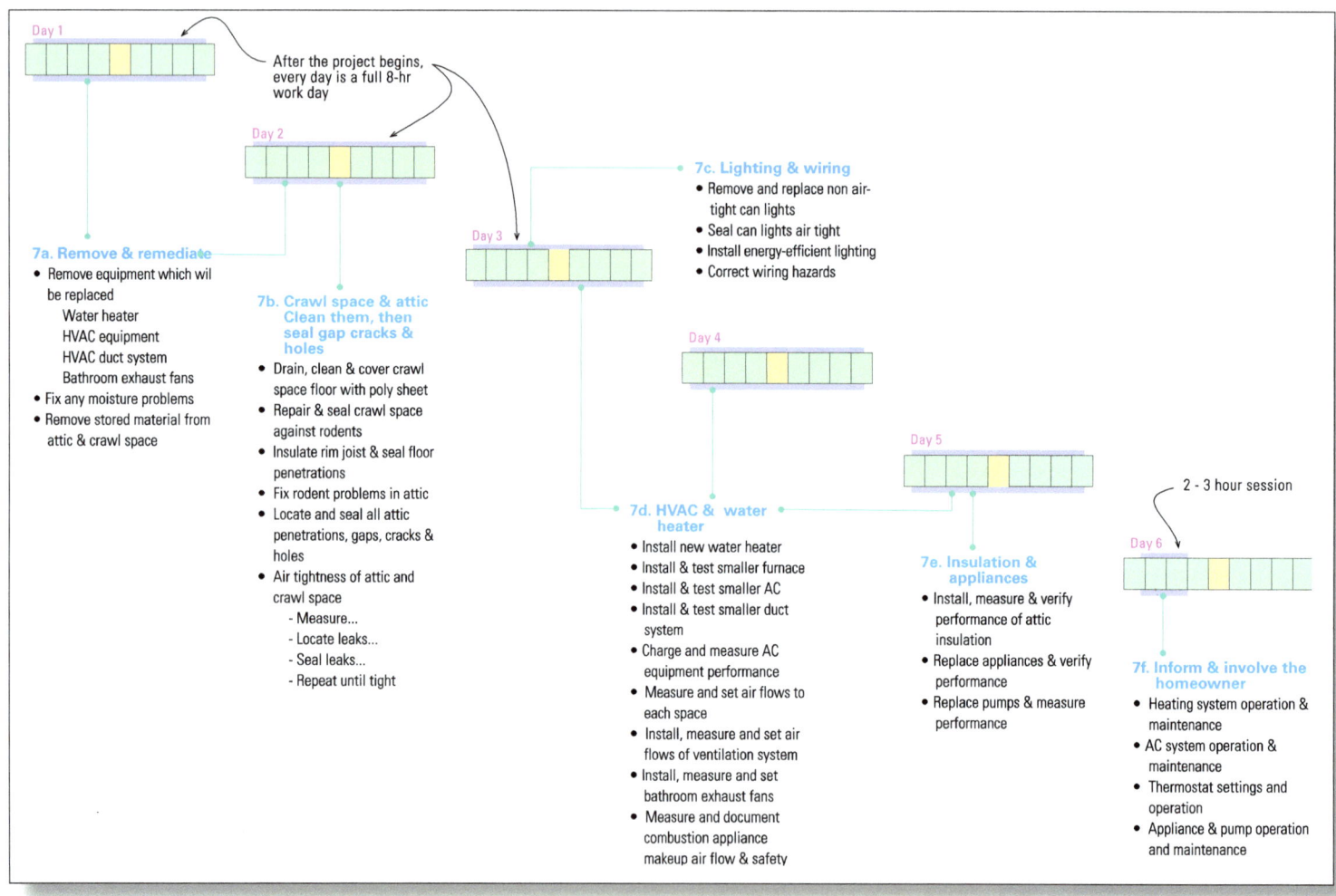

Fig. 3.6 Doing the work - Typical work sequence

7. Do the work

Once the project begins, everything must be designed and installed correctly, as a system. And during installation, key results must be measured to make certain that energy-saving goals will be achieved.

To achieve 40 to 60% energy savings, super-human technicians with impressive certifications are not necessary. All that's required are good crews, working with effective in-process inspection tools like blower doors, thermal cameras, duct blasters and fog generators.

These tools provide motivated workers with the visual clues which help locate shortcomings, and the measured values which document success or the lack of it. Using those tools, the good-but-not-super-human crew will identify, locate and fix the usual problems—right away. With every job, the measurements, when taken during the actual work, provide the contractor with "self-training" crews. These are motivated employees who know with certainty, at the end of each day, that they've done an excellent job. And the homeowner benefits from that excellent job.

The key to success is not flawless quality, nor rigid adherence to a government-approved protocol nor even post-process testing by highly-experienced energy professionals. What has allowed Building Performance Contracting to save so much more than other energy programs is the in-process test measurements which prompt the crews to correct the major defects before the project is complete.

7a. Remove equipment & remediate deficiencies

To provide clear work spaces, the contractor first removes any equipment that's going to be replaced. This could include HVAC equipment, duct work and perhaps the water heater. The exact timing depends on whether the home will be occupied during the project (the typical case), or whether the occupants will be away while the contractor works. When occupants remain in the home, the removal will be phased so that they will have heat, cooling and hot water when they need it. Without occupants, a project can usually move more quickly because the contractor can work steadily without interrupting the client's activities.

Also in the first part of the project, work begins on remediating any moisture problems, or problems with rodent or insect infestation. The comprehensive survey of the building often identifies problems that need fixing such as mold, moisture damage or siding problems, or gutters and perimeter drainage which needs repair or replacement. That work is usually done up front, so that the energy-related improvements can be installed into a more robust and durable home.

7b. Attic and crawl space cleaning & sealing

After the contractor relocates any stored materials and removes any existing insulation, the attic and crawl space are cleaned and prepared for energy-related work. In some cases, rodents have found a home in those spaces. They'll be evicted, and the space will be cleaned of their leavings by either the contractor or a subcontractor licensed to deal with such issues.

Fig. 3.7
Air sealing the assembly that separates the attic from the living space below.

Fig. 3.8 Blower door for in-process measurements as the workers are sealing the attic and crawl space

In the summer, as hot air in the attic cools in contact with air conditioned surfaces, it "falls into" the occupied spaces through those same gaps, cracks and holes, pulling more hot air into the attic as it falls into the house.

So for comfort and energy savings in both seasons, the base of the attic must be sealed up, air-tight. The same goes for the crawl space, when there is one.

Air entering and leaving the house through the crawl space is not what you want to be breathing. That air carries humidity, mold spores and objectionable particles upward into the home, unless the top of the crawl space is sealed up air tight, just like the attic.

When the home has a crawl space, the contractor will first make sure it's dry by fixing any perimeter drainage problems. Then a layer of vapor retarder material will be laid over the dirt in the crawl space to keep water vapor from drifting up and condensing on the cool, air conditioned surfaces at the top of the crawl space. Then the contractor will air-seal the top of the crawl space, just like what was accomplished in the attic. Any penetrations of that "pressure boundary," such as drain pipes, electrical wiring or penetrations for HVAC ducts will be sealed using an expanding bead of "gun foam." (That's trade jargon which describes the plastic foam sprayed into crevices and over seams using a hand-held foam injector. The result is shown in figure 3.7.)

As the sealing operations proceed, the crew will use a blower door to test the air tight integrity of their work, usually about once an hour or more. It's not necessary to make a hermetically-tight air seal. But when the crew has a blower door and thermal camera to locate the remaining leak points, they can easily reduce the original air infiltration rate by 50% or more, making a tremendous reduction in the building's heating and cooling loads.

It's true that all of the components of the energy retrofit work together to achieve the comfort and energy cost reductions which are so impressive. However, air sealing of the assembly which separates the house from the attic, and sealing the top of the crawl space are

In the attic, the task is to seal up all the gaps, cracks and holes which allow air to flow upwards and escape out of the house through the attic. Sealing the assembly which separates the house from the attic is like putting a lid on a pot. The conditioned air is retained inside, so the homeowner saves energy and the house is more comfortable during both the summer and winter.

With a leaky attic, during the winter any warm air escaping out through the attic drags in outdoor air behind it, pulling that cold air into the home and creating the uncomfortable drafts which make occupants want to turn up the thermostat.

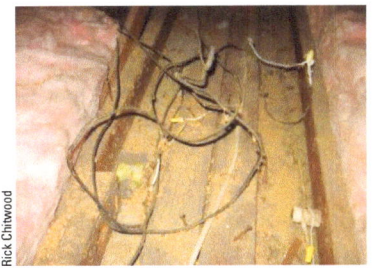

Fig. 3.9 Wiring deficiencies like this one are a fire hazard, and *must* be corrected before filling the attic with insulation

probably the most fundamental building blocks of that success. That's why the crew will take care to measure progress during the process, using the blower door and thermal camera to find and seal the gaps, cracks and holes.

7c. Correct wiring deficiencies and replace lighting

Over time, the wiring in houses can become less than safe. This may be result of "informal" wiring efforts by previous homeowners, or because the wiring is old enough that it cannot be safely covered by insulation. You don't want loose connections or rodent-chewed wire insulation under thick layers of insulation. Under insulation, heat can build up at worn connections and cause a fire.

So for safety reasons, it's quite important for the contractor to correct the shortcomings in wiring and the electrical system as a whole before adding insulation or installing any new equipment.

Lighting rework is also done at the same time as correcting potential electrical problems. A typical target of lighting retrofits are the "can lights"—any recessed fixtures which penetrate the base of the attic and light the upper floor of the home. These penetrations must be sealed up air tightly, to keep conditioned air from escaping upwards into the attic. Also, the attic will be filled with much more insulation, burying the entire light fixture. So the warm metal enclosure of those can lights must be rated for full contact with insulation (FIC-rated) to avoid creating a fire hazard.

Contractors and homeowners usually prefer replacement of older can lights. For reasons of cost, speed, safety and potential liability, new fixtures are usually best. Typically, installing new air tight, IC-rated fixtures is less than the cost of labor and materials to be sure existing fixtures are safe for insulation contact, air-tight and will tolerate the heat which accumulates in the fixture after it is made air-tight and covered with insulation.

7d. Install new HVAC system & water heater

While there are exceptions, most Home Performance Contracting Projects will include replacement of the HVAC system and water heater, even if the existing equipment is relatively new. For the homeowner, this may be the most puzzling aspect of the project. Why should new equipment be replaced? It seems like a business development plan for the contractor rather than a real need. But there are good reasons why existing equipment and duct systems will no longer be appropriate for the retrofitted home. Here are the typical components in the HVAC portion of the project.

Smaller HVAC equipment

After air sealing and insulation, the heating and cooling loads will be much lower than the pre-project loads. Also, past practice in the HVAC trades have led to gross oversizing of equipment, even for the original larger load. Most homeowners and HVAC contractors opted

Fig. 3.10 Usually the entire HVAC system must be replaced
In most cases, the duct work must be re-sized and reinstalled, because the HVAC loads will be much smaller. And in many cases the original system is so poorly designed and installed that there's not much worth preserving.

to install the "next larger" unit for the estimated load, to cover installation uncertainties, and uncertainties about the appliances and loads that may appear in the home over time. But with Home Performance Contracting, the loads are substantially reduced, and there is no uncertainty about either the loads or the installation quality—both will be measured by the contractor.

Leaving oversized equipment in place and expecting energy savings would be like hopping into your new Boeing 747 to zip over and pick up a few items at the supermarket. It is certainly a powerful and impressive vehicle and may even be an effective choice for large loads and long distances. But for short trips, a bag of groceries and a single passenger, it's tough to keep a 747 from flying way past the local supermarket, and it uses an awful lot of energy to get there and back. Oversized HVAC equipment is similarly difficult to control. It quickly overshoots the target temperature, creating too-hot or too-cold conditions in spite of its impressive capacity. And it uses a great deal of energy while creating that discomfort.

So to achieve significant energy savings and much better comfort, the contractor almost always needs to downsize both the heating and cooling equipment to fit the newly-lowered loads, and then install that equipment into a new duct system.

Smaller supply duct work with more return air

To provide comfort as well as energy savings, the cooled or heated supply air must leave the duct system with a high-enough velocity to properly blend and mix the room air, eliminating the hot and cold spots which lead to discomfort and increased energy use. At the same time, that necessary high velocity must not blow onto the room occupants, or they will be quite uncomfortable. Also, if not done right, high velocity air generates an annoying amount of noise as it enters the room.

To provide high velocity without noise, discomfort or high energy consumption, the duct work will need to be smaller. It will also need new diffusers selected for the new air flow, with its necessary high velocity but without perceptible noise. Finally, the diffusers will need to be relocated and aimed in a direction which provides good air mixing, rather than jets of air onto occupants.

Then there's the very important matter of return air. Imagine blowing air into a soda bottle. If you cover the bottle with your mouth, allowing no air to escape as you blow, you won't be able to get much air into the bottle. It runs into a dead end. The same problem occurs in most HVAC systems. There's not enough open area to let the incoming air flow out of the space and back to the system—so the incoming air is restricted or blocked from entering the room in the first place. That's often why oversized HVAC equipment still does not provide comfort—the air from the system can't flow smoothly into and out of the spaces it's supposed to heat and cool.

The solution is to figure out how much air must return back to the system, and design and install fixtures that let the air flow out of each space and back to the return air inlets of the HVAC system.

Finally there's the matter of duct insulation. To avoid wasting heating or cooling capacity as the ducts pass through unconditioned attics or crawl spaces, the heat transfer through the duct surface will be reduced to nearly zero. This will be accomplished by first insulating the duct to much higher standards than in the past, and then burying that well-insulated duct in a thick layer of additional insulation in the attic.

So for all of these reasons, the contractor will redesign and reinstall the duct systems as well as the HVAC equipment itself.

Seal duct connections & measure system air tightness

In past practice, loose duct connections wasted somewhere between 25 and 60% of the system's capacity because the air leaks out before it reaches the conditioned space. (That's another reason why in the past, HVAC installers often selected oversized equipment.)

In a Home Performance Contracting project, after the duct work and new equipment is installed, all the connections and seams will be sealed with mastic. As the duct connections are being sealed, the

Fig. 3.10 - Measuring duct tightness
*The standard is less than 20 cfm combined supply and return air leakage. But keep in mind that the **goal** is zero cfm leakage.*

installation crew will have blocked all the system's inlets and outlets and connected the system to a calibrated fan. That fan pressurizes the system and measures any outward air flow. While the fan keeps the system under positive pressure, the crew keeps finding and sealing cracks, drill holes and seams until the calibrated fan shows that the system's air leakage is nearly zero.

Measure and set air flows to each space

It's not enough to set the system air flow as a whole. What matters is exactly how much air flows through each of the conditioned rooms. Too much supply air in one room will starve a different room of the air flow it needs to maintain a comfortable temperature. Also, each room has different loads, and therefore needs different amounts of supply air.

After the new system has been installed, the contractor will measure the air flows to each room, and set the position of control dampers to make sure each space has the amount of supply air it needs to stay comfortable year-round.

Charge AC system & and measure cooling effectiveness and efficiency

In the past, the refrigerant circuit of most air conditioning systems was simply connected and the unit turned on. But having the right amount of refrigerant in the system is critical to achieving both comfort and energy cost reduction at the same time—instead of just one or the other, or neither.

Fig. 3.11
Measuring and setting air flows to each room
It's critical to comfort—and therefore to energy reduction —to measure and set all air flows. This process ensures that the air flows to each room are large enough (and are delivered at a high-enough velocity) to remove the heating and cooling loads while keeping the air in the room well-mixed and comfortable.

Fig. 3.12 Measuring and adjusting the refrigerant charge of the AC system, based on its operating load

After the rest of the system has been installed, tested and balanced, the contractor will trim the refrigerant lines to the appropriate length, connect the cooling side to the heat rejection side of the system and then measure its combined performance. Given the variability of systems and their match to the home, in nearly all cases these measurements will indicate that refrigerant needs to be added to or subtracted from the system. The contractor will accomplish this task, and then record the key performance indicators of system air flow, condenser subcooling and evaporator superheat. When these are appropriately matched through adjustments to the refrigerant charge, they provide the necessary certainty that the system will perform at peak efficiency as loads change.

Install, measure and set ventilation air flow

When the building is tightened up to reduce air leakage and energy waste, the home will need a controlled amount of filtered outdoor air. This air will dilute the pollutants generated by normal occupant activities and therefore ensure adequate indoor air quality.

In some cases, ventilation is provided by a combination of an exhaust fan and a filtered outdoor air inlet on the return side of the HVAC system. In other cases the contractor installs a dedicated ventilation system which may include a heat recovery ventilator (HRV). But no matter what the plan, the contractor will take measurements to ensure the home is being properly ventilated after completion.

Install sealed combustion water heater

If the water heater is gas-fired and is not a new, well-insulated unit, in most cases it makes economic sense to replace it with a modern unit which has improved insulation and a high-efficiency sealed combustion system. That means the unit will draw combustion air directly from the outdoors rather than from inside the house, and will also exhaust its combustion products using a small fan instead of relying on the stack effect. Such water heaters are not affected by the pressure differences created by exhaust fans in the kitchen, or in the bathrooms or the clothes dryer. Also modern water heaters are highly insulated, so they don't loose much heat in standby mode. Finally, for further energy cost savings modern units can be more easily integrated with both the heating components of the HVAC system and also solar hot water panels.

When the project includes replacement of the hot water heater, the contractor will make sure it is integrated smoothly with both the HVAC system and the solar hot water system when those are part of the re-designed thermal system of the home.

Often, the contractor may redesign and reinstall the hot water distribution system as well. If those pipes are not insulated, water is wasted as the occupants run the tap to get warm water before stepping into the shower. Short piping runs which are well-insulated reduce not only energy consumption, but also reduce water use as well—always an important consideration.

Measure combustion efficiency and adjust air flow for safe operation

When the home has combustion appliances indoors such as a gas-fired fireplace, or gas cook tops or a gas-heated clothes dryer, it's very important to ensure that these appliances have enough air for safe and efficient combustion. This is critical in homes which have been air-tightened to reduce their heating and cooling loads.

Fig. 3.12 Combustion efficiency testing
Testing is critical for safety and energy efficiency of any cobustion appliance. And special attention must be paid to those which do not have a sealed combustion circuit, as in the case of this older-style natural-draft water heater.

Fig 3.13 The last step - Attic insulation
*After **everything** else has been completed, tested and measured, insulation can be added in the attic. Note how after completion, the insulation entirely covers the duct work, so that virtually no AC or heating capacity is lost.*

After the HVAC systems have been installed and the building enclosure has been tightened, the contractor will use a micromanometer and combustion analyzer to make certain the appliances are getting an adequate supply of air and are operating safely and efficiently. This series of tests is called the "worst case depressurization." All the home's combustion appliances and all of its exhaust fans will be turned on at the same time. The combustion efficiency and exhaust stack draft pressure differences of each appliance will be analyzed under these worst-case operating conditions to make sure all appliances can operate safely in the newly-tightened home. If the combustion efficiency or exhaust stack draft is not adequate, the contractor may have to reduce the resistance to air flowing to these appliances by installing louvers in closet doors, or by resetting the amount of air from exhaust fans.

7e. Replace appliances and install insulation

The last parts of the installation include adding insulation to the attic and replacing any major appliances that have been agreed in the contract. It is usually more convenient and less disruptive to replace any appliances like the refrigerator, clothes washer and dryer or dishwasher at the end of the project rather than in the middle.

Attic insulation cannot be installed until the base of the attic has been sealed up air tight (in step 7b) and after the HVAC systems and its duct work has been installed, sealed and tested. It's not possible to accomplish air sealing or to install the new HVAC system when insulation is in the way. So adding insulation must be done as the *last* step—not the first.

8. Inform & involve the homeowner

The final step in a typical project is to inform and involve the owner in the operation of the new systems installed in the home. Owners who are used to the typical poorly-designed and poorly installed HVAC system in most homes are not usually prepared for the very different behavior of a system designed and installed for optimal comfort and energy use. Homeowners accustomed to a reassuring blast of hot air in the winter and cold air in the summer will be surprised to learn that this familiar pattern is not the behavior of efficient systems.

The big differences are that the new HVAC system will be nearly silent... and it is not a good idea to switch the system on and off as occupancy changes. In fact, if a optimally-sized system is turned off and on, it will have difficulty warming up a cold house, or cooling down a hot one. The familiar but annoying need to fiddle with the thermostat is a sign of a problem in design, installation, or both. When a correctly designed and installed system is simply let alone it operates at peak efficiency, and the home stays comfortable and economical all the time *without* adjusting the thermostat or using setback.

Chapter 3

Pre-visit Preparation

Fig. 4.1 Pre-visit preparation
Before the site visit, there's information you can gather to assess the oppportunity for both your client and your company.

Pre-visit Preparation

A Home Performance Contracting (HPC) project starts with an assessment of the client's needs, wants, motivations and potential savings. After these are confirmed and quantified by the test-in site visit, you'll build a preliminary proposal and suggested budget.

Pre-visit preparation for a typical project will probably average an hour or less for an experienced contact person. Goals for pre-visit preparation include understanding:

- The clients' initial wants and expectations.
- How much they spend for all forms of energy per year.
- The size of the house and therefore the clients' cost of energy per ft2 per year.

Phone interview : Understand client needs, wants, motivations and expectations

HPC projects begin and end with your client. Nothing else is as important as understanding their needs, wants and expectations. Without that understanding, you either won't get the job, or you'll waste time for your company or do a poor job for the client. Here are some questions which can help you engage the client to find out what they need and expect.

What can we do for you?

You want to know what the client wants to accomplish. In most cases the client will have one goal in particular, with several other goals which emerge through the conversation. Your task is to draw out the most complete list possible of how the client will probably judge success, after your project has been completed.

Do they just want to have solar panels on the roof? Or do they want to make Grandma more comfortable in the 3rd bedroom? Or do they want to do their part to save the planet by preventing global warming? Or do they want new windows paid for by a community energy efficiency subsidy? Have there ever been any problems with squirrels in the attic? Damp basement or mold ever been an issue at all?

In short, what is the full list of what the client has in mind before he's spoken with you. Chances are good that there are many items or benefits that the client is not aware you can provide. But begin by figuring out what he or she had in mind when they called, and keep track of that list. You'll use that list later, as you generate the proposal.

Have you made other recent home energy investments?

You'll need to understand any recent expenditures. For example, if the original 1965 AC unit has just been replaced by a shiny new ground-source heat pump, you'll want to keep that fact in mind when looking at the utility bills, and in thinking about how to structure a project that won't seem like a needless expense to the client. On the other hand, if installing a whole-house fan in the attic has been the extent of recent home energy modifications, you know you have a different set of opportunities.

Fig. 4.2 Check Numbers

Check numbers are sometimes useful as an initial "ballpark estimate" for assessing the reasonableness of either an opportunity or your intended result.

These check numbers come from the collected experience of several long-time California Performance Contractors. They are not set in stone. So feel free to use them as a starting point. Then apply your judgement and experience to the always unique specifics of each situation.

Check Number	Description
$0.05 to $0.10 • ft²/yr	Annual heating and cooling costs for a state-of-the-art energy-efficient home in Southern California or The Valley
$0.10 to $0.24 • ft²/yr	Same check number for a home in Northern California or in the mountains
$0.80 • ft²/yr	Below this annual utility cost, savings after Performance Contracting may not entirely self-fund the project.
$1.50 • ft²/yr	Above this annual utility cost, savings with Performance Contracting will almost certainly be very attractive.

Have you had experience with other Home Performance Contracting projects?

What has the client heard about HPC? How much do they understand about what a typical project entails? Are they already prepared for a large and complex project, or were they expecting that home performance improvements can take place during a single morning or an afternoon? Do they already understand that a test-in visit will require them to be on-site to tour the building with the technician and provide access to the attic and crawl space?... or will you need to explain that fact to them during this conversation?

What size project are you thinking of?

That's another way of asking about their budget expectations. Are they thinking that $700 would be a lot to spend for just a project to install some insulation and caulk... or are they planning to invest their recent $100,000 inheritance from Uncle George?

After you visit the site you'll know what the opportunities are. But if the client doesn't expect to spend more than a few hundred dollars, it's better to find that out quickly. Then you'll know if you need to change the customer's understanding of the opportunities and costs, or if you should refer the client to a different organization which can meet their more urgent needs within a limited budget.

We'll need copies of your electric and gas bills for 12 months. Do you have those, or shall we get them from the utility companies directly?

There's not much you can do for the client until you have a clear idea of where the energy money is being spent and in which months. That will be the basis of project costs and benefits. It's critical for the client to understand there's no way you can prepare a credible proposal until you have all 12 months of heating and electric bills.

In some parts of the State, utility companies make it easy for the client to obtain his monthly energy consumption and dollar costs. In other places, it's more of a challenge. Obtaining permission from the client to collect monthly consumption data on his behalf is sometimes a possibility, depending on the utility and the client. That's the preferred option, because there's less opportunity for errors in transcribing the data.

Asking for this data is a key moment in the relationship between the contractor and the client. It has the potential to be awkward. This is private financial data. But it's also the first moment when the contractor's standard procedures begin to demonstrate that measurements—not guesses—are the basis of Performance Contracting. Gently pointing out that fact sometimes helps overcome awkwardness if the client hesitates in providing 12 months of utility bills.

Quantify the opportunity - Utility bill disaggregation

After the interview, you'll review the utility bills to help quantify the opportunity. Three simple calculations tell you a great deal about which energy saving opportunities are the most promising, and also what you'll need to check more carefully during the site visit. That's why it's important to do the utility bill disaggregation before the site visit.

The word disaggregation just means "pulling apart." In these simple calculations, you'll pull apart the bills to figure out the size of the four major energy uses in the home: heating vs. hot water and air conditioning vs. other electrical loads. That will tell you which are the larger targets and which are smaller opportunities for savings and comfort improvements. Then you'll total all the costs to get an annual cost per square foot.[1]

If the combined total of annual energy consumption is less than $0.80/ft2/yr, then energy cost savings probably won't be a major motivator for the client (although for some, saving energy in general may still be a motivator regardless of the actual dollar savings.) On the other hand, if the total annual energy costs are over $1.50/ft2/yr, that cost savings can be an attractive part of the project.

Domestic hot water, cooking and clothes drying vs. heating costs

To identify the monthly expenses for domestic hot water, find the average of the heating fuel consumption figures for the three summer months: June, July and August. That's when there's little or no heating load, so the remaining base load expense is mostly for domestic

---

Note 1: For homes which are audited under the new California HERS II criteria, utility bill disaggregation is performed automatically by the software which is used to satisfy the HERS II procedures.

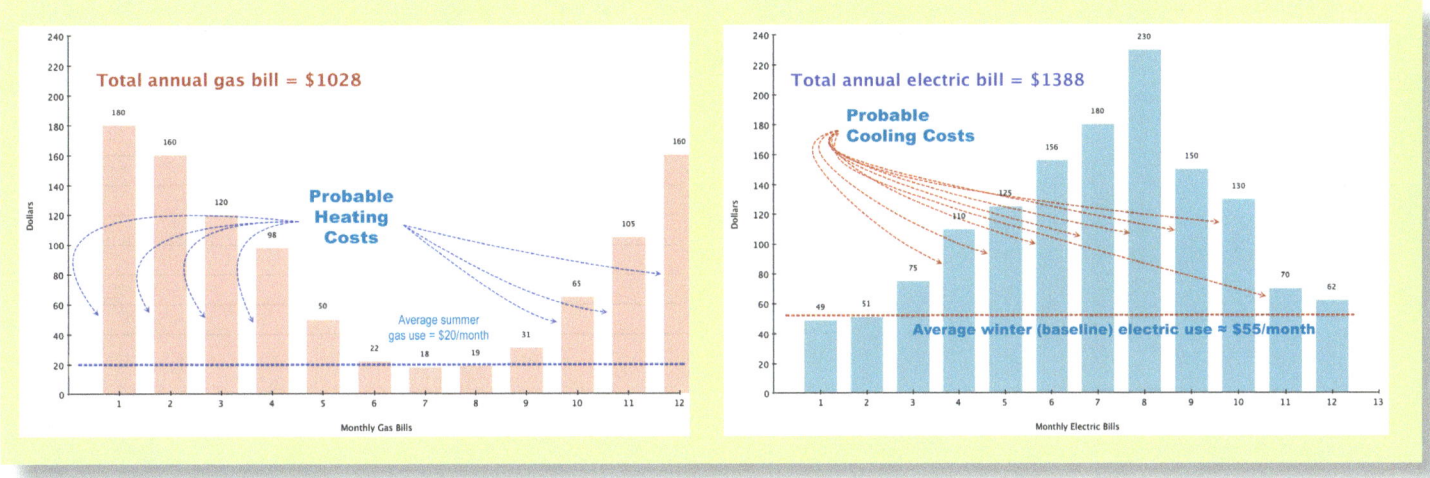

Fig. 4.3 Disaggregating utility bills
With a full 12 months of utility bills, you can estimate the heating and air conditioning expenses compared to other uses. Find the average of the off-season utility costs for gas and electric. Subtract that average from the bills for the other months, to find the approximate heating and air conditioning costs.

hot water (and for cooking and/or clothes drying if those are accomplished with gas appliances).

To find the probable annual heating costs, subtract the average summer base load cost from the monthly bill for every month in which that average is exceeded. Then sum the results for all of those months. That total is the probable cost of heating the house for a year.

For example, look at figure 4.3. The annual total gas bill was about $1028. The average of the monthly gas bills for June, July and August is $20. So subtract $20 from the gas bills for September, October, November, December, January, February, March, April and May and total the result. In the case shown in figure 4.3, the annual energy bill for heating is probably about $790 per year, while the annual bill for hot water and gas appliances is probably $20 x 12 months or $240.

Based on this example, the more interesting opportunity is in improving the space heating efficiency rather than hot water efficiency or other gas use. If the non-heating costs were more like $400 per year, then the gas appliances might deserve closer attention.

Base electric load vs. space conditioning costs

Now consider the base load electrical costs compared to the cost of running the air conditioning. Look again at the example in figure 4.3. Take the average of the electrical costs for the three winter months; December, January and February. Subtract that number from the electrical bills for the other nine months. Sum the results of that subtraction for those other nine months. That total is the probable cost of running the air conditioning for a year.

In figure 4.3, the total electrical cost is $1388. The example shows that the baseline (winter month) electrical costs are probably about $55.00, making the annual baseline costs 12 x $55.00, or $660. The non-baseline electrical costs for the year are then $1388 - 660 = $728. So that's probably close to what it costs to run the air conditioning for that year. Those numbers are fairly high. They suggest that for this example, there may be opportunities for monthly cost savings by improving air conditioning, and also by reducing other forms of electrical consumption.

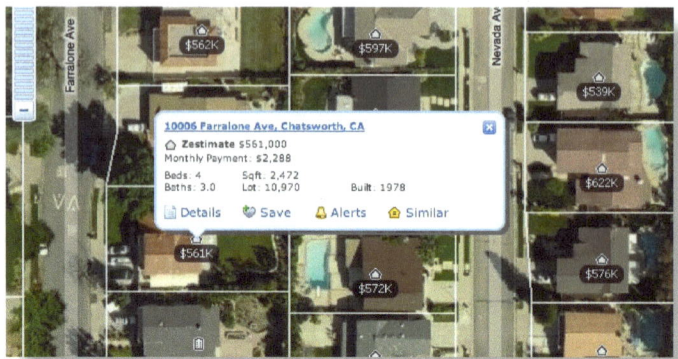

Fig. 4.4 Estimating square footage - Zillow.com
For many houses, Zillow.com provides approximate sq. ft. of living space quickly, without the delay of seeking tax records.

Fig. 4.5 Bing.com provides a bird's eye view of the neghborhood
This view allows an informal visual assessment of business potential of other homes in the neighborhood.

Total annual costs per ft2 per year

Next, assume that the house in the example shown in figure 4.3 has 1400 ft2 of finished living area. The utility bills (for space conditioning alone) are $740 for cooling and $790 for heating, for a total of $1,530. So the combined annual energy consumption is $1,530 ÷ 1400 = $1.09 • ft2/yr.

A state-of-the-art well-sealed home, with a well-insulated attic, properly sized and installed heating, air conditioning and hot water systems will use about $0.05 to $0.10 per ft2 per year in Southern California and about $0.24 per ft2 per year in Northern California. So in the example shown in figure 4.3, set in the Central Valley and totalling $1.09 per ft2, there's probably a significant opportunity for savings with heating gas use, as well as improved air conditioning efficiency or reduced air conditioning loads, or probably both.

Gather and document the real estate facts

The client does not usually know how many square feet of occupiable area are in the home. But you need that number, or at least a reasonable estimate to complete the simple calculations described above. You can get the approximate occupiable square footage from public tax records. But often it's easier and faster to look up that property characteristic using a web-based real estate record search. One service which provides much of the public record data at no charge is zillow.com.

Zillow.com data

Figure 4.4 shows a screenshot of a typical record from zillow.com. The data on file for that house suggest it has about 2,472 ft2 of occupiable space. So if you know the street address of the home in question, it's quick and easy to obtain a reasonable approximation of its floor space. That's certainly good enough for the purpose of scoping out the project, and for estimating the annual energy costs per square foot.

Google Earth + Bing.com bird's eye view

It's also useful to know, before you go to the site, what sort of a neighborhood surrounds the house as well as some idea of what the house looks like from the outside. These days, it's quite simple to obtain an aerial view of millions of buildings from either Google Earth (available at no cost at Google.com), or from the "Bird's Eye View" provided at no charge by the mapping functions within Bing.com.

Figure 4.5 shows an example of the visual information available from Bing.com for a neighborhood in Southern California. The level of detail is quite adequate for assessing what sort of buildings are around the home in question. The Bing.com view also shows the fact that nearby homes have swimming pools. Filter pumps for pools provide an opportunity for energy savings beyond air conditioning. Based on this useful visual data, swimming pool energy use becomes an item for further investigation during the test-in site visit.

Tips and Traps for Pre-visit Preparation

Don't forget the husband, or brother-in-law, or daughter.
Keep in mind that usually, there is more than one person involved. It's quite important to understand the needs, wants and motivation of all of those who will influence project decisions.

Use the client's words (whenever possible)
Keep track of the words the client uses to describe the results he wants, or the problems he wants to correct. Those are the words you'll want to keep in mind as you write the proposal, to help make your plans easily understandable and persuasive for the client. Using industry terminology is important for internal communication within your organization for clear communication. Using words the client understands is important to demonstrating that you've listened carefully to their needs and wants.

Understand the neighborhood potential
The Bing.com and Google Earth maps and aerial views also help you assess the neighborhood's business potential even before you travel to the site. If the houses are all very similar in design, and if the income level of the owners appears similar, then you'll know that the savings potential vs. the costs of a given project are also likely to be similar. This can affect the desirability—from your company's perspective—of doing an initial project in a given neighborhood.

Understand local incentives
As of the writing of this guide, there are a wealth of utility, community and State and Federal financial incentives for energy conservation retrofits. These will probably fade away over time. So it's important to base your proposal on the comfort improvement and energy-savings opportunities more than on the reduced cost of the project as supported by temporary incentives.

At the same time, these incentives may well be what prompted the client's interest. So it's rather important to your credibility to have a clear understanding of any financial incentives which could apply to the project your client has in mind. Check those with your local utility companies and your local municipality as well as the State and Federal energy offices. Finally, the US Department of Energy funds the website at DsirUSA.org (Database of State Incentives for Renewables & Efficiency) It provides a superb and current database of utility incentive programs, plus federal, state and local tax incentive programs. The coverage is nationwide, and it is searchable by ZIP code.

Chapter 5

Test-in Site Visit

Test-in Site Visit

When you leave the site after your test-in visit, you will:

a. Know exactly what is important to the client, and what is not, with respect to the project.

b. Have listened respectfully to any client misimpressions about energy-saving technologies, so you understand the client's motivation and knowledge base, allowing you to tactfully correct any such misimpressions, later.

c. Have all the detailed information and measurements you need to prepare a proposal for a project that will save energy, satisfy the client's needs and wants, and be both practical and profitable for your company.

d. Have demonstrated to the client (through your sympathetic, attentive, methodical and comprehensive information-gathering) that they can trust your company to do an excellent and cost-effective retrofit of their home.

Site inspection while driving up to the home

There's a wealth of important information to gather before you even knock on the door. All of this information will help you assess both the business potential and the relative importance of each potential item in your eventual proposal. Make note of:

1. Regional considerations. Is groundwater an issue in this neighborhood? Does the soil emit gasses like radon or industrial vapors which must be kept out of the home? Is the site exposed to constant wind or shaded by tall trees nearby? How many heating and cooling degree days are typical at this location?

2. Neighborhood economics. Are most of the homes alike? Might they have similar problems and opportunities—or are they all different? How about relative affluence of the homeowners? Will the projects be modest in scope, focusing only on a few major items, or are these large houses with utility bills which are probably also large?

3. Site microclimate. Is the home shaded, or highly-exposed to solar heat including nearby acres of hot parking lots? Is the north side heavily sheltered with plantings, and therefore its siding likely to have a higher risk of moisture damage? Is the site irrigated, and therefore might the home have a higher risk of moisture damage near the foundation slab? How is the neighborhood's rain drained—near the homes or well-away from them? Do nearby trees offer a path for squirrels to enter the attic?

Fig. 5.2 Neighborhood & Context
Each house is different. And the surrounding neighborhood also gives you important information about the business potential, and the probable needs of the homes.

The proposal for the home in the woods will necessarily be a more modest one, not only because of the lower loads, but also because it's probably worth less, and therefore the homeowner's budget will probably be more modest.

Such "clues from the curb" are never certain... but they do provide a starting point to help focus your on-site investigations.

4. Clues from the curb. What is the approximate age of the home? What is the condition of the roof, and the type of shingles? Does the roof have gutters and downspouts? If so, how far away from the foundation do the downspouts drop the rainwater? Can that rainwater drain away from the building freely—or is it held at the foundation by a decorative border around shrubs or flowers? Are there vents visible for combustion appliances, and are these terminated properly? If not, make a note to investigate carefully. What is the type and age of the car(s)? Have there been any obvious recent additions to the home? What is the condition of the siding, trim and windows—do they show signs of extreme age, wear or deterioration?

5. Solar exposure. Maximum heat gains are from west-facing unshaded windows. Which way do the windows face, how many are there, how big are they, and are they shaded?

Occupant interview

The test-in visit is the first major face-to-face interaction your company will have with the client. It's incredibly important to walk the walk and talk the talk. As the saying goes: "You'll never have a second chance to make a first impression."

If the test-in crew is sloppy and disorganized, the client will rightfully assume there's not much difference between contractors, and the best price should rule. If the crew is respectful, listens carefully, asks good questions, takes well-organized notes and gathers relevant measurements, the client will understand that Performance Contracting may cost more, but provides a superb value.

Basic principles for the occupant interview

Here are a few principles to follow during the interview:

1. Be prepared. Have your paperwork, forms and tools physically well-organized and ready for discussion and testing. Review the preliminary information gathered over the phone so the client does not have to repeat him/herself.

2. Show extreme respect for client's home and possessions. Don't touch anything you don't need to, and ask before you do. During the test-in procedures, wear shoe covers. And never lay down tools on any surface other than a clean drop cloth placed on the floor.

3. Listen carefully—all the time. There's a reason you have two eyes and two ears, but only one mouth. If you know what's important to the client, you can react accordingly. If you don't learn what's important to the client, you can't explain what's important about your proposed work in terms which will be relevant and understandable.

Fig. 5.3 The all-important homeowner interview
Here's when you learn what's important from the perspective of the people who control the decisions... if you listen carefully.

4. Explain what you're going to do before you do it. After you have listened and gathered the key information from the client interview, describe your test-in work plan, taking care to explain why that work plan is relevant to the results that the client is seeking.

Keep in mind that the more you learn about the home, its history and occupants, the more closely your proposal can match the client's needs and wants. In short, you want and need lots of information, lots of photos and lots of measurements. In case there's any misunderstanding on this point, it's quite important to make this clear to the occupants early, so they understand that they'll need to be with you for part of the time you'll be on site, which will be hours—not minutes.

Info which is only available from the occupant

On-site measurements will follow soon. But before those operations, establish a productive and cordial working relationship with the occupants. They will be the only source for some of the most critical information you'll use to generate a relevant, affordable and compelling proposal. Important questions for occupants include:

1. Energy-saving strategies and equipment - Misimpressions vs. correct understanding. You need to know what they have heard about different ways to save energy and improve comfort. Later, you'll reinforce all of their correct understanding (and tactfully adjust any misunderstanding) about what saves energy in a home and what does not.

2. Occupancy and use patterns. How many people occupy the home? When are they home and for about how long during a typical weekday and weekend day? How about ventilation? Do the occupants just open windows occasionally?.. or do they use bathroom and kitchen fans every day?

3. Seasonal comfort. Who's comfortable and who's not, at what times of the year and in what parts of the house, exactly? (Ask them to think about the hottest days of summer and the coldest days of winter). Does one of the occupants sometimes disagree about thermostat setting? If so, when during the year and for how many weeks of the year does the disagreement occur?

4. Health concerns or IAQ problems. Does any member of the family (or visitors) have breathing difficulties when inside the house, but not when outside? How about musty or chemical odors or chronic coughs or runny noses? Any issues with indoor condensation on windows during the winter? Any problem with flooding or water intrusion during different seasons? (Ask about musty odors or stains, and note any that you can smell or see.)

Fig. 5.4 "Well, now that you mention it... our bedroom does stay pretty cold in January unless we turn on our space heaters."
Comfort is probably more important than energy to most people. Be sure to ask about seasonal problems that might be a concern to those who spend more time in the home than others.

4. Client goals for the project. Find some way to get an answer to this question: "Assuming you're very happy with our project after we get done, what will be the three improvements that will have made the greatest contributions to your satisfaction?"

Whole house inspection tour

The more information you record, the better and more relevant a proposal you can provide. You want lots of information, and you'll need to take lots of pictures. Make sure the occupants understand this before you start snapping those dozens of photos.

The information you need is outlined on the worksheets which are available to members of the California Building Performance Contractors Association (CBPCA.org).

First, tour the house with the owner. Later, after the occupant loses interest in your testing you can come back to the key locations and take the photos and measurements you'll need for the proposal.

Your agenda for the whole-house tour should be thought out ahead of time. It will be based on the information gathered during the pre-visit phone interview and on the results of the utility bill disaggregation. From the utility bill, you should have a reasonable idea of which components will need the most attention during your site visit.

Here's a suggested sequence for the all-important initial house inspection tour (you must be accompanied by the occupant).

1. Known problem areas. First, ask the occupant to show you areas which he or she reported as problem areas. This includes areas where the home is not comfortable during the summer or winter, or areas where there have been odors, or where water stains have been noticed by occupants. Later, be sure to take photos of these areas and of any visual evidence which could help you diagnose factors which may have contributed to the reported problems (or problems which you notice that the occupant may not have noticed).

2. Attic. Have the occupant show you the attic access. (Later, you'll get up there, inspect the conditions and take the pictures you know you'll need for the "before" photos for the proposal.

3. Room-by-room. Begin at the top of the house and proceed downwards. Looking at each specific room together gives your potential client an opportunity to remember and describe problems that might have been forgotten during the initial interview. Also, note locations of fireplaces and other penetrations that may need to be sealed before testing the building's air tightness with the blower door.

4. Mechanical spaces. Be sure the occupant shows you the mechanical spaces and the equipment they contain. Again, showing you the equipment itself often prompts the occupant to remember problems or important conditions that may not have come to mind during the initial interview. You need to see into the locations of the heating equipment, the cooling equipment and the water heater. Also, don't forget about the pool-related mechanical equipment, if there is any. Later during this test-in visit, you'll come back and gather the name plate information and photos you need for the proposal.

Fig. 5.5 Tour the home, with the homeowner as your guide
Look at the entire home, to identify and visually inspect all concerns

Fig. 5.6 The outside of the home is also important
Don't "let loose" of the homeowner until the tour is complete. Walking around the exterior sometimes reminds the owner of water penetration issues that need to be fixed before other priorities.

Fig. 5.7 Detailed meaurements after the tour
When the walkaround tour is complete, the homeowner can turn his or her attention to other issues. You can go back and get the nameplate data and detailed measurements you need by yourself.

4. Garage. Be sure to look through the garage. Often there are air leakage paths from the garage to the home. If that is the case, sealing off those air paths will be an important part of the proposal. Keeping auto exhaust from entering the home is unfortunately a common (and potentially life-threatening) issue.

5. Exterior. With the occupant, walk around the exterior of the building, noting any apparent moisture problems, drainage problems or areas of the roof or siding which look as though they may need attention. Note the location and relative size of the windows and any shading, for later attention in gathering the data you'll need for the HVAC load estimates. If there is a crawl space, ask the occupant to show you the exterior access to that space so you can inspect it in detail, after the occupant leaves your tour.

6. After the tour is complete. The occupant can return to other activities, leaving you alone to go back and collect the detailed information you'll need for the proposal.

Test-in Procedures and Sequence

The test-in measurements you gather will depend on the nature of the opportunity. Not every home will need a full inspection of the AC units. And some homes will need either more or less inspection of moisture problems or pest infestation.

But there are at least two tests which every home will require to meet the minimum due-diligence standards set by the Building Performance Institute.[1] These include the combustion appliance safety test and the whole-house air leakage test using a blower door. Beyond these two tests, most homes will also benefit by a measurement of duct leakage, and of air flow measurements when the central AC and heating systems are operating. With the numbers from these tests, the Performance Contractor will have a sturdy foundation for the recommendations in his (or her) proposal.

Direct-vent Combustion Appliance Tests

Modern direct-vent appliances draw air directly from the outdoors through a dedicated and hard-connected duct, and they vent their combustion by-products back to the outdoors with a small fan, through a second hard-connected duct. Because this air path is almost entirely isolated from air inside the house, safe operation won't be affected by air-sealing the home. There's no need to test modern direct-vent combustion appliances (if they are properly installed) beyond a quick test of CO concentration at the vent discharge. Focus instead on older appliances which need to pull air out of the house to operate safely (natural draft combustion appliances). If all combustion appliances are the direct-vent type, skip this next section and move on to blower door testing.

Natural Draft Combustion Appliance Tests

Note 1: BPI standards are minimums. Only reaching the minimum requirement is not something to be especially proud of. Just as a student would not expect praise for D+ work, most Home Performance Contractors are not content to only satisfy BPI's minimum standards. The best practices outlined in this booklet are for those who want to achieve superior and admirable results. That's why the procedures and check numbers described in this document are not always the same as minimum BPI requirements.

Figure 5.8 Tests are important to avoid backdrafting and spillage from natural draft appliances after the house is tightened up

If the area around an operating natural draft combustion appliance is too depressurized, backdrafting (air flowing down the stack instead of up) creates a safety hazard. The air coming down the stack forces products of combustion out into the home through the draft diverter opening. In the photo above, a backdraft is forcing the tracer smoke away from the draft diverter and into the room. In nomal operation, the tracer smoke would be pulled into the stack at the draft diverter.

When a combustion appliance is operating, you don't want to have backdrafting (spillage) which lasts for longer than one minute. This is because if a combustion appliance is not operating properly, its exhaust gases could include carbon monoxide, which would be hazardous if it built up to high concentrations.

That's why the test procedures described in tables 5.1 through 5.7 are so important. The home must always be safe, even under worst-case operating conditions, after it is tightened up.

In existing homes, older water heaters and furnaces rely on the stack effect to lift the products of combustion up and out of the home.

Relying on natural draft to exhaust combustion by-products from water heaters and furnaces was safer in the past. Houses have been so leaky that until now there has been plenty of excess air leakage into the home to help the stack effect work effectively without an exhaust fan. But in energy-efficient homes, buildings must be more air-tight.

After the enclosure is tight and when interior doors are closed, the HVAC system fan and exhaust fans in bathrooms, clothes dryers, central vacuum systems and kitchen range hoods create negative

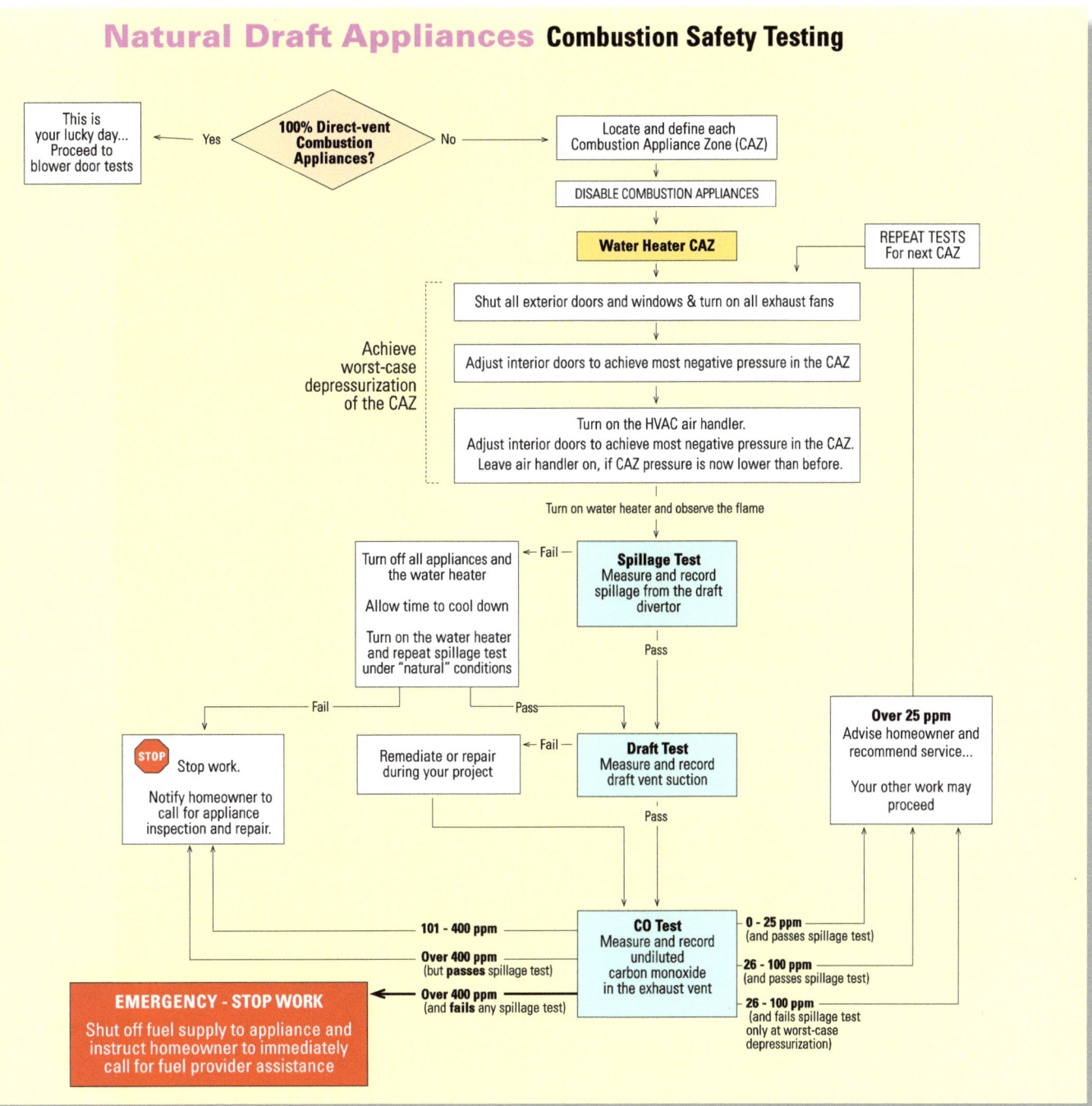

Fig. 5.9 Natural draft appliances - Mandatory combustion safety testing

pressure (suction) inside the home. That suction may be too high to allow the stack effect to exhaust the gasses up though the vent and safely out of the house.

To check for this potentially serious life-safety concern, three combustion safety tests must be run on each natural draft combustion appliance. Tests are performed in the following sequence:

1. **Spillage**. If the suction indoors is too high, exhaust gases which should go out the vent stack may instead "spill" out into the home through the draft diverter. This is only a problem if it happens for more than one minute. But if it continues for longer periods, spillage is a safety risk.

2. **Draft**. If indoor suction is too high, there won't be enough buoyancy difference between the hot exhaust and the cool air outdoors to lift combustion by-products up and out of the home. You'll need to measure the pressure difference between the stack and the room to be sure the draft pressure (stack pressure) is low enough to safely exhaust by-products of combustion.

3. **Carbon Monoxide**. If the combustion appliance is producing carbon monoxide, it's not operating properly. If it's producing excessive amounts of carbon monoxide, and spillage or back-drafting of the exhaust gases pulls carbon monoxide into the home, we have an unsafe situation. CO is toxic, and odorless. So each natural draft appliance must be tested to make sure it's not producing excessive CO when it's operating.

Before running these three tests, you'll locate and define each combustion appliance zone (CAZ) and then turn on fans and open and close doors until you have achieved the "worst-case depressurization" in each of those zones. Fact of life: achieving worst-case depressurization in all CAZ's can be time-consuming.

Establishing the worst-case depressurization of the combustion appliance zone (CAZ)

Tight homes will always be under a negative air pressure if they have natural draft appliances and other exhausts such as kitchen range hoods, clothes dryers and bathroom exhaust fans. Negative pressure is not necessarily a problem. It depends on the amount of negative pressure in the zone immediately around the heater, furnace, wall furnace or water heater.

Figure 5.9 shows the sequence of tests that ensure each combustion appliance is operating safely under all normal operating conditions. Note the fact that each CAZ must be brought to its worst-case depressurization separately. One must work through each CAZ one after another. Achieving worst-case depressurization in one zone does not mean that all the other zones will automatically be at their worst-case depressurization at the same time. Each zone is a separate set of circumstances, and must be brought to its worst-case depressurization separately from the other zones.

First, locate each appliance. Then identify the limits of the space that encloses each appliance. Those are your combustion appliance zones.

Before establishing the worst-case depressurization, measure the baseline pressure difference between each CAZ and the outdoors. To do this, close all exterior windows and doors (and the fireplace damper, if there is one). Then, measure and record the baseline CAZ pressure with respect to outdoors. Establish the "worst-case depressurization" by:

1. Turning on all the appliances which have exhausts, such as the clothes dryer, the central vacuum system, the kitchen range exhaust hood and the toilet exhaust fans and...

2. Then, while keeping track of the pressure difference between the CAZ and outdoors, open and close interior doors until you have reached the lowest depressurization with respect to the outdoors.

3. Turn on the furnace and/or the AC system air handler and...

4. Repeat step 2: while keeping track of the pressure difference between the CAZ and outdoors, open and close interior doors until you have reached the maximum possible depressurization with respect to the outdoors.

5. Subtract the original baseline pressure reading and then record the resulting net worst-case depressurization and compare that value to the limits shown in table 5.1.

Table 5.1 shows the prudent limits for worst-case depressurization of the combustion appliance zone. If the negative pressure exceeds these limits, there are five choices:

1. **Replace the natural draft combustion appliances with modern direct-vent units. (Preferred approach)**

2. Remove and reinstall the combustion appliance to outside of the home's pressure boundary (usually to the garage or attic).

3. Install "jump ducts" or transfer grills which allow air to flow more freely into and out of rooms when the HVAC system is operating. If opening the door to any given room reduces the depressurization of the CAZ, this strategy can be effective. With jump ducts or transfer grills, the same improvement can be achieved without the need to leave that room's door open.

4. Design and install two independent paths for combustion air to reach the appliance zone directly from outdoors. Then air-seal and insulate these paths, and also insulate and air seal the appliance zone itself. (Table 5.2)

5. Enlarge the combustion appliance zone by removing obstructions like interior partitions and doors, so that air can flow freely into the zone from other parts of the house.

Of these, appliance replacement is usually the most practical and least expensive. It provides energy savings plus safe operation.

The 4th alternative is rarely practical or cost-effective. Not only will you need two independent ducts to the outdoors, but you'll also need to insulate and air-seal that entire path, including the combustion appliance zone itself. That's because the air path, including the zone itself, is connected to the outdoors—so it's now outside the thermal boundary of the home. On the other hand, in some situations this approach may be a practical alternative. That's why we include the information in table 5.2. It will help you assess how large these two paths must be, and where they must be located.

MAXIMUM CAZ DEPRESSURIZATION (NOTE 1)	
Check Number	Description
-2 Pa	**Independently-vented natural draft** water heater
-3 Pa	Natural draft boiler or furnace—**when vented through a combined stack with a natural draft water heater**
-5 Pa	Natural draft boiler or furnace **equipped with a damper**—when vented through a combined stack with a natural draft water heater
-5 Pa	Natural draft boiler or furnace—when vented by itself. Also "orphan" water heaters connected alone to a large stack intended for two applicances
-5 Pa	**Induced draft** boiler or furnace—when vented with a water heater.
-15 Pa	**Power-vented or induced draft** boiler, furnace or fan-assisted water heater—when vented by itself.
-50 Pa	Chimney-top, powered draft-inducer, or direct-vented or sealed combustion appliances or high static pressure, flame-retention-head oil burners

Note 1: These values are established by the Building Performance Institute for Building Performance Contractors to use as minimum standards for safe operation.

They are the maximum allowable negative air pressure between the combustion appliance zone (CAZ) and the outdoor air—when the CAZ is at worst-case depressurization.

Based on standards set by BPI.org

Table 5.1 Maximum allowable CAZ depressurization

COMBUSTION AIR PATHS

Check Number	Description
50 ft³ per 1,000 Btu/h of burner input	Minimum volume of the area in which the combustion appliance is located. (Known as the combustion appliance zone: CAZ) This volume must not be reducible by closing any doors. If the CAZ volume is less than this standard, code-compliant safe operation requires the construction of two dedicated air supply paths from other spaces in the building, or directly from outdoors or from a ventilated attic. (See check numbers below)
One opening within 12 in. of the ceiling One opening within 12 in. of the floor	Minimum number and locations of unobstructed openings to the combustion appliance zone (CAZ) from either other areas of the house, or from outdoors, or from a ventilated attic (when the CAZ does not have sufficient volume, as required above).
1 in² per 1,000 Btu/h of burner input	Minimum code-compliant unobstructed open area for each of the two required dedicated supply air paths to the combustion appliance zone when air is taken **from inside the building**.
1 in² per 2,000 Btu/h of burner input	Minimum code-compliant unobstructed open area for each of the two required dedicated supply air paths to the combustion appliance zone when air is taken **directly from outdoors**.
1 in² per 4,000 Btu/h of burner input	Minimum code-compliant unobstructed open area for each of the two required dedicated supply air paths to the combustion appliance zone when air is taken **from a ventilated attic**.

Based on California Title 24

Table 5.2 Minimum combustion air paths for small combustion appliance zones

Fig. 5.10 Spillage testing
The smoke test shows a strong, safe draft in this equipment. Some "spillage" back out of the draft divertor is permissable for a maximum of one minute, but such risky spillage must not continue for longer periods. (Table 5.3)

The 5th alternative (enlarging the combustion appliance zone) is also seldom desirable from the homeowner's perspective. It requires, for example, removing or installing vents in the closet door if the furnace or hot water heater is stuffed into a hallway closet. Most occupants don't want to stare at the hot water heater every time they walk past the closet. If they put the door back on because it looks better that way—the appliance becomes hazardous again. So usually, appliance replacement is the preferred choice.

In any case, after the worst-case depressurization has been achieved, the tests for the appliance in that CAZ can be started.

Test 1 - Measuring "spillage" of exhaust gasses from natural-draft water heaters and furnaces under worst-case depressurization conditions

When the draft suction is really inadequate, exhaust gasses can actually be pulled back down the stack and spill into the air around the furnace or water heater. With natural draft appliances, one can expect a certain amount of this spillage when wind pressures outdoors combine with worst-case depressurization indoors. The key is that such spillage should not last very long—one minute at most. (See table 5.3)

To measure spillage, you'll need a mirror (or a smoke puffer, as shown in figure 5.10) and a stopwatch. Bring the CAZ to worst-case depressurization. Turn on the appliance and place the mirror near

Table 5.3 Maximum spillage period

MAXIMUM SPILLAGE PERIOD (NOTE 1)	
Check Number	Description
1 minute	**Natural draft** water heater, boiler, forced-air furnace or gravity furnace
1 minute	**Space heater**

Note 1: These values are established by the Building Performance Institute for Building Performance Contractors to use as minimum standards for safe operation. They are the maximum allowable amounts of time that exhaust gasses can spill back out of the exhaust stack and into the combustion appliance zone during worst-case depressurization.

Note 2: If spillage exceeds one minute during worst-case depressurization, turn off the appliance and allow the flue to cool down. Then re-test under "natural" conditions. Note the pressure difference between worst-case depressurization and "natural" conditions.

Based on standards set by BPI.org

the draft diverter of the exhaust stack. Whenever fog forms on the mirror, it's an indication that spillage is occurring. Note the length of time the spillage occurs, and record its duration. Then refer to table 5.3 for any required action.

Test 2 - Measuring draft suction of natural-draft water heaters and furnaces under worst-case depressurization conditions.

To safely exhaust by-products of combustion, there must be adequate draft (enough suction) in the vent system (one to two feet above the draft diverter). To be sure the suction is adequate, the technician will measure the negative pressure in the vent system of the natural draft appliance. The check numbers in table 5.4 indicate what draft is adequate to safely exhaust combustion by-products at all outdoor temperatures.

At lower levels of suction (less negative pressure), the stack effect will not be adequate to safely remove carbon monoxide and other products of combustion. When testing shows the draft suction is insufficient, the Home Performance proposal will need to include measures to either:

1. Replace the appliance with a modern sealed-combustion unit, or...

Fig. 5.11 Measuring exhaust vent draft suction
Consult table 5.4 for minimum vent draft suction levels

2. Remove and reinstall the combustion appliance outside of the home's pressure boundary (usually to the garage or attic).

3. Add jump-ducts or transfer grills between "compartmented spaces" to reduce the pressure differences created when the HVAC system's blower is operating. (Compartmented spaces are rooms with doors, but without an air outlet to relieve pressures created by the HVAC system.) Or...

4. Add a ventilation air system to the area where the appliance is located (the combustion appliance zone), or...

5. Add some type of powered fan to increase the force which exhausts products of combustion.

MINIMUM EXHAUST VENT DRAFT SUCTION (NOTE 1)

Check Number	Description
-2.5 Pa	Minimum acceptable draft test result when the outdoor temperature is 10°F or below.
$(°F_{outdoors} \div 40) - 2.75$ Pa	Minimum acceptable draft test result when the outdoor temperature is between 11°F and 89°F
-0.5 Pa	Minimum acceptable draft test result when the outdoor temperature is 90°F or above.

Note 1: These values are established by the Building Performance Institute for Building Performance Contractors to use as minimum standards for safe operation.

They are the minimum acceptable test result for the pressure in the exhaust stack of the combustion appliance, compared to the pressure in the surrounding combustion appliance zone—at worst-case depressurization.

In other words, the exhaust stack pressure test results must be at least this negative—or more negative—to provide safe venting of the exhaust gasses from the appliance.

Based on standards set by BPI.org

Table 5.4 Minimum exhaust vent draft suction

Of these alternatives, appliance replacement with direct-vent units is by far the preferred alternative. It saves energy through much-increased heating efficiency and provides an opportunity for further energy-saving synergies with other heating and cooling components.

Test 3 - Carbon monoxide measurements

Under BPI standards, the background indoor concentration of carbon monoxide should be less than 9 parts per million. (Ideally, it will be near-zero ppm) If the CO concentration is near 9 ppm without any appliances operating, it's an indication that there's some form of combustion taking place that has not been identified. Find that source and stop the combustion, so you can then measure the CO concentration of the exhaust gas of each appliance with as near-to-zero background as possible.

As these appliances are operating, record the measured CO values on the worksheets provided in the appendix to this guide, and compare those values with the check numbers in table 5.6 and 5.7.

CARBON MONOXIDE ACTION LEVELS - INDOOR AIR

CO Concentration in open air (Note 1)	Effects and action (Note 2)
1 to 3 ppm	Typical outdoor levels - No known negative effect for healthy people
5 to 8 ppm	Elevated. Levels between 5 and 8 ppm should signal concern. The source of the problem should be located, to ensure it does not generate CO for extended periods.
9 ppm and above	**Stop work and fix the problem.** For healthy adults, this is the maximum acceptable time-weighted average for 8-hours of continuous exposure in *outdoor* environments. (U.S. EPA and the World Health Organization)
25 ppm	Threshold limit value (TLV) - Maximum recommended time-weighted average concentration *indoors*, for 8 hours of continuous exposure for healthy adults. (ACGIH)
35 ppm or above	Maximum acceptable average concentration for 8-hours of continuous exposure for healthy adults in *outdoor* air (U.S. EPA)
70 ppm	A good residential CO detectors should alarm
200 ppm	Flu-like symptoms—headache, nausea fatigue—within 2 hrs in healthy adults.
800 ppm	Headache, nausea, dizziness and convulsions in healthy adults within 45 minutes. Death within 2 to 3 hours.
1600 ppm	Death of healthy adults within one hour of continuous exposure.

Note 1: These values refer to measurements taken indoors, in well-mixed air, away from any operating combustion appliances.

Note 2: Nationally, the US has not yet established any regulatory limits for this toxic gas in indoor residential environments. The US Occupational Safety Administration has established only one limit, and that is for the work environments of healthy adults—a maximum time-weighted average of 50 ppm for an 8-hour work day. The U.S. EPA has established levels of concern for carbon monoxide in outdoor air, but not yet for indoor air.

Table 5.5 Limits for carbon monoxide concentration indoors

CARBON MONOXIDE ACTION LEVELS - EXHAUST STACKS

CO Concentration in the exhaust stack (Note 2)	And/Or	Maximum spillage and minimum draft tests	Allowable or required action
0 - 25 ppm	And	Passes	Work may proceed
26 - 100 ppm	And	Passes	Technician must advise homeowner of the elevated carbon monoxide level and recommend that the CO problem be fixed for reasons of efficiency.
26 - 100 ppm	And	Fails only at worst-case depressurization	Technician must advise homeowner of the elevated carbon monoxide level and recommend a service call for the appliance and/or building modifications to correct the problem for reasons of both efficiency and safety.
101-400 ppm	Or	Fails under natural pressure conditions	**STOP WORK** No work may proceed on the system until it is serviced and the problem is corrected.
Over 400 ppm	And	Passes	**STOP WORK** No work may proceed on the system until it is serviced and the problem is corrected.
Over 400 ppm	And	Fails under any conditions	**EMERGENCY** Shut off fuel supply to the appliance and instruct the homeowner to immediately call for appliance service or fuel provider assistance to investigate and correct the problem before the fuel source can be reconnected.

Note 1: These limits have been established as minimum standards by the Building Performance Institute. As such, they do not have the force of law. But they do represent a minimum standard of care for Home Performance Professionals with respect to the safety of workers and homeowners.

Note 2: These values refer to measurements taken in the exhaust gas flue, after approximate steady-state operating conditions have been achieved. These readings must be taken in the exhaust stack just below the draft divertor, so that the exhaust gasses are not yet diluted by the room air which is also entering the exhaust stack.

Table 5.6 Carbon monoxide action levels for natural draft combustion appliances

If the levels reach high enough, take the actions described in that table. If they are below the levels of concern, simply note them for the record and for the benefit of the homeowner.

As you test gas appliances, keep in mind the general rule that when you see yellow flames instead of blue flames, you should be suspicious. Yellow flames result from poor combustion, and excess carbon monoxide may result.

Natural-draft water heaters and furnaces

Place the combustion analyzer probe (or carbon monoxide tester probe) into the exhaust stack below the draft diverter, as shown in figure 5.12. The exact placement is important, because you want to measure the concentration of the undiluted exhaust gases. Above the draft diverter, ambient air will dilute the combustion by-products and make your CO reading useless.

Gas cook top and Open combustion space heaters

Take the reading above the operating appliance, with all burners operating. Convert the raw reading to the "air-free" reading and check the result against the values of the check numbers in table 5.7.

CO Air-Free (CO A/F) is a calculation that allows a carbon monoxide reading to be stated as an undiluted or absolute reading in PPM. For this reason, this is the method used most commonly to measure appliance and heating equipment emissions.

The CO A/F measurements is computed from the CO and O2 measurements. It allows you to determine the relevant amount of CO present in the air above the cook top by compensating for the amount of excess air provided by the burner. Instruments can now determine the CO A/F reading automatically, or you can measuring the CO and O levels and then solve this equation:

$$(20.9 \div (20.9 - O2\text{ ppm})) \times (\text{measured CO ppm}) = CO\text{air-free ppm}$$

Fig. 5.12 Carbon monoxide probe location
Note how the probe is inserted slightly downwards into the exhaust stack. In that location, there's not yet any ambient air diluting the gas and distorting the reading, as would be the case just an inch higher up in the stack.

Gas ovens and clothes dryers

Place the combustion analyzer probe into the vent sleeve at a location which ensures that dilution air has not yet entered that vent sleeve.

Consult the check numbers in table 5.7 for the permissible limits of CO concentration in vent sleeves of ovens and ranges. But again, keep in mind that a properly-functioning combustion appliance does not generate carbon monoxide. If you have an ambient reading above the suggested limit for background concentration (9ppm), it might be that something's wrong with the appliance. It would be wise to have it checked and tuned by an appliance repair technician, even if the CO concentration does not exceed the limits in table 5.6.

Gas leak detection

The last combustion safety test is to check all gas line connections for leaks. The quick way is to use a gas leak detector, placing the probe

CARBON MONOXIDE - RANGE & OVEN VENT SLEEVES

CO Concentration in the vent sleeve (Note 1)	Description and Action (Note 2)
Less than 100 ppm	Acceptable. No action required.
100 to 300 ppm	Elevated. Before additional work, technician must advise homeowner of the elevated carbon monoxide level, install a carbon monoxide sensor in the appliance zone, and recommend that the appliance be serviced for reasons of safety.
Over 300 ppm	Excessive. Before additional work, the appliance must be serviced and the problem corrected. If retesting after service continues to show vent sleeve carbon monoxide over 300 ppm, exhaust ventilation must be installed with 25 cfm capacity if its operation will be continuous, or 100 cfm if operation will be intermittent.

Note 1: These values refer to measurements taken in the vent sleeve, at a location **before** the dilution air also enters that vent sleeve.

Note 2: These limits have been established as minimum standards by the Building Performance Institute. As such, they do not have the force of law. But they do represent a minimum standard of care for Home Performance Professionals with respect to the safety of workers and homeowners.

In a perfectly-performing appliance, the CO concentration of the undiluted exhaust gases would be nearly zero ppm (or no greater than the outdoor background concentration.) So these limits should not be seen as indicators of ideal operation.

Fig. 5.7 Maximum acceptable carbon monoxide concentration in exhaust vent sleeves of ovens and ranges

close enough to each of the joints in turn to "sniff out" any gas leaks. If the detector indicates a gas leak, then brush on a detergent solution over the joint to help locate the problem, and to provide a sense of it's magnitude.

Gas leaks are surprisingly common. All leaks must be repaired. Notify the homeowner and recommend that he or she contact the local utility's emergency desk to schedule the repair.

Chapter 5... Test-in Site Visit

Fig. 5.13 Electronic gas leak detector - Audible indicator

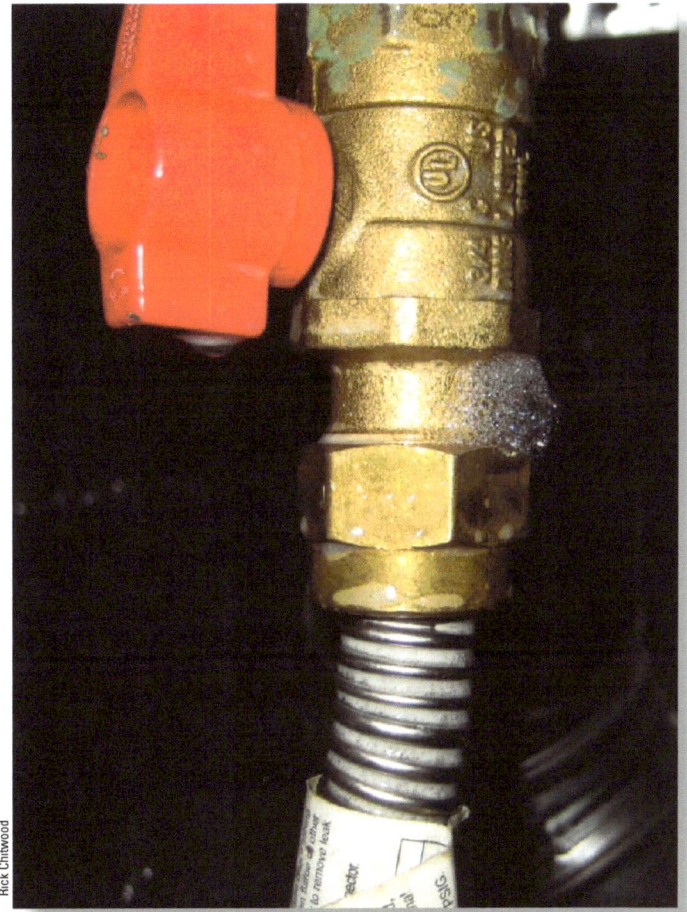

Fig. 5.14 Detergent solution - Visual gas leak detection

Whole-house air leakage test with the blower door

Before you begin the blower door test, complete these six tasks:

1. Vacuum up or cover any ashes in the fireplace with a layer of newspaper. (Otherwise, you'll spend an unpleasant afternoon cleaning up the ashes that you've blown over all over the furniture after the blower doors pulls air down the chimney.)

2. Explain to the occupants that you'll now need to seal up the building and close all the doors and windows. So they should be prepared to stay inside—or outside—for the duration of the blower door test, and don't open any windows or doors during the test. When there are younger occupants who may be less-receptive to this message, blue painters' tape placed across doors temporarily can be an effective reminder to keep them closed during the tests.

WHOLE-HOME AIR TIGHTNESS	
Check Number	Description
1 cfm$_{50\,Pa}$ • ft² (of conditioned space)	Typical maximum air leakage for an energy efficient home. Test values above this level (more than 1 cfm$_{50}$ • ft²) may call for better air-sealing of the building enclosure.
1 cfm$_{50\,Pa}$ • ft² (of conditioned space)	Maximum prudent air tightness for passive ventilation. Test values below this leakage rate (less than 1 cfm$_{50}$ • ft²) save energy, but may also call for a mechanical ventilation system to provide adequate indoor air quality. Also note: ASHRAE Standard 62.2 requires ventilation beyond passive infiltration. Check to see if local codes require compliance with that standard for retrofit

Table 5.8 Field check numbers for whole-home air tightness

Fig 5.16 Blower door testing

Fig. 5.15 Avoid decorating the home with ashes
Get rid of ashes or cover them with newspaper before starting the blower door. You'll avoid embarrassment, and save a lot of cleaning.

Fig. 5.17 Thermal camera
For the average homeowner, images are more convincing than air infiltration rate numbers.

3. Make sure you've got everything you need for all other work inside the home while the test will be in progress. (It's embarrassing when you have to remove the blower door to go outside to get something in the truck, after you've made the reminder speech to the occupants).

4. Close all the exterior doors and windows.

5. Open all interior doors.

6. Turn off the HVAC system and reset the water heater to pilot-only operation.

The blower door test is usually quite interesting for the homeowner. This is an excellent time to demonstrate the value of measurements. Don't pass up this opportunity for education and meaningful interaction with the homeowner.

It's also wise to have a thermal camera ready, so you can make the point about the volume of air leakage not only with the blower door numbers, but also with visually powerful thermal image. (Fig. 5.18.) A thermal camera image is usually more compelling to the owner than numbers from the blower door tests. (But of course you'll also need those air leakage numbers, to establish the baseline air leakage when you begin the air sealing part of your project)

The check values in table 5.8 help you interpret, for the owner, the relative importance of the values you eventually measure. That table also helps you explain the implications of those values.

Convert air leakage rates from CFM_{50} to ACH_{50} and $ACH_{(Natural)}$

You'll need to know the "natural" air leakage rate, to be able to estimate the savings from tightening up the enclosure and duct connections. The leakage rate under a test pressure of -50 pascals is much higher than what one should expect when there's no powerful fan pulling a large suction on the building.

This difference has been carefully measured by the Lawrence Berkeley Laboratory, in homes throughout the country. Their results showed that the average annual natural air leakage rate is 10 to 30 times less than the leakage rate at a test pressure of -50 Pa, depending on where the home is located, how well it is sheltered from wind and how many stories the home has.

Factors to adjust the 50 Pa test pressure leakage air flow to a probable annual average natural air leakage rate are shown in table 5.9.

Zone	# of stories	1	1.5	2	3
1	Well-shielded	18.6	16.7	14.9	13.0
	Normal	15.5	14.0	12.4	10.9
	Exposed	14.0	12.6	11.2	9.8
2	Well-shielded	22.2	20.0	17.8	15.5
	Normal	18.5	16.7	14.8	13.0
	Exposed	16.7	15.0	13.3	11.7
3	Well-shielded	25.8	23.2	20.6	18.1
	Normal	21.5	19.4	17.2	15.1
	Exposed	19.4	17.4	15.5	13.5
4	Well-shielded	29.4	26.5	23.5	20.6
	Normal	24.5	22.1	19.6	17.2
	Exposed	22.1	19.8	17.6	15.4

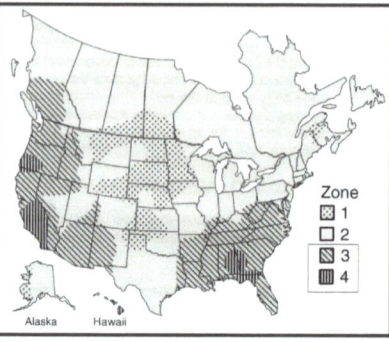

Table 5.9 "LBL numbers"
Divide the test pressure leakage values by these numbers to obtain the average annual natural air infiltration rates. (The leakage rates when fan pressure is not applied). These factors are based on measurements from tests by Lawrence Berkeley Laboratory (LBL).

rate to the whole-house air change rate per hour (ach) using this equation:

$$(cfm(Natural) * 60\ min/h) \div house\ volume\ ft3 = ach(Natural)$$

Implications of whole-house leakage rates

Air tightness is a double-edged sword. If the house leaks, it will waste energy. But if the house is tight, it won't automatically provide adequate indoor air quality through leakage.

Based on research and field measurements performed by the Lawrence Berkeley Laboratory for the U.S. Department of Energy, a test pressure leakage rate of less than 0.35 air changes per hour indicates the cost-benefit ratio of further sealing in an existing home would be poor, because the home is already fairly tight.[1] That's good news. However, keep in mind that when the home is that tight, leakage won't provide adequate dilution of indoor contaminants. So when the house is that tight, it's wise to propose an engineered ventilation system.[2]

On the other hand, when the test pressure leakage rate is more than 0.35 ach, there's significant potential to save energy by air sealing the enclosure. But again, after the building is tightened to a lower leakage rate than 0.35 ach it will need a dedicated ventilation system.

So based on your blower door test results, your proposal should include one of two items: either air sealing and a dedicated ventilation system if the home is leaky, or a dedicated ventilation system alone if the home is already tight.

All of California falls into either zone 3 or zone 4 of the LBL factor table. After selecting the most appropriate factor from the table, solve this simple equation to convert the air leakage rate at test pressure to the natural air leakage rate:

$$cfm50 \div LBL\ factor = cfm(Natural)$$

Next, to show the owner a meaningful comparison between this home and others in the area, you'll need to "normalize" the leakage rates by converting the air leakage flow rate in cubic feet per minute (cfm) to an air exchange rate for the whole house (ach, which means air changes per hour). That way you can compare the leakage rates of different houses, even though they may have different floor areas.

First, calculate the interior volume of the building except for the attic—the occupied portion of the home. (Don't waste too much time on precision with this calculations An approximate air volume will be sufficient for purposes of comparison.) All units are in feet. The volume of the bulk of the house below the roof line is simply:

$$Height\ to\ the\ roof * Home\ width * Home\ depth = volume\ ft3$$

After you have the volume of the home, normalize the natural leakage

---

Note 1: Even if the building is fairly tight, don't stop looking for the leakage. Whole-house air tightness below 0.35 ach/50 is often seen in slab-on-grade homes. But it's still important to find the *location* of the remaining air leakage. If (as usual) there is substantial leakage between the home and its attic, it's important to to seal those leaks even if the overall leakage is below 0.35 ach/50. If air continues to leak to and from the attic, the attic insulation won't be effective.

Duct Leakage Testing

Duct leakage testing is partly accomplished by using the blower door. So we'll discuss it now, before you remove the blower door and turn your attention to the rest of the HVAC system. There are two parts to the test: total duct leakage and duct leakage to the outdoors.

Fig. 5.18
Seal off the HVAC system before starting the duct leakage test.

Fig. 5.19 Duct blaster, used in combination with the blower door for measuring duct leakage to the outdoors

Testing total duct leakage

Begin the duct leakage test by making sure all of the supply air diffusers are tightly sealed with plastic sheeting and tape. Next:

1. Connect a duct blaster to the return air grille.

3. Start the duct blaster, and increase its air flow until the pressure inside the duct system reaches 25 Pa (with reference to the pressure inside the house).

4. Read and record the air flow through the duct blaster after the duct pressure reaches 25 Pa. This air flow is the total air leakage from the HVAC air distribution system, including leaks from the air handler and all of the connections to diffusers, grills and other HVAC components.

Testing duct leakage to the outdoors

Testing duct leakage to the outdoors is similar, but you'll need the assistance of your blower door.

1. Leave the duct blaster in place, attached to the return air grille.

2. Use the blower door to positively pressurize the house to +25 Pa with respect to the outdoors (Blow air into the home instead of pulling it out. In other words, reverse the direction of blower door flow compared to your earlier whole-house leakage testing).

3. Increase the duct blaster fan speed until there is essentially no pressure difference between the duct system and the inside of the house. (The micromanometer should now read less than 1 Pa pressure difference between the duct system and the inside of the house.)

4. Read and record the air flow through the duct blaster. That air flow reading is the total air leakage from the system to outdoors.

HVAC SYSTEMS - CAPACITY AND AIR LEAKAGE

Check Numbers (Existing Systems)	Description
40,000 to 60,000 Btu/h per 1,000 ft² (Conditioned space)	In existing homes, heating capacity of over 60,000 Btu/h per 1,000 ft² strongly suggests the system is grossly oversized and can be redesigned and downsized to improve comfort. (A new system in a well-sealed home would only need about 15,000 Btu/h per 1,000 ft².) But, if heating capacity is less than 40,000 Btu/h/1,000 ft², redesign would only be practical if equipment needs replacement.
1 Ton per 450 to 600 ft² (Conditioned space)	In existing homes, cooling capacity of more than 1 ton per 450 ft² strongly suggests the system should be redesigned and downsized to save energy and improve comfort. But if each ton of capacity serves 600 ft² or more, there is less benefit to replacing the system. (A new system in a well-sealed home would only use about 1 ton for every 1,000 ft².)
250 to 350 cfm of supply air per ton of AC system capacity	In existing homes, air flow rates below 250 cfm/ton strongly suggests the AC equipment and duct system are wasting energy. Above 350 cfm/ton, there is less to be gained by replacement (New systems in a dry climate supply about 500 cfm per ton.)
6 to 15% of total supply air flow	In existing systems, duct leakage rates of less than 6% of system flow suggest there is little to be gained by duct redesign and reinstallation. But leakage rates of over 15% strongly suggest redesign and replacement. (A new system should leak less than 1/2 of 1%... less than 20 cfm_{25})

Rick Chitwood

HVAC System Assessment

HVAC assessment begins with visual inspection of the state of the equipment and air distribution system. If the equipment and it's duct work is old, obviously deteriorated and needs replacement, detailed testing may not be useful. If the homeowner already plans to replace the entire system, there's no need for more than visual assessment.

On the other hand, when it's not clear if the entire system needs to be replaced, a comprehensive set of tests and measurements is appropriate, as described in this section.

HVAC comfort effectiveness & energy consumption

Seven factors reduce the HVAC system's ability to deliver comfort at a reasonable energy cost. From most to least effect, these are:

1. Duct air leakage losses (Compared to a target of zero)

2. Duct conduction losses (Compared to a target of zero)

3. Insufficient air flow across the AC evaporator coil (Compared to a target of about 500 cfm/ton for a dry climate)

4. Inadequate or excessive refrigerant charge (Measured against superheat and subcooling targets)

5. Inadequate room-by-room air flow, delivery velocity and delivery location (Compared to each room's heating and cooling loads, a delivery velocity between 500 and 700 fpm and delivery locations away from occupied portions of the rooms)

6. Excess cooling and heating equipment capacity (Compared to both current loads and reduced future loads after air sealing and insulation)

7. Equipment efficiency (AFUE and SEER)

Table 5.10
Check numbers for evaluating the sizing and installation quality of existing air-based heating and cooling systems.

Note that the equipment's lab-tested efficiency is the last and least important factor in the list. Installation quality and equipment sizing are what really determine the system's comfort effectiveness and energy efficiency. That's why you'll inspect, test and measure the first six factors to assess the HVAC system.

Installed AC capacity
Table 5.10 provides check numbers for quick assessment of installed cooling and heating capacity. The ideal target for well-built new homes would be about 1 ton of cooling for every 1,000 ft2 of conditioned floor space. Less space than 1,000 ft2 per ton means the cooling loads are higher than they should be if a home is tight and well-insulated, and has reasonably good windows. But with existing homes, if the installed capacity is in the range of 1 ton per 450 to 600 ft2, the equipment is probably not so grossly oversized that it would cause a major comfort problem after air sealing and insulation.

On the other hand, if the existing AC system has 1 ton of capacity for less than 450 ft2, it's already much too big for the home. Leaving a unit that large in place will create comfort problems after the loads are reduced through air sealing and insulation of attic and duct work.

When you see that level of oversizing, you'll want to begin preparing the client for the idea of replacement of not only the unit, but also the duct system.

Installed heating capacity
Table 5.10 also shows the range of reasonable installed capacity for heating equipment in California. In the colder climate zones, one can expect higher installed capacity. But in Southern California and the Coast, the heating load is so small that conventional furnaces are not available in small-enough capacities to provide effective comfort.

In any of our California climate zones, if the installed heating capacity is over 60,000 Btu/h per 1,000 ft2, it's time to think about equipment and duct replacement, because it's simply too oversized to work properly. (By "working properly," we mean it should provide reliable, comfortable, well-mixed, warm-but-not-overheated rooms, without noticeable noise and without excessive energy costs.)

In Southern California or on the Coast, heating capacity of over 40,000 Btu/h would be similarly excessive, and make it difficult to provide comfortable rooms, no matter how "advanced" the equipment might appear from its combustion efficiency rating (AFUE).

Total system air flow measured at the return grill
Moving on to measurements of the system performance, table 5.10 also shows the range of reasonable amounts of supply air per ton of cooling capacity. (There's no need for similar numbers for heating, because if the AC air flow is within a reasonable range, the heating capacity will also be reasonably well-matched to the air flow.)

In California, a reasonable target supply air flow would be close to 500 cfm per ton of AC capacity. Below 500 cfm/ton, in the California climates you can save money and reduce energy consumption by increasing the supply air flow rate.[3] This is different than in most other parts of the country, where a target of about 400 cfm per ton would be a good compromise between the competing needs of cooling efficiency and dehumidification effectiveness.

Less air per ton means the system will cool the supply air more deeply, removing more moisture. But in California, the humidity loads are so low that the greatest benefits for cooling and energy efficiency are gained at a flow rate of 500 cfm/ton.

Although the target range for new homes would be near 500 cfm/ton, the realistic check number range is between 375 to 350 cfm/ton for existing homes. Above an air flow rate of 320 cfm per ton, the benefits of smaller equipment and duct redesign and replacement are

Note 3: Cooling airflow of 500 cfm/ton is indeed optimal in the dry California climate, PROVIDED that the rest of the system does not chew up so much fan horsepower that the benefit of 500 cfm/ton is lost. To avoid problems, watch out for high efficiency filters. If these are installed, the resistance they create makes it difficult to obtain full flow without excessive fan HP. Also, if the return ducts are too small or if there's not enough return grill area, boosting the system flow to 500 cfm/ton will waste energy rather than conserve it. So the check number of 500 cfm/ton is right for new construction with properly-sized ducts, diffusers and return grills. In existing homes, use moderation. Don't boost the flow up as high as 500 cfm/ton unless a. the rest of the system is capable of handling that flow or b. you're going to replace the existing duct system and do it right. Chapter 8 has more information on this issue.

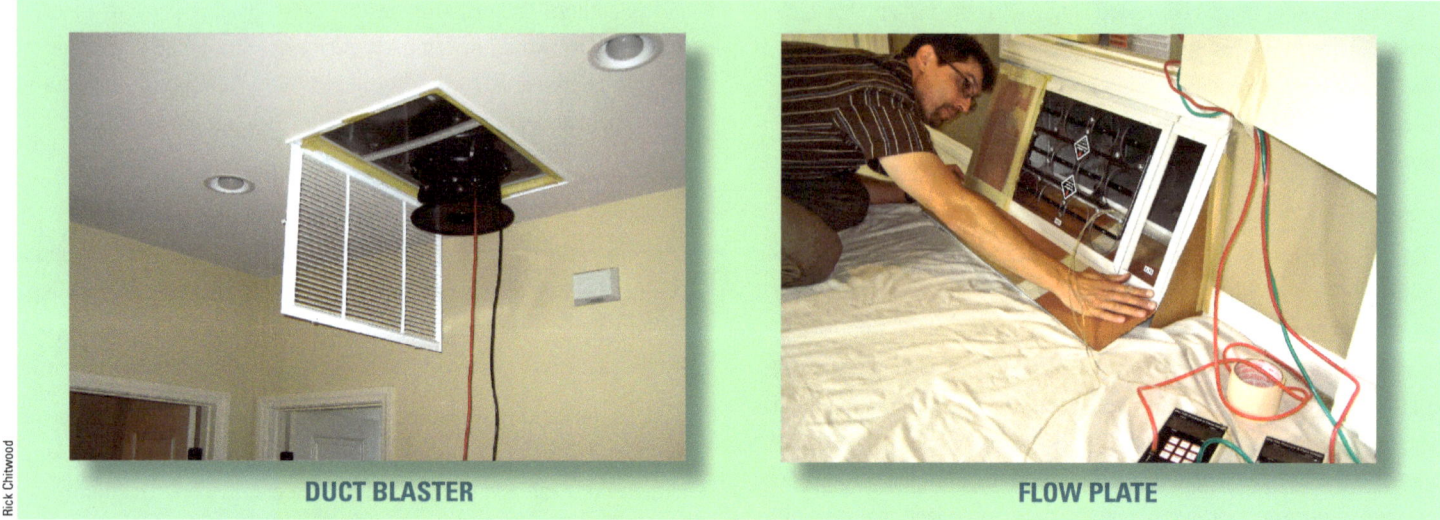

DUCT BLASTER   **FLOW PLATE**

Fig. 5.20 Measuring total system air flow
A duct blaster or flow plate attached to the return air grille. These instruments arrangement is used to measure the system's total air flow at the return grill—a relatively convenient location to access.

modest compared to the retrofit costs. But below 250 cfm per ton, existing equipment is probably so oversized and/or the return-side duct system is so undersized that both comfort and energy consumption will improve significantly when the equipment is downsized and it's duct work is replaced. Replacement equipment and a new duct system will be much smaller, use less energy and provide better comfort, because it will match to the low post-retrofit cooling loads.

However, note that there are many reasons why the existing air flow could be below the target range. The most typical reason is that there are high resistance "high efficiency" filters installed in the system instead the equipment's original standard filters. Most homeowners are not aware of the energy cost and system capacity and operational problems and sometimes equipment damage that come from replacing standard filters with "high efficiency" filters. If your inspection uncovers dirty high efficiency filters, part of the solution to the low air flow problem may be to replace those filters with clean, standard efficiency filters. (Instant energy efficiency improvement!)

But if the filter is relatively clean and don't have the crippling resistance of a high efficiency filter, other reasons for low air flow may be leaky ducts (which waste supply air) or a duct system that creates too much resistance to allow adequate air flow. (Poor duct design often results from complex architectural design, which forces the HVAC ducts into complex and leak-prone contortions. These chew up fan energy and reduce net air flow) In any case, when the supply air flow is below about 350 cfm/ton, the technician needs to look through the system to determine the cause of the low air flow.

See figure 5.20 for equipment usually used to measure the total air flow rate through the system by measurements taken at the return grill. The total flow, along with measurements of evaporator superheat and condenser subcooling allows the technician to assess the state of repair and effectiveness of the current system.

First, the AC system is put into normal operation. The micromanometer is arranged to measure the normal system operating pressure (NSOP). That value is entered or stored in the micromanometer.

Next, the duct blaster is mounted on, sealed to the return grille and also connected to the 2nd channel of the micromanometer. The system is started again. Then the duct blaster is started and it's speed

Fig. 5.21 Semi-automatic superheat and subcooling calculations
Modern digital refrigerant guages calculate subcooling and superheat semi-automatically, based on temperature and pressure measurements and their built-in refrigerant property tables. This saves time and improves both accuracy and consistency of these critical measurements.

increased until the pressure in the return duct is the same as the NSOP measured before the duct blaster was attached. When the NSOP is reached, the micromanometer displays the total system air flow.

Evaporator superheat[4]

Adequate superheat is important because the AC system's compressor will literally blow its gaskets if liquid refrigerant reaches its inlet. This is called "slugging." It happens when cooling coils are not absorbing enough heat to evaporate all of the liquid refrigerant into a gas before that refrigerant leaves the cooling coil on its way to the compressor. That's why cooling coils are set up to heat the refrigerant gas above

Note 4: Superheat is the degree to which the refrigerant is "superheated" beyond the saturation temperature for its current pressure inside the cooling coil (the evaporator—where the refrigerant evaporates). But more important than that definition is the context and *meaning* of the superheat measurement, which is what we've focused on in this guide.

In field practice, the refrigerant gas temperature and its pressure are measured not in the cooling coil, but instead as the refrigerant gas arrives at the inlet to the outdoor unit (the condenser). That's the most practical location to take the measurements—at the service port.

AIR CONDITIONING SYSTEMS - REFRIGERANT CHARGE

Check Numbers for Existing Systems	Description
5 to 10° F (Ideal)	**Evaporator Superheat (TXV systems only)**
15° to 30°F (Typical)	Target range of refrigerant superheat, measured at the inlet to the condensing unit (the outdoor unit). Less superheat than 5°F suggests there may be too much refrigerant in the system. More than 30°F of superheat suggests there may not be enough refrigerant and/or other significant problems which require diagnosis and repair. (All such problems waste energy and impair comfort)
Over 30°F (Significant problems)	
Consult manufacturer's installation manual	**Evaporator Superheat (Fixed orifice or capillary tube systems)** The appropriate superheat varies widely depending on load and mnaufacturer's design. It may be as high as 45° or as low as 5°F in normal operation, or those values could indicate a significant problem. Consult the manufacturer for appropriate superheat troubleshooting values.
Within 3°F of Mfrs target range (Ideal)	**Condenser Subcooling (TXV systems only)**
9 to 17° F (Typical)	Target range of refrigerant subcooling, measured at the refrigerant outlet from the AC condenser (outdoor unit). Between 9 and 17°F is typical—not optimal but not a major concern. Below 6°F the system has major problems—not enough refrigerant, or similar major problems. Above 21°F of subcooling means there may be too much refrigerant or similar major problems. (Superheat outside of the manufacturer's recommended range means energy is being wasted and comfort is needlessly impaired)
Under 6°F or Over 21°F (Significant problems)	

Table 5.11 Check numbers for evaluating installed air conditioning equipment

it's saturation temperature. "Superheating" the refrigerant gas is accomplished by holding it in the coil longer and forcing it to absorb more heat from the supply air. That extra heat makes certain that all the refrigerant is in a gaseous state before it leaves the coil. That way, no liquid will reach the compressor.

Measuring the evaporator superheat is the second of three measurements that tell the technician how effectively the AC equipment is operating (system air flow, evaporator superheat and condenser subcooling). Superheat measurement follows the determination of the supply air flow, because superheat depends on the cooling load—and the load depends on how much air is being cooled. So you need the supply air flow measurement in order to figure out if the superheat is too high or too low for the load.

The amount of superheat essentially indicates how well the refrigerant flow matches the current cooling load. But the appropriate range of superheat depends on the type of device which meters the refrigerant into the evaporator coil. There are two basic types: modulating valves or fixed devices. First we'll discuss what's normal for systems with modulating valves.

Systems with TXV's

Thermostatic expansion valves (called "TXV's") control the evaporator superheat within a relatively narrow range. Reasonable check numbers for TXV systems are superheat values of at least 5°F, but not much higher than about 10°F (or different values based on the manufacturer's instructions). In a TXV system, if the superheat is above the higher end of the target range, the system may not have enough refrigerant, or there may be some form of contaminant in the refrigerant such as moisture, or cruddy bits of corroded copper or dirt. Or there may be something clogging the system's refrigerant expansion valve, or its filter-dryer might be clogged, or you may be testing when there is a very low load on the system. (We need a pressure difference of at least 125 psi across the TXV to ensure adequate refrigerant flow. If the load is low, the pressure inside the evaporator coil may be too high to ensure full refrigerant flow.)

In any case, in a TXV system, when the superheat is above about 10°F there's not enough refrigerant flowing through the cooling coil. So the system needs servicing.

The most common reason for high superheat is that the system is not charged with enough refrigerant. That sometimes happens because of refrigerant leaks. But more frequently, the installing technician did not add enough refrigerant to fill the "line set" (the liquid line and suction line which connects the indoor cooling coil to the outdoor condensing unit). Manufacturers provide information about how much refrigerant should go into the condenser and evaporator, but they generally assume a short line set between those two components. (Usually the assumption is 25 ft). In most houses, the line set length is much longer—sometimes as long as 150 ft. If the technician did not add extra refrigerant to fully charge the line set as well as the evaporator coil, the system as a whole will not have enough refrigerant, and the superheat will be high.

When the superheat is below the lower end of the target range (below 5°F), there's not enough heat being absorbed by the refrigerant flowing through the cooling coil. That may be because there's too much refrigerant in the system, or because the supply air flow is too low. In either case, low superheat means there's a risk to the compressor, because the gas/liquid mixture in the coil is too close to its saturation temperature. The gas mixture could still contain some liquid when it reaches the compressor. The compressor would then try to compress that liquid and fail, blowing its seals and gaskets apart in a catastrophic failure.

Systems with fixed refrigerant metering devices

Less expensive AC systems don't usually have TX valves. Instead, they have either fixed-size orifices or capillary tubes which restrict the flow of refrigerant to the evaporator coil. The orifice is sized (or the length of the capillary tube is determined) by the desired refrigerant flow at some combination of AC load and refrigerant pressures that the manufacturer has decided will provide the best combination of capacity and efficiency over a wide range of operating conditions. But

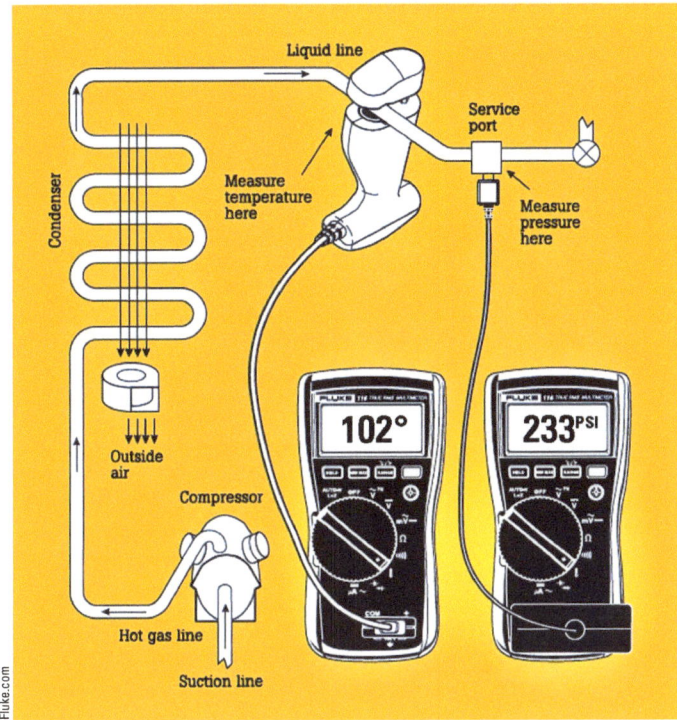

Fig. 5.22 Measuring subcooling using meters which don't have built-in refrigerant tables
Place the pipe clamp or Velcro probe on the liquid line. Note the liquid line's temperature. Then attach the pressure/vacuum module to a port on the liquid line and measure the liquid line pressure. Based on that pressure, determine at what temperature the refrigerant in the condenser would be saturated (by consulting the temperature-pressure chart for the refrigerant in use). The difference between the line temperature and the saturation temperature is the subcooling value.

because those operating conditions will vary so widely, and because the orifice or capillary tube has a fixed resistance to refrigerant flow, the range of superheat values in such systems will be very broad.

At high loads, the superheat can be as high as 45°F. At low loads, the superheat might fall as low as 5°F. So to know what's normal and expected for superheat in fixed orifice or "cap tube" systems, the technician must consult tables provided by the manufacturer of the equipment and the manufacturer of the specific refrigerant installed in the equipment.

Condenser subcooling[5]

Subcooling is important because as the refrigerant leaves the condenser, you want it be a liquid (and to remain a liquid) until it reaches the evaporator. If it is so warm that it flashes to a gas as it travels though the liquid line before it reaches the cooling coil, you've lost cooling capacity, and you will also have problems in the valve or capillary tube which meters the liquid into the coil. That's why the condenser is set up to subcool the refrigerant below its saturation temperature—after it leaves the condenser, refrigerant will not gain enough heat to flash to a gas before it reaches the cooling coil (unless the line lacks it's normal insulation).

Fixed orifice and cap tube systems - No need to check subcooling

If the system has a fixed orifice or a capillary tube refrigerant control device, there is no benefit to checking the subcooling at the condenser. The flow of refrigerant is not controllable, so the condenser subcooling is what it is, and there's no need to adjust it.

In TXV systems, on the other hand, measuring the condenser subcooling is necessary to check and adjust the charge.

Checking subcooling in TXV systems

In systems with TXV's, if the subcooling is below the target range (6°F or below) it means the refrigerant was not cooled enough as it passed through the condenser. That could be because there's not enough refrigerant in the system, or because of some other problem.

It's easy to check to see if air flow is blocked through the condenser, and to fix the problem. Just remove the obstruction. But more commonly, when subcooling is below the target range it's because the system does not have enough refrigerant, or because there's something blocking the flow such as a clogged filter-drier, or some form of dirt or corrosion inside the refrigerant circuit.

Note 5: Subcooling is the amount of cooling below the saturation temperature of the condensed refrigerant, based on it's average pressure while it's in the condenser. Again, this definition is correct, but not very useful. Understanding that definition is much less important than understanding what the measurements really mean in the context of your test-in evaluation.

Other common reasons for low refrigerant charge include a refrigerant leak, or because the original technician did not add enough refrigerant to the system to fill the line set, as discussed earlier.

When the subcooling is too high (either 3°F above the manufacturer's recommended range, or over 21°F), it means the refrigerant has been cooled too much as it passed through the condenser.

Excessive subcooling is seldom a result of excess condenser air flow (they rarely have too much air flowing through them). More likely, it's because there is too much refrigerant in the system.

With excess refrigerant, there's so much refrigerant condensing in the condenser that it can partly fill up with that liquid. Extra liquid in the condenser increases the resistance to refrigerant flow. That resistance makes the compressor work harder, wasting electricity. When the refrigerant charge is really excessive, the liquid resistance in the condenser is so high that the compressor could switch off automatically because its operating pressure is too high.

Significance of AC equipment measurements

Measurements of supply air flow and refrigerant superheat and subcooling are important, because they help you determine if the system is installed and operating properly.

In theory, any AC system installed in California in the last 10 years will have been carefully tested, and all of these measurements recorded and placed on file by the installing company. In practice, this seldom happens, even in new construction. And for systems which have been retrofitted, fewer than 6% of replacement installations have these measurements on file. That's one of many reasons why field measurements have consistently showed that installed systems in California, on average, deliver only 55% of their rated capacity. That shortfall also helps explain why wasteful oversizing is so common in all parts of the country. (If systems weren't oversized, they couldn't cool the house properly because they are usually so poorly installed). But the more pleasant consequence of that sad situation is that there are wonderful opportunities for improving comfort and reducing energy.

Fig. 5.23 Flow hood
Room-by room measurements of HVAC system supply air flow are necessary to explain comfort problems, and also to plan either remediation or system replacement.

Room-by room supply air flow measurements

Next come the measurements of supply air flow at each of the supply air grills in the HVAC system. When the homeowner knows there are comfort problems, these measurements are one of the easiest ways to explain the cause of those comfort problems.

These measurements are taken with a flow hood, as shown in figure 5.23. The flow from each diffuser is recorded, along with the dimensions of the diffuser itself. You'll need those flow rates and dimensions when you get back to the office to diagnose the extent of system problems, and to plan either remediation or system replacement. Some technicians prefer to note the dimensions and flow rates on the floor plan sketch that comes next in the list of tasks for the test-in visit.

Floor Plan Sketches and Data Gathering for Load Calculations

Increasingly, Home Performance Contracting firms use tablet computers. Technicians enter the data needed for heating and cooling load calculations directly into a load calculation program, while they are still on-site.

Real-time data entry and electronic sketches of the home's floor plans are certainly the wave of the future. These save time and reduce the opportunities for errors in communication. A "running total" load calculation in real time also provides immediate feedback to the technician gathering the data, which in turn allows early error correction.

But regardless of the method of data collection and data entry, here are some considerations and reminders for technicians gathering data for load calculations during the test-in visit.

Floor plan sketches

Dimensioned sketches of the floor plans of the house are helpful in estimating the cost of various aspects of the project, as well as for recording the key aspects of the home which govern the HVAC loads. In particular, keep in mind that at some point you'll need to know these items, for the load calculations. The floor plan sketches are an excellent place to record:

1. The compass orientation of the building. If you are in doubt, consult the aerial views on either Bing.com or Google Earth.)

2. The window locations and their dimensions.

3. Existing HVAC supply air diffusers and return air grills, and their dimensions and current air flow rates.

4. Location of exhaust fans, such as clothes dryers, and kitchen and toilet exhausts.

Fig. 5.24 Floor plan sketch with key data for load calculations
These days, such data is often recorded on tablet computers so it can be entered in load calculation programs directly. But hand sketches also work fine. Simply record the orientation of the building and dimensions of windows and walls—the key variables for heating & cooling loads.

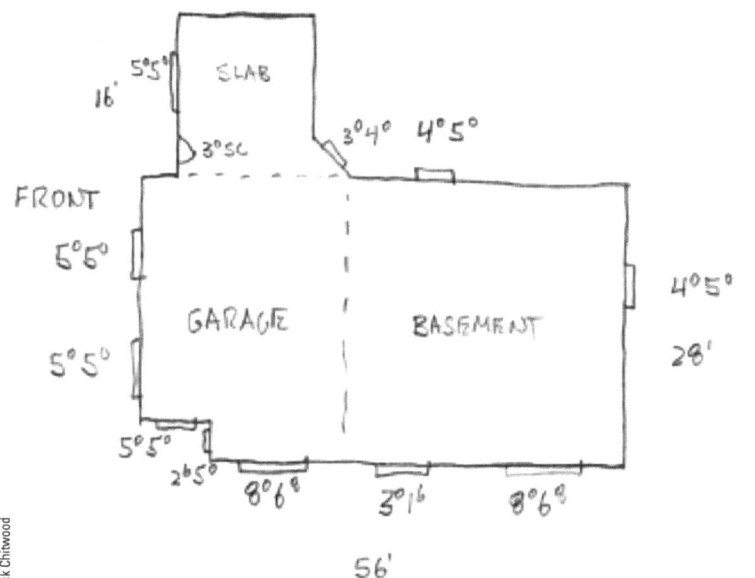
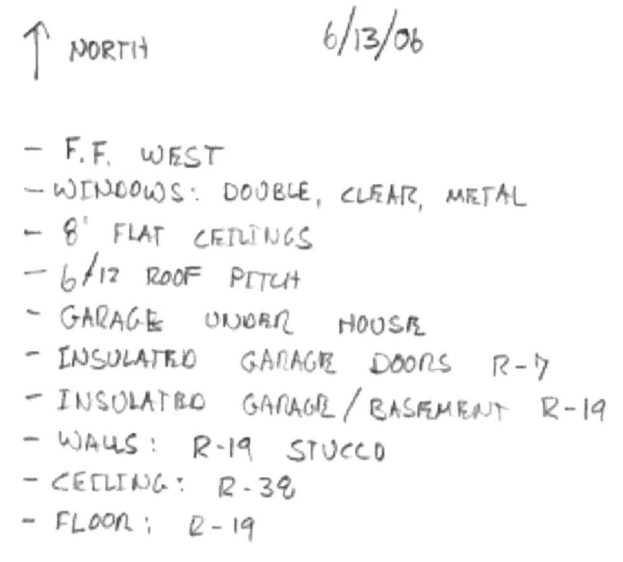

Photos, photos and more photos

The more photos, the better. It's quick and easy to take photos, compared to the time needed to make detailed sketches and notes. In particular, remember to take photos of:

1. Each exterior elevation of the house, from the outside.

2. Each exterior wall, from the inside, showing the location and relative size of windows and doors.

3. All combustion appliance zones

4. Each major component of the HVAC system, from a distance showing the whole installation context and its relative condition of repair, and another shot, close up, of the nameplate data (For that one, don't forget to use the "macro" setting on your camera to make sure the close-up shot is clear enough to read the nameplate data)

5. The water heater, from a distance showing the installation, and also a close-up shot of the name plate

6. The attic. Take several overall shots, and at least one shot which clearly shows the type, thickness and extent of attic insulation.

7. The crawl space, if any. Take photos with enough detail to indicate the need for repair, reinsulation, moisture remediation, drainage, pest removal or structural repair, if any.

8. Photos of any conditions you believe will have to be addressed during the retrofit, such as disconnected ducts, gaps or cracks in exterior walls, open soffits, lack of toilet exhaust fans, moisture damage, deteriorated siding or roofing, exterior drainage, pest infestation, etc.)

All of these will be helpful for both the proposal, and for planning the actual work.

Room-by-room data collection for room-by-room supply air requirements

Each of the ACCA-approved, Manual-J-compliant HVAC load calculation programs asks the technician to enter the house characteristics in a different way. But they all end up needing the information outlined on the data input sheets developed by the CPBCA. Consult those sheets for a reminder of the essential elements needed for load calculations. But here are a few tips and traps about gathering data for heating and cooling load calculations:

1. Room-by-room data gathering is fundamental to achieving comfort. The loads in each conditioned space can vary widely. To design a system which will really achieve comfort, it's critical to know how much supply air each room needs. To know that, you'll need to know the load elements in each room—not just in the house as a whole. In particular, the locations and sizes of windows, and lighting.

2. Window characteristics are critical to load calculations. Windows are a very large contributor to heating and cooling loads. So it's important to know what's really installed, rather than just guessing. In most of California, single-glazed windows are quite common. But if the windows are double-glazed, they transmit much less heat, and if they have a low emissivity coating, they transmit even less heat. If you assume the windows are all single-glazed and it turns out they are in fact double-glazed with a low-e coating, your load calculations will result in the hugely oversized equipment that is so problematic for comfort and energy efficiency. So be sure to check if the windows are double-glazed or single-glazed, and if they have a low-e coating. (See fig. 5.25 for an example of an instrument which helps you measure the reduction in solar heat gain achieved by a given glazing system.) The larger the net window area, the more important it is to have them properly characterized.

OPEN WINDOW = 100% SOLAR HEAT GAIN (SHGC = 1.00)   CLOSED WINDOW = 58.2% SOLAR HEAT GAIN (SHGC = 0.582)

Fig. 5.25 Solar power meter meaasures solar heat gain coefficient (SHGC)
The meter measures the amount of solar energy coming through the window opening when the sash is up. That value is set as 100%. Then the sash is lowered while the meter is held in the exact same position. The display shows the approximate beneficial effect of the glazing system in reducing the solar heat gain. In this case, the net solar heat gain coefficient of the glazing is 58.2. In other words, 41.8% of the solar heat is excluded by this glazing system. Devices like this one help you avoid assumptions which would oversize equipment and lead to comfort problems and energy waste.

3. Floors over crawl spaces: keep in mind they are like exterior walls. In the colder California climate zones, crawl spaces are common. Although they do not add much load to the air conditioning system, they do face winter winds and temperatures. So for heating load calculations, make sure you know the layers of construction and insulation, if any, which separate the crawl space from the first floor.

Lighting & Appliance Inventory

Lighting power is a large component of a typical home's annual electrical consumption. Also, during most of the year in the warmer climate zones of California, the lighting power consumes power twice: once to light the space, and a second time when the heat generated by those light must be removed by the air conditioning system.

Even more important, the air leakage through "can lights" is another waste of energy, especially when they penetrate the ceiling between the house and the attic. Around and through those fixtures, air leaks into and out of the home.

So for all of these reasons, it's important to make an inventory of the number of lighting fixtures, the wattage of the bulbs they contain and their exact locations. And you'll need to know the total number of can lights which penetrate the ceiling between the home and the attic because you're probably going to want to replace them before you insulate the attic.

Usually, it's less expensive to replace leaky can lights with modern air-tight fixtures rated for full contact with insulation rather than retrofitting them with air-tight, insulated covers. Such custom covers require a lot of time, expense and liability risk compared to simply replacing the fixtures with units designed by the manufacturer to be both air tight and safe when buried under the attic's insulation.

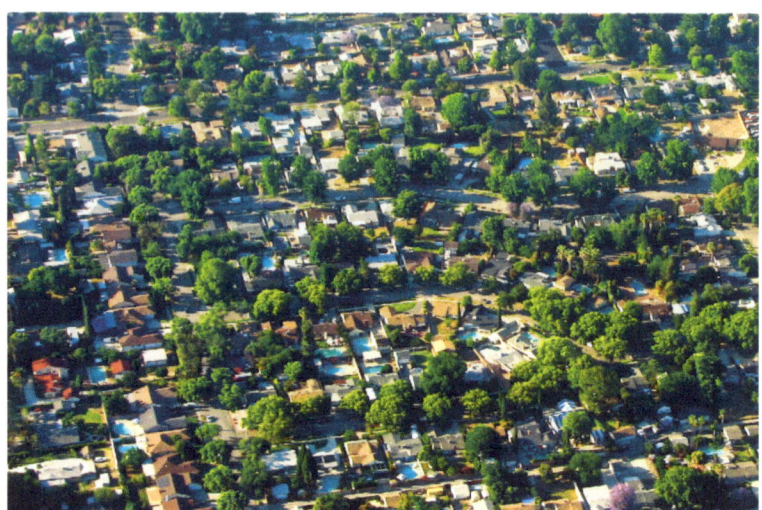

Swimming Pool Pumps, Sweeps & Lighting
By Steve Easley

When we think about building performance and making homes more energy efficient, Home Performance Contractors gravitate towards making improvements in the building envelope, the HVAC systems, water heating and maybe even appliances and lighting. Surprisingly one of the biggest energy users can be swimming pool pumps. They are huge energy users and are not always on the radar screen of Home Performance Contractors.

In California there are over 1½ million in-ground residential swimming pools. Pools require filtering. Pumps have to circulate the pool water to filter it. These pumps can have 1 to 2 horsepower motors that run 5-6 hours per day. PG&E engineers estimate that the power required to run these pool pumps simultaneously in California is the equivalent of six (6) 500 megawatt power plants!

Pool pumps

A typical pool pump draws about 1,500 to 2,500 watts. These motors often run 4 ½ to 6 hours a day, 7 days a week, 365 days a year. That's 10.5 kilowatt hours per day, or about 3,800 kWh per year. Many pools also have pool sweeps with booster motors than can add another 1,200 to 1,500 Watts, and these run about 3 -1/2 hour per day or 1,500 kWh per year. The grand total for pool pump operation can be over 5,300 kWh per year. This can account for 1/3 or more of total home electricity usage, when the house has a swimming pool.

Fig. 5.27 Pools, pools, pools
The baseline electrical load of many homes is high, because of the power consumption of pool pumps, sweeps and lights. Assessing these loads—and the retrofit opportunities—should be part of your test-in visit.

It's also important to keep in mind that California has a tiered electric rate structure that penalizes high energy use. The first few kilowatt hours we use are in the lower cost tier, at 12¢ or 14¢ per KWH. Pools with constantly-running pumps and sweeps consume that low-cost power, forcing the owner to use high-cost power for lights, clothes dryers, dishwashers and all the other electrical appliances. Higher tiered electrical rates can be 25¢ to 40¢ per kWh.

It's easy for a pool to consume 5,000 kWh a year at 25 cents per kWh. The result is a whopping $1,250 per year for pump operation. Even smaller systems can use 2,600 kWh a year plus another 1,500 kWh for the sweep. These loads also have a strong effect on the State's electrical capacity. Pool pumps are typically running during the peak hours of the day, placing a big burden on the entire electric grid.

Some pool-related electrical consumption can be reduced by education alone. The owner may especially appreciate this service when the Contractor is charging for the extensive work required during the test-in visit. No-cost power reduction strategies include:

1. Check out the time clock. Make sure the pool pump and sweep are not running longer than they need to, especially in the winter, when lower water temperatures and fewer hours of sunlight naturally reduce algae growth. The pool industry recommends 6 to 8 hours per day to ensure all the water gets at least one pass through the filter daily. PG&E did a survey of pool owners and found that their customers average about 4 ½ hours per day for filter pumps and their pool sweeps 3 ½ hours per day.

2. Be sure that the pool filters are cleaned regularly and replaced when worn out.

3. Also make sure that skimmer baskets are kept clean, reducing the flow restrictions which lead to needless power consumption.

Potential retrofit solutions - Variable speed pumps

There are now high efficiency, variable speed, low flow pumps that are electronically controlled and can save 50 to 75% on electricity bills. The traditional pool pump motor is a single speed induction motor and has typical efficiencies of 35 to 70%... not very efficient. Since these also operate at high speed, single-speed pumps consume more energy than variable speed pumps.

Modern variable speed motors have permanent magnets and are similar to the electric motors used in hybrid cars. These motors have efficiencies in the 90% range. Also, they can vary their speed and water flow rates. High efficiency, variable speed pool pump motors running on low speeds draw between 180 and 400 watts. They average about 2 kWh per day… compared to between 10 and 12 kWh per day for the typical high speed pool pump. Some of the efficiency gain comes from motor efficiency. But the major gain is because power consumption goes down at a nonlinear rate as you reduce pump speed and water flow. When you cut the flow rate and the speed of the motor in half... the power consumption is cut to 1/8th of the power consumed at full speed.

Since you cut the flow in half you now have to run the pump twice as long to get the same filtration. But the net result is you are using ¼ of the energy compared to an outdated pool pump. Bottom line— you run your pump at a slower speed for longer periods of time, but it's far more efficient and costs less to operate. Also variable speed pumps are higher quality motors, so they last longer. Manufacturers estimate a 15 year life, based on advanced aging tests.

Other advantages are that variable-speed pumps are very quiet compared to standard pumps. And they put less stress on the pool's piping systems because they are working at lower pressures and velocities. Finally, the longer filtration time (combined with slower water velocity through the filter) provides more effective filtration.

Pool sweeps

Another potential energy improvement is to configure the variable-speed pump so that you eliminate a 2nd pump for the pool sweep. This could save an additional 1,000 to 1,500 kWh per year.

Alternatively, robotic cleaners can also reduce energy use by eliminating the booster pump motor of the pool sweep. Robotic cleaners rely on a self contained low voltage motors to propel and sweep the pool. These are very efficient compared to the traditional sweeps, which use a motor to pump water for propulsion and cleaning.

Pool lights

Another big potential energy user is the decorative pool lighting. Pool lights are 300 to 500 watts. Often, pool lights are used for dramatic effect, to supplement landscape lighting. During the test-in visit, it's important to ask home owners how many hours per day they use their pool lights.

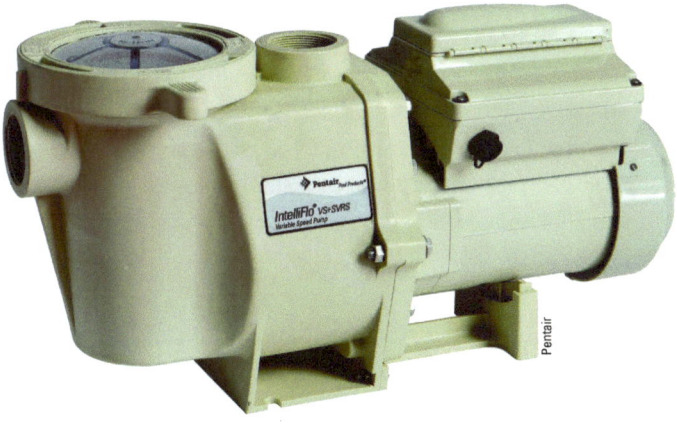

Fig. 5.28 Variable-speed Pool Pumps
In one recent project, the original constant-speed pool pump drew 2000 to 2200 Watts. After replacement by a variable-speed model similar to that shown here, the pump draw was measured at 220 to 250 Watts—for the same filtration duty.

Fig. 5.29 Exterior lighting
Ornamental pool lighting often compliments landscape lighting. Both provide opportunities for energy reduction, through relamping with LED fixtures.

Consider replacing the traditional pool lighting with LED lamps. A traditional pool light is 300-500 watts. New LED lights use 70 watts and last much longer. (You can even program them to change colors.)

Pool pumps and filters may be outside your scope

Reducing the energy consumed in the pool may or may not be something you want to include in your Home Performance Contracting Proposal. If not, refer home owners to knowledgeable pool contractors that have a solid understanding of variable speed pump technology and have the skills necessary to install and commission a system that works as intended.

Regardless of who designs and installs the retrofit, it's important that any replacement pumps for in-ground residential pools meet California requirements, which are described in Title 20 and 24. In particular:

1. **Pool filter pumps §150 (p)** – All residential pool pumps used to filter water must be in the CEC Appliance Efficiency Database.

2. **Multi-speed pool filter pumps §150 (p), §1605.3 (5) (B)** Pool filter pumps with a "Total Horsepower" of one or larger must be multi-speed (two-speed, three-speed, or variable-speed).

3. **Controls §114 (b)** – A time switch or similar control mechanism must be installed with the pool filter pump to be set or programmed to run only during the off-peak periods. Pool filter pumps 1 Total HP or larger, must be installed with controls capable of defaulting to a low-speed setting after running at a higher speed for some other purpose, like running a cleaner or water feature.

Chapter 6
Tips & Traps for Proposal Preparation

Fig. 6.1 Generating your proposal

Your Proposal

An effective Home Performance Contracting proposal will:

1. **Result in a signed contract** which you know will...
2. **Satisfy the client's needs and wants**, in ways which...
3. **Save significant amounts of energy** and...
4. **Make a profit** for your company.

Measured energy savings are what distinguish HPC projects from other home improvement projects. That's why it's so common to focus on that 3rd point above. But you don't get the opportunity to save that energy or to make a profit unless you get the job. That's why the most effective proposals have the three-part structure described by figure 6.2.

The effectiveness of the 1st and 2nd parts of the proposal are what nearly always sell the job, and sell it at a price which allows you to make a profit. It's a lot of up front work to understand the customers needs and wants so clearly that you can articulate them and connect them to the measurements and observations of your test-in visit. But that connection between needs, wants and measured results is what makes your proposal better than your competition, which in turn allows you to win a higher percentage of projects at economically-sustainable prices.

Part I - Client's Concerns, Needs and Wants

In the first section of your proposal simply restate what you heard from the client about their needs and wants with respect to comfort, energy, appliance replacement and home repairs.

This should not be an exhaustive essay. You're simply generating a bulleted list of concerns that need to be addressed by your proposal. This section is very brief—a few sentences or one page at most. It demonstrates that:

a. I listened carefully to what you said, and I didn't forget any of your concerns.

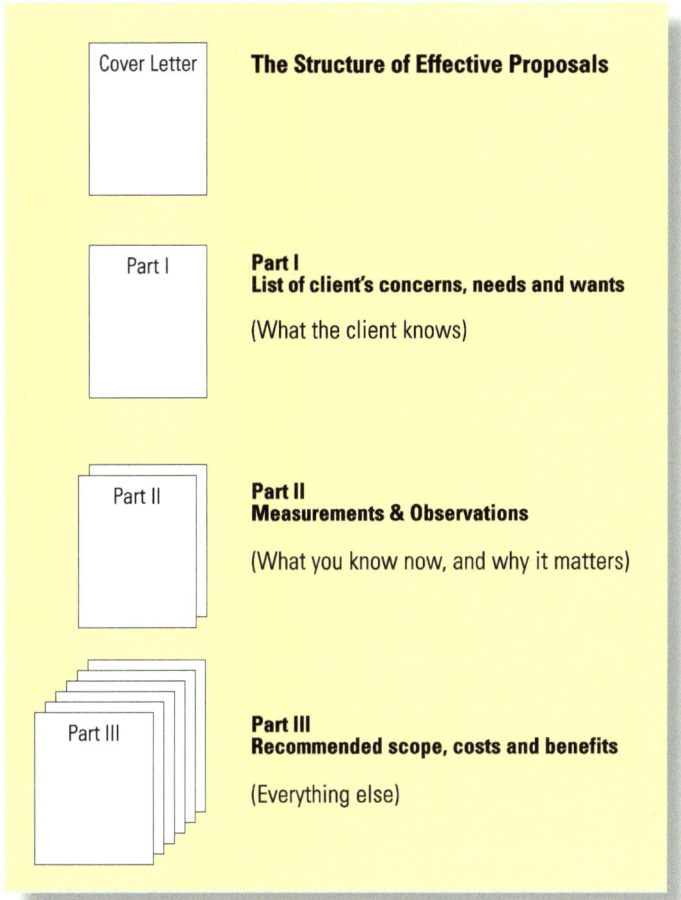

Fig. 6.2 Suggestions for proposal structure

b. I understand each of your concerns clearly, and I understand what's most important from your perspective.

A clear, simple list of concerns, needs and wants also helps avoid last-minute changes. The list often reminds the client of other issues or other priorities that may have come to mind after your test-in visit. This initial list is the basis of the project's scope and costs, so it's important that the list be complete, and that you understand the client's priorities within that list.

Good and bad examples of items on a list of concerns

In section I, you don't want lots of words, but you do want enough detail so both you and the client remember what the issue is, and where and when it occurs. Here are some examples how three different Performance Contractors might write up the same items of concern to the homeowner.

Not enough detail
- Bathroom exhaust fan problems

OK. That's a start. But what are these problems, exactly? Which bathroom exhaust fan is bad and in what way? How extensive are these problems—annoying, energy-wasting or life-threatening? Without more detail, neither the client nor your work crew will have any clear picture of what the project needs to accomplish to remove these problems and address the client's concerns.

Details which don't help you understand the concern
- Master bath fan model B-1622, 120v, 0.4 Amp humidity-initiated exhaust fan is not installed in accordance with manufacturer's instructions and has been damaged. Improper flow, moisture and odor problems. Fan balance issue also needs to be considered for night time operation.

What sort of installation shortcomings are there? What are the moisture and odor problems? Is the flow to high or too low? Why would it matter? Why would any homeowner care about fan balance, for heavens sake? Also... what does "be considered" mean, exactly?

At least we know where the problem occurs, and there's more detail in this description. But none of it helps the owner and contractor remember the nature, extent and urgency of the problem. This description is nearly as useless as ones which are too brief, even if this one sounds more impressively technical.

Just right
- Master bath exhaust fan problems. Corrugated aluminum exhaust duct work is too long, and has been stepped on in the attic, crushing it. Excessively long duct run and crushed duct has the exhaust air flow to nearly zero. Consequently, excess humidity and odors remain in the bathroom, with the result that paint is peeling and microbial growth is visible on the ceiling. Also, the low-cost fan is noisy, and wakes up Ms. Client when the fan turns on at night. Both fan and exhaust duct should be replaced to provide low-noise and adequate air flow. New fan and duct work will also allow the master bath to comply with current codes and best practices.

This description uses more words, but each one is relevant to the issues at hand. To judge the effectiveness of Part I of your proposal (the client concern list) ask yourself these questions as you read through your list:

1. Does the list describe all the issues raised by the client?

2. Can somebody who is not familiar with the house understand what each issue is, where it occurs, why it probably matters to the client and what probably needs to happen to correct it?

Part II - Measurements and Observations

Part II is where you connect what the client knows to what you have learned about the house during your test-in visit. To make that connection in the most effective way, use the measurements you've taken, along with photographs of specific conditions. Measurements and photos are convincing evidence that you understand the problems. As the client reads this list, it should become quite clear why your Part III (proposed scope, costs and benefits) includes the items you have selected.

Part II is more extensive than Part I, because you'll need to explain a few things, and you'll also be using photos and perhaps graphs to save words and help make the explanation clear. So there are usually many more pages in Part II than in Part I.

As in part I, the writing needs be both clear and accurate. Beyond accuracy, your text should always provide evidence of the need for the solution you have in mind.

Here are two ways to describe the same issue. The first description makes no connection between what you know (the measurements) and what the customer knows (she's uncomfortable and pays a lot for air conditioning). The second example does a better job of making that connection, while also pointing towards a solution.

Measurements without meaning

"The whole-house leakage was measured at nine (9) ACH at 50 Pascals. Duct leakage to the exterior was measured at approximately 32.7% of the supply air flow @ 25Pa. These are high values."

This description has numbers, which proves that you took some measurements. But why do these number matter? How do they explain the concerns that the customer has told you about? What's an "ACH?" is 9 a high number or a low number? What's the average air leakage for other homes? What does "high" mean in this context... is "high" a good thing or a bad thing? This description adds confusion rather than reducing it.

Measurements which explain problems the customer cares about

Here's a description that takes those same test results and makes a better connection between what you know and what the customer knows.

"Our test data shows that on average, about half of the air in this home leaks out every hour. (0.45 air changes per hour under natural conditions) That amount of leakage is about twice as much as average houses of similar size. The incoming air which replaces that leakage must be heated or cooled to the indoor conditions, which helps explain why the heating and cooling bills are so high."

"Our test data also show that about 33% of the HVAC system's air leaks out of the duct system and out to the weather. (Total supply air is about 800 cfm for this 3-ton system, but duct leakage to the weather was measured at 265 cfm.) In other words, about 33% of your conditioned air is being wasted."

"Duct leakage also explains why the Mother-in-law apartment is never comfortable. The duct that leads to Mrs. Mom's apartment is not sealed to the main supply trunk line (see photo number 6.xx below) Since that connection leaks, the system blows a great deal of conditioned air into the attic instead of into her apartment."

"Our proposed project will provide year-round comfort for the entire home at much lower energy costs, even after you adjust the thermostat to more comfortable temperatures."

Fig. 6.2 Photos, photos, photos
*In Part II of the proposal, photographs provide compelling visual evidence which helps the customer understand **why** problems must be fixed to provide safety, comfort and savings. The more photos, the better.*

Horizontal side wall vent does not provide safe exhaust of combustion gasses

Open gaps allow expensive conditioned air to escape the living space

Some old wiring presents a fire hazard. All wiring problems must be fixed.

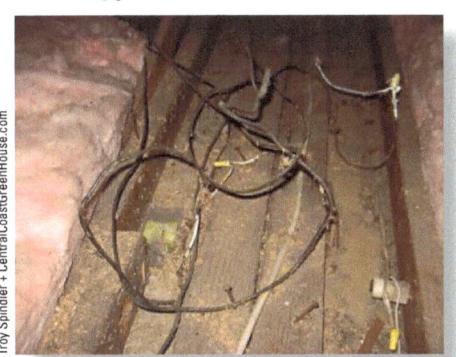

Part III - Project Scope, Costs and Benefits

The project scope, costs and benefits will vary widely, depending on the opportunities of each home, and the budget challenges for its owners. Also, the amount of detail at this stage will depend on your business model. When deciding what to include in your proposal, here are a few tips and traps to consider.

Safety first, last and always

"First, do no harm" That's the most important part of the Hippocratic Oath taken by doctors. Home Performance Contractors will be making major repairs to the home, similar in some respects to major surgery on the human body. And like major surgery, things can go wrong in spite of the best of intentions, if you're not careful.

There's an obvious moral imperative to keep both workers and home occupants safe. So as you generate the proposal, keep in mind that there are a few non-negotiable safety features that must be included in the work plan, and therefore in the cost of the project.

Combustion appliance safety measures

If natural draft combustion appliances like furnaces, water heaters and space heaters will remain in the home after the project is completed, they must have adequate and unrestricted supply of combustion air. And the zone they occupy (the Combustion Appliance Zone - CAZ) must be either very large, or vented directly to the weather as outlined in chapter 5. This is likely to be time-consuming and costly, but it's mandatory. After the home is air-sealed during a Home Performance project, natural draft appliances won't be safe without extensive modification.

So instead, you might consider replacing the water heater and furnace with a high-efficiency, sealed-combustion water heater along with an air handler with a hot water heating coil and a DX cooling coil. This configuration is usually called a "combined hydronic air handler", or "hot water furnace." Given the amount of work needed to make natural draft appliances safe in a tight home, a new sealed-combustion water heater with a hydronic air handler may turn out

Fig. 6.4 Replace knob-and-tube wiring
With knob-and-tube wiring it's not safe to properly insulate the attic. Old wiring connections heat up under insulation, creating a fire hazard. Replace such wiring with modern, code-compliant electrical work before covering it with insulation.

to be the lowest-cost safe alternative. And of course new equipment, when properly installed, will be more efficient and save energy, which existing appliances will not, even after they are made safe.

Replacement of knob-and-tube wiring in the attic

It's not safe to bury knob-and-tube wiring under a layer of insulation. That would be a fire hazard. So if the home has such wiring in the attic, make sure you include the cost of wiring replacement in your project.

Correction of wiring deficiencies

Apart from knob-and-tube wiring, older houses often have other wiring deficiencies which must be corrected to keep the occupants safe. When your project uncovers wiring deficiencies, you have an obligation to either fix them, or to inform the homeowner of the problem so that others can fix the problem.

Replacement or safe modification of can lights

Older can lights that penetrate any ceiling allow a great deal of energy-wasting air leakage. Also, any of can lights which stick up into the attic will be buried under insulation at the end of your project.

To avoid a fire hazard, older can light fixtures must either be replaced with modern fixtures which are both airtight and rated for full contact with insulation, or covered with airtight, insulated enclosures that the original manufacturer will agree is safe.

Nearly always, the more certain and less costly alternative is to replace older fixtures with modern airtight, IC-rated units. Also, when can lights must be replaced, it's a good time to consider replacement with either airtight compact fluorescent fixtures (CFL's) or even light-emitting diode fixtures (LED's). But regardless of the replacement or modification method chosen, for the fixtures which stick up into the attic, heat buildup is a safety issue. You will be installing a great deal of insulation in the attic, so don't forget to include the cost of replacing or safely modifying can lights so they can be buried safely under that insulation.

Beware of equipment replacement without load reduction

Sometimes, the customer's original motivation for calling a Home Performance Contractor is to replace an old AC unit or old furnace with a modern "high efficiency" model because the old unit is at the end of it's useful life.

Customers usually expect that modern equipment alone will save lots of energy. You know it won't, for all the complex reasons discussed in chapters 2,3,4 and 5. But if all the customer really wants to do is replace equipment, and the test-in interview has confirmed that preference, it might be better to back away from the project than to be forced into a project you know will neither improve comfort nor save energy. Alternatively, you might consider a more bold approach: guarantee the energy-saving result—but only if the customer is willing to fund all of the measures you know will need to work together to achieve energy savings. Here are some suggestions for those clients who cannot fund everything at once.

When the project must be "phased for budget reasons"

A full Home Performance retrofit project is not a low-cost investment. Anticipating homeowner sticker shock, the HPC technician may be tempted to present the project in phases, so the homeowner can finance the project over time, as budgets allow. That's not an all-bad approach, but it's important to keep in mind that to ensure safety and ensure measurable energy and comfort improvements, some parts of the project will have to remain together. Specifically, if you need to consider proposing a phased project, here are some recommendations for what needs to stay together, and what can be separated without running a safety risk or damaging the success of the project.

Phase 1 - Consumer education and base-load electrical reduction

a. Low-cost consumer education (eg: Fans don't cool the house—they only cool people. So it makes no sense to run fans if nobody's home, etc.)

b. Lighting replacement with CFL fixtures

c. Replace power strips with "smart strips" which automatically turn off accessories when computers or the TV is switched off.

d. Replace major electrical appliances with energy-efficient models (clothes washer and dryer, refrigerator and dishwasher)

Phase 2 - Enclosure and HVAC (Health, safety and comfort)

a. Crawl space & drainage remediation

b. Any necessary siding & roof repair

c. Air sealing (Crawl space, plus the assembly which separates the house from the attic)

d. HVAC equipment and water heater replacement or remediation, plus air distribution system replacement or remediation

e. Insulation (attic, crawl space and duct work)

f. Window replacement (if the budget allows)

Phase 3 - Supplemental renewable energy systems

a. Solar PV generation

b. Solar hot water

Window replacement and renewable energy systems

Note the order in which the phases are arranged, with windows and renewable energy at the end of the list of priorities. Often the original motivation for the homeowner's interest in Home Performance is an eagerness to either replace windows or to install some form of renewable energy generation such as solar photovoltaic panels or solar hot water panels.

These are big investments that, unfortunately, seldom provide an attractive return in either cash or improved comfort. But that does not stop them from being very appealing to many of us.

If you need to respond to the customers' desire for these features, you might consider separating the cost for them out from the rest of the project, in case the customer has sticker shock when considering the project as a whole.

Chapter 6... Proposal Preparation

Chapter 7

Proposal Presentation, Discussion And Adjustment

Fig 7.1 Making the connection
Success depends on explaining why and how your proposal meets the customer's needs. Your measurements and your on-site observations provide assurance that you really understand those needs, and that you have the solutions to meet them.

Presenting & Adjusting Your Proposal

Each company and each salesperson will have different ways to present the Home Performance Contracting Proposal. There are many models for managing this delicate discussion, and all of them can achieve the primary goal: agreement on the scope and cost of the contract.

But to satisfy the other goals of the Performance Contracting business, there are four best practices can which help you and the client agree on a contract is reasonable in cost and profitable, and which will provide year-round comfort at greatly reduced energy cost. Successful Performance Contractors make the connection between what the customer knows and what the Performance Contractor has learned about the house. Specifically:

1. **Describe how test-in measurements help explain what the customer has observed and experienced.** Your customer's concerns are always the center of a successful project; first, last and always. Your test-in measurements and observations provide assurance that you really understand those concerns.

2. **Explain how your proposed project scope will meet your customer's stated needs and wants**, and also how your project will correct any problems you noted and discussed with the customer during your test-in visit.

3. **Confirm the customers' correct understanding of potential solutions to the problems and challenges of the home**—but also tactfully correct any misimpressions. Ensure that the customer now really understands what saves energy and provides comfort, and what does not.

4. **Be responsive to customers needs for budget adjustment**—but not in ways which compromise the essential elements of Home Performance Contracting: safety, comfort and energy reduction.

Connect Customer Concerns to Test-in Results

Performance Contracting is more effective than other home energy improvements because it relies on measured results. As you present your proposal, demonstrate why measurements are so important. Take the time to describe, briefly, how the measurements taken your test-in visit explain the problems that the customer has been concerned about in the past. For example, here are two ways to describe your test-in results:

1. **Distracting technospeak:** "Mr. Jones, our blower door test showed that the air exchange rate of your home is 9.6 at 50 Pascals. The Pascal is named for Blaise Pascal, a famous French Mathematician in the 17th century. We use those units for our test, even though in this country we usually use the old English inch-pound system, which for pressure would be inches of water column. But in Home Performance Contracting we use the metric system—at least for pressure. In any case, that rate of air exchange wastes energy, even in metric units. So we propose air-sealing your home to bring down the air exchange rate to something we can all be proud of."

2. **Connecting results to customer concerns**: "Mr. Jones, remember how you told me that your Mother's room always seems too cold in the winter and too hot in the summer? Well, our blower door testing shows that her wing of your house leaks air at a rate of about one air change per hour. In other words, to keep her comfortable the heating and cooling system has to cool and heat all that leakage air every hour. That amount of air leakage is about three times the typical leakage rate of other homes in California. You can keep her more comfortable (and use less energy than you do now) by air sealing the building enclosure. Air sealing saves energy by reducing the air infiltration load on the heating & AC systems. It's like closing the refrigerator door instead of leaving it open." Here's another set of contrasting approaches to describing the results and implications or air flow measurements:

3. **Confusing data** "Mrs. Jones, remember when we used our flow hood to measure the air flowing into each room and our flow plate to measure the air flow through the furnace? Well, those are accurate to about ±7% of actual flow. After we correct actual cfm to standard cfm's, we find that the mass flow is about 60% of target. Also the living room only gets 45.6 cfm's while the bathroom gets 87.2 cfm's. No wonder your utility bills are so high! We'll fix that."

4. **Useful information** "Mrs. Jones, we know you're concerned about summer cooling costs. So we measured the air flow to each room and the total air flow through your HVAC system. Without full air flow, the system can't actually deliver the heating and cooling capacity that the equipment is designed to produce. Our measurements show that your system is only delivering 60% of it's rated air flow. The other 40% is lost to leakage out of the duct connections and lost because of resistance caused by twists and turns. Because of the way the system is designed and installed, you're paying to move and to heat and cool 100% of the air, but the system is only delivering 60% of what you're paying for.

Building science and HVAC jargon are just confusing and annoying to normal people. The average customer just wants to make problems go away and save money. The discussion should begin with what the customer has said is important, and then use the measurements to help the customer understand why the problems are happening.

Relevant and Supportable Project Scope

Performance Contracting Projects often require a very broad scope for successful results. So they sometimes cost the same or more than popular non-energy home improvements such as bathroom and kitchen upgrades. Whenever costs are near or above other benchmarks the customer may have in mind, it's important for that customer to understand why the costs are what they are, and that the costs are actually quite low compared to the benefits.

Unlike kitchen and bathroom upgrades, most successful Home Performance Projects save money and are even "cash-flow positive" every month. In other words, after the project is complete the owners' monthly costs go down—not up. That includes the cost of any loans necessary to finance the project. The result is an appealing prospect any customer: better comfort and a more valuable home—for less money per month than what they currently pay. Plus, many customers like the fact that energy improvements conserve resources for future generations. The same can't be said for kitchen and bathroom improvements.

All the same, when dollars are large, each item in the cost proposal needs an explanation. And those explanations are most convincing when supported by relevant evidence. Namely:

1. A clear connection to the customer's needs and wants, and...

2. ...objective and repeatable measurements which ensure that the expected benefits will be achieved.

For example, consider these two ways to describe the scope of a proposed project:

1. Trust me—I'm a professional: "Mr. Jones, to air-seal the house, install insulation, replace the HVAC system and hot water heater, the cost will be $25,600. Assuming you can get a loan for the full amount, our computerized building energy model (which complies with California's Title 24 energy regulations and is endorsed by the Air Conditioning Contractor's Association) tells me you'll have your money back in about 23 years.

2. We understand your concerns, here's what we recommend and why we know it will work: "Mr. Jones, I know that comfort has been a real issue in the summertime for your mother. And that you've mentioned that utility bills are putting a strain on the monthly budget. Even so, we're suggesting a large project, and here's why. First, we'll reduce the overall heating and cooling

loads by about 35%. We'll do that by air-sealing your home and adding insulation. Reducing the loads will let us take out the existing HVAC system and design one which is matched to the lower load, and then install it so you don't lose air to leaky duct work. The indoor temperature will stay between 70 and 73° year round. Also, because the new mechanical system will be twice as efficient as your existing system, the net effect is that your heating-cooling bills will go down by about 70% each month. That means you can afford the cost of the loan to pay for the project, and still save a few dollars per month beyond the cost of paying off the loan. We know this will be so, because we have measurements and utility data from more than 10 houses like yours. Because we always hit our targets for air tightness and HVAC installation quality, we've always delivered the energy savings we've promised—or better."

Supportable project scope

Here's a good general rule to follow when preparing to discuss your proposal with your customer: be ready to explain why each and every item is in your proposal.

If you can't explain to yourself why each item is essential to meeting the customers stated needs, either take out that item—or take the time to figure out how and why it really is essential to meeting the customer's goals for your proposed project.

Here's a second useful general rule. Make sure that every item of concern that the customer has described to you is addressed by an item in your proposal. If you don't have items in your proposal that address each of the customer's concerns, then perhaps you've left out something important and you need to re-think the proposal.

Responsible Budget Responsiveness

In any consumer business, there's a natural resistance when total project costs become clear. This is especially true with Performance Contracting because the projects are large, and because the customer may have begun with the impression that by simply changing out equipment, energy savings would happen automatically.

So to stay in business, every Performance Contractor must deal effectively with initial consumer misunderstandings and the resulting cost pressures. As you respond to the natural pressure to reduce costs in your proposed project, keep in mind that some components are more essential than others.

Big budget reductions without big consequences

Often, the initial motivation for a Performance Contracting project is to reduce the monthly energy bills by replacing windows or installing renewable energy features like solar photovoltaic panels or solar hot water panels. But those are seldom the big energy savers that homeowners imagine them to be. Removing these from the budget often makes the rest of the project much more economically practical.

But if the customer really wants those features, it's certainly possible to install the balance of the project with connections for renewable energy generation, so it's easier to install those features later, after their costs become more in line with the benefits they provide.

Smaller budget reductions

Appliance replacement is another area where energy savings don't always balance the costs. A new kitchen range or a new clothes washer will certainly save energy, but not very much compared to the more essential aspects of the Home Performance project.

On the other hand, replacing the hot water heater with a high-efficiency, sealed combustion model is usually the least-cost way to keep the house safe after it is made more air-tight. (The alternative is to vent the combustion appliance zone, and in most houses, that's an expensive and awkward process.)

Also, if an appliance is near the end of it's useful life, it's usually wise to replace it as part of a Home Performance Project, because skilled workers will be on-site rather than just an appliance delivery crew from the local discount store. The appliance will be installed correctly and safely, and early replacement can avoid emergency replacement when the old appliance fails at an awkward time. And speaking about refrigerators in particular, if the unit was installed before 1993, chances are good that by replacing it, the new refrigerator's energy use will be less than half that of the old unit.

So appliance replacement is a mixed bag. It can save money in the budget... but often, the total dollars saved are not that large, and in the case of combustion appliances, replacing them may be the least-cost safe alternative. Nevertheless, if appliance replacement is part of your proposal and the budget is tight, you can discuss the benefits vs. costs of each replacement with the customer.

Improving rather than replacing the HVAC system

In most cases, the supply duct system and air diffusers are oversized and the return air system is undersized. Also, both are generally so leaky that, when combined with the nearly-always oversized equipment, the system as a whole is completely ineffective. In most cases the most economical alternative is to take out the existing system, then redesign and install a new system using measured test results. On the other hand, that's not always necessary.

The tricky bit is knowing for sure what costs are involved in repairing rather than replacing the system. The equipment must be matched to the loads (the new, lower loads). And the supply air must reach each space in the right amounts in the right location, and at a velocity high enough to ensure mixing and comfort.

You can use the check numbers shown in table 7.1 to make a quick assessment about system replacement vs. system repair. If the existing system is close to meeting the check numbers, then perhaps it can be made efficient and effective by repair, air sealing and rebalancing instead of complete replacement. However; a word of caution. Partial replacement and system repair does not usually work well. Half-way measures may save money in construction, but they seldom achieve the key benefits of a Home Performance Project: better comfort with lower monthly costs.

HVAC SYSTEMS - CAPACITY AND AIR LEAKAGE

Check Numbers (Existing Systems)	Description
40,000 to 60,000 Btu/h per 1,000 ft² (Conditioned space)	In existing homes, heating capacity of over 60,000 Btu/h per 1,000 ft² strongly suggests the system is grossly oversized and can be redesigned and downsized to improve comfort. (A new system in a well-sealed home would only need about 15,000 Btu/h per 1,000 ft².) But, if heating capacity is less than 40,000 Btu/h/1,000 ft², redesign would only be practical if equipment needs replacement.
1 Ton per 450 to 600 ft² (Conditioned space)	In existing homes, cooling capacity of more than 1 ton per 450 ft² strongly suggests the system should be redesigned and downsized to save energy and improve comfort. But if each ton of capacity serves 600 ft² or more, there is less benefit to replacing the system. (A new system in a well-sealed home would only use about 1 ton for every 1,000 ft².)
250 to 350 cfm of supply air per ton of AC system capacity	In existing homes, air flow rates below 250 cfm/ton strongly suggests the AC equipment and duct system are wasting energy. Above 350 cfm/ton, there is less to be gained by replacement (New systems in a dry climate supply about 500 cfm per ton.)
6 to 15% of total supply air flow	In existing systems, duct leakage rates of less than 6% of system flow suggest there is little to be gained by duct redesign and reinstallation. But leakage rates of over 15% strongly suggest redesign and replacement. (A new system should leak less than 1/2 of 1%... less than 20 cfm$_{50}$)

Table 7.1 Check numbers for existing HVAC systems

Budget reductions which ruin the project

There are several budget reductions that seem logical to the customer—but in fact ruin the project. By "ruin the project" we mean that the customer spends money, but does not get either better comfort or lower utility bills.

Here are a few examples of "false hope" budget reductions. If the customer insists on these reductions, you may still want the business. But it's not good to describe the work as a Home Performance Project, because the home won't perform well after you finish the job.

AC equipment replacement without attic air sealing and insulation

If the loads don't go down, there's only so much that new equipment can accomplish. With proper, well-measured reinstallation of new, high-efficiency equipment, it's likely that comfort and energy will be "less bad" than before, but if the loads are the same, the energy consumption probably won't change much.

Mike Dater

Figure 7.2 "But, but but... my Brother-in-law said I could save money by replacing only the engine!"
Replacing HVAC equipment without improving the system as a whole is like putting a new engine in an antique car... the car might be more powerful, but it won't use less energy or provide a comfortable ride. Everything needs to work together as a balanced system. "Replacing the engine alone" is not a Home Performance Retrofit—because the home won't in fact perform well if the HVAC equipment is replaced without also improving the other parts of the system.

AC equipment replacement without air distribution redesign and reinstallation

Duct improvements take time and cost money, but air leakage, convective heat losses and tortuous duct design influence the energy consumption of the system far more than combustion efficiency or the AC system's SEER rating. For a visual analogy of this strategy, see figure 7.2. You can put a shiny new high-powered engine in an old car with a beat-up transmission, bad shock absorbers and worn-out brakes—but don't expect it to perform like a sports car. It won't.

Attic insulation without air sealing

Attic insulation seems like such a good idea by itself. But it's not. If the first step is installing more insulation in the attic, the insulation becomes an obstacle to making any of the other necessary improvements to the HVAC system and the home at a later date. All that insulation will have to be pulled out of the attic so that technicians can air-seal the assembly which separates the attic from the rest of the house, and so that they can re-work the HVAC system to make it efficient. Imagine trying to do that work when everything is buried in a blanket of loose insulation. It can't be done. Any existing insulation has to be removed before any work can proceed in the attic. That's why attic insulation should always be the last item to be installed—never the first.

Safety is non-negotiable

Many other types of contractors are comfortable with increasing potential safety risks in homes, but Measured Home Performance Contractors are not.

If the owner's budget simply cannot stretch far enough to ensure safety, it's time to tactfully and respectfully withdraw the proposal and find a different customer. Make no mistake; there are life-safety issues with Home Performance Retrofits.
Examples of expensive but non-negotiable items include:

1. Adequate venting of combustion appliances as described in chapter 4, or replacing them with high-efficiency, sealed-combustion appliances.

2. Replacement of any knob-and-tube wiring in the attic before insulation.

3. Adapting can lights to make them air-tight and safe for full insulation contact, or replacing them with new fixtures which meet those criteria, before the attic is insulated.

4. A complete set of test-out measurements.

Chapter 7... Presenting & Adjusting Your Proposal

Chapter 8

Tips & Traps For HVAC Design

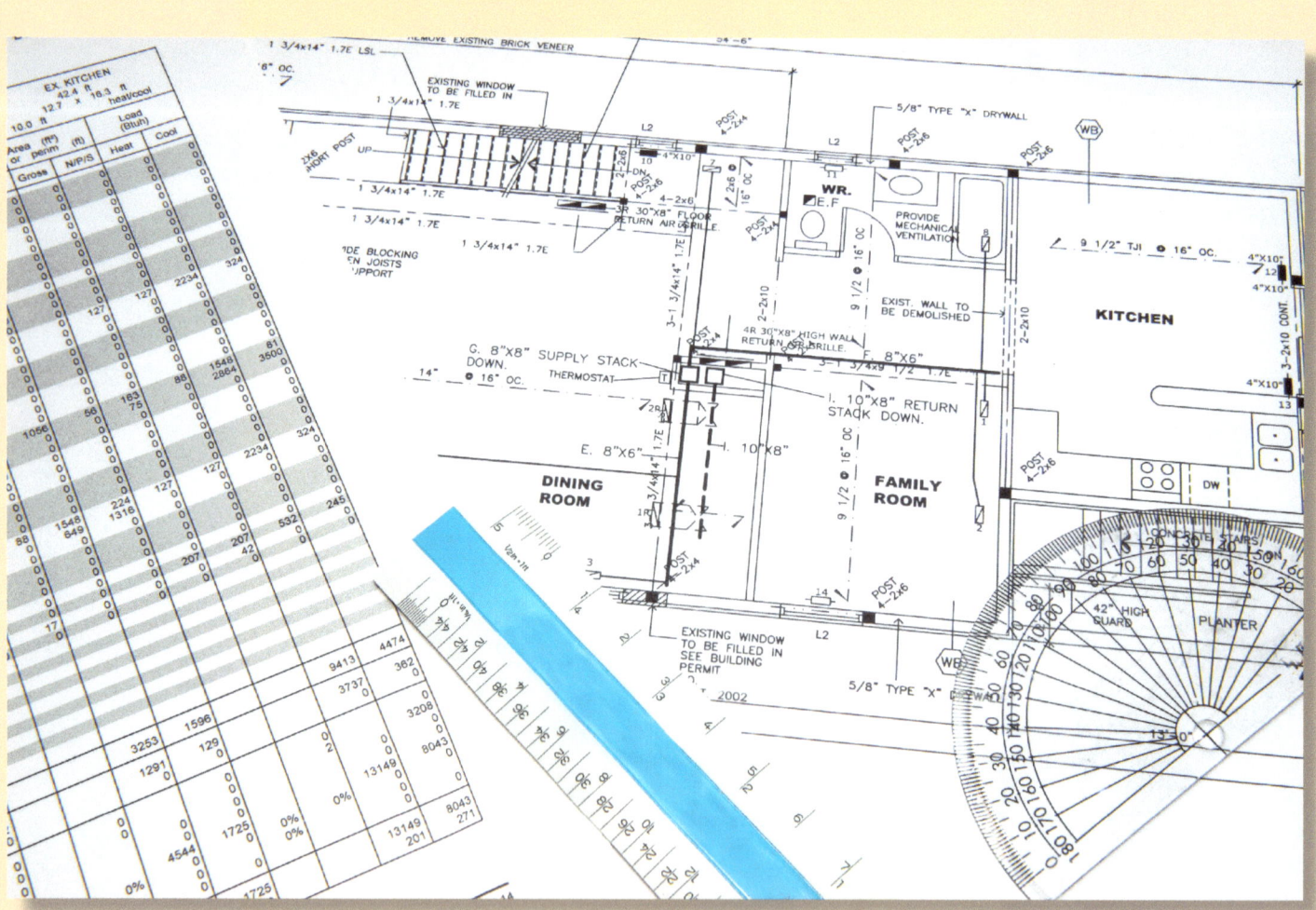

Fig. 8.1 Room-by-room load calculations are the foundation of excellent HVAC system design

Tips and Traps for HVAC Design & Renovation

A complete course in residential HVAC design is beyond the scope of this publication. HVAC design is a big topic. Critical details of implementation depend on the home, the budget, local fuel options and the type of system selected. In order to be helpful to the greatest number of readers, this chapter will focus on several best practices which are especially important for the most typical system used in California homes: the all-air, central heating and DX cooling system.

Better HVAC Design Goals and Assumptions

A perfectly-designed HVAC system has just enough heating and cooling capacity to keep up with the loads, provided that it's allowed to run continuously. In other words, it's a system with no excess capacity. It provides comfort without wasting either capacity or energy.

With a well-designed and properly installed HVAC system in a well-insulated and sealed thermal envelope, there's no need to set back the thermostat to save energy. In fact there's no need to touch the thermostat at all. The system just runs and provides comfort, no matter what the outdoor weather, year-round. Also, it's so quiet that the occupants may not even realize it's operating, especially since they never feel any uncomfortable blasts of either hot or cold air, because there's never any significant temperature difference between their ankles and their head. The house is comfortable all year long. So the homeowner simply never thinks about the HVAC system. It just works.

This is quite different from most of the HVAC systems installed in California homes. Traditionally, residential HVAC systems have been designed with too much cooling and heating capacity, because most designers have assumed (based on their bitter experience) that the building will be leaky and poorly insulated, and that the HVAC system will be installed badly. In other words, past HVAC design practice can be summarized as "When in doubt, use a bigger hammer."

In order for Performance Contracting to deliver reliable year-round comfort while also saving energy, it's critical to take a different approach; namely, design the HVAC system based not on failures and shortcomings of installation, but rather on what you know will be accomplished (and validated by in-process measurements) during the Performance Contracting project.

HVAC EQUIPMENT CAPACITY

Check Numbers (New Systems)	Description
15,000 Btu/h per 1,000 ft² (Conditioned space)	**Target maximum installed heating capacity.** Lower Btu/h per 1,000 ft2 are better, because the higher Btu/h of furnace capacity needed to heat 1,000 ft2, the less effective is the current heating system. (Greater potential for improvement)
1 Ton per 1,000 ft² (Conditioned space)	**Target maximum installed cooling capacity.** Lower # of tons per 1,000 ft2 are better, because the higher the tons per 1,000 square feet, the less effective is the current cooling system. (Greater potential for improvement)
450 - 500 cfm per ton of AC system capacity	**Target minimum total supply air flow** Lower flow rates are not efficient in the dry California climate
60°F	**Lowest desirable coil-leaving air temperature** during cooling operation
90°F	**Highest desirable coil-leaving air temperature** during heating operation

Table 8.1 Check numbers for HVAC equipment capacity

Calculate Loads After Assuming Correct Installation of Energy Features

Among HVAC designers, there's a natural inclination to select equipment and design the system based on the assumption that duct work will leak, that the loads will be higher than expected and that the system won't be installed quite right. But with Performance Contracting, such major problems don't happen. So it's very important not to allow old assumptions about arbitrary load estimates and poor installation to sneak into the designer's thinking. If they do, the system won't work well, and it certainly won't save energy.

To avoid problems of poor comfort or excess energy use, check your load calculation assumptions and results against the values shown in table 8.1. More explanation of those numbers follows:

Total cooling load about 1 ton per 1,000 ft²

If the total calculated cooling load is more than 1 ton per 1,000 ft² of occupied floor space in most of California, there's something wrong with either your assumptions or the scope of your project. Examine both closely. Adjust either your assumptions or your project scope, and then recalculate the loads. (The exception is in the desert, where you can expect higher cooling loads.)

Total heating load under 20,000 Btu/h per 1,000 ft²

If the total calculated heating load is more than 20,000 Btu/h per 1000 ft² of occupied floor space in most of California, there's something wrong with either your assumptions or the scope of your project. Examine both closely. Adjust either your assumptions or your project scope, and then recalculate the loads. (For most of the State, 15,000 Btu/h per 1,000 ft² of occupied space would be ample for a well-insulated air tight new house. The exceptions would be in snow country, where you can expect higher heating loads.)

Duct leakage near zero

The duct work and the duct connections will be air tight. The system won't lose more than 50 cfm total from the supply air flow through leakage at a test pressure of +25 Pa. In fact, a total leakage of 20 cfm_{25} and below is quite commonly achieved by well-trained crews.

Ducts with near-zero conductive losses

The duct work will be insulated to R-8, and then in the attic will be mostly buried by cellulose or glass fiber insulation. That level of insulation effectively reduces conductive duct losses to near zero for much of the year and only rises to the values shown in table 8.2 during the hottest and coldest hours.

Attic insulation that really performs

The attic will be insulated to R-40 and the crawl space (if there is one) will be insulated to R-19. The depth of the insulation will be verifiable quickly and easily, as shown in figure 8.2

Real-world walls and windows

Assume walls and windows will contribute to the loads according to their field-measured dimensions, locations and insulating

Fig. 8.2 Design the HVAC based on insulation values you *know* will occur with Measured Performance Contracting

PAST PRACTICE... INSULATION IS "MISSING IN ACTION"

BEST PRACTICES - R40 IS *MEASURED* & *VERIFIED*

AIR DISTRIBUTION DESIGN

Check Numbers for New Systems	Description
500 - 700 fpm	**Minimum and maximum discharge velocity** from supply air diffusers
250 fpm	**Maximum velocity through return air grills and filters**
0.35" to 0.45" wc	**Duct design target - Max external static pressure for the air handler's fan.** (Maximum combined resistance of supply and return duct systems, including coils, filters, supply diffusers and return grills)
50 cfm_{25} or 5% of measured fan flow, whichever is less	**Maximum combined total air leakage from supply and return sides of the system.** (The real goal is zero air leakage, and 20 cfm_{25} is commonly achieved in practice by well-trained crews)
4,250 Btu/h per 1,000 ft^2 of occupied floor space	**Cooling load from attic duct work** Maximum conductive heat gain from attic duct work per 1,000 ft^2 of occupied space (Based on R-8 insulation, 40% of occupied floor space as duct surface, attic temperature of 140°F and supply air temperature of at least 55°F)
2,500 Btu/h per 1,000 ft^2 of occupied floor space	**Heating load from attic duct work** Maximum conductive heat loss from attic duct work per 1,000 ft^2 of occupied space (Based on R-8 insulation, 40% of occupied floor space as duct surface, attic temperature of 40°F and supply air temperature of no more than 90°F)

Table 8.2 Check numbers for air distribution design

SUPPLY AIR DUCT & GRILLE SIZING

Air flow (cfm)	Duct Diameter	Curved Blade Ceiling Grille[1]	Floor Grille[2]	High Sidewall Grille[3]
50	5"	4" x 4"	10" x 2.25"	4" x 4"
75	6"	6" x 4"	8" x 4"	6" x 4"
100	7"	6" x 6"	10" x 4"	8" x 4"
125	7"	6" x 6"	12" x 4"	10" x 4"
150	8"	8" x 6"	10" x 6"	8" x 6"
175	8"	10" x 6"	10" x 6"	10" x 6"
200	9"	8" x 8"	12" x 6"	10" x 6"
250	10"	14" x 6"	12" x 8"	10" x 8"
300	10"	14" x 8"	14" x 8"	12" x 8"

1. Typically a commercial-grade extruded aluminum grille
2. Simple bar-type grille (non-diffusing)
3. Typical residential double-deflection type grille

Table 8.3 Check numbers for supply air ducts and grilles
*Note that the grilles are the no-diffusing type. Leaving the grille, the air flow is straight or angled, but **not** interrupted by the turbulence of either a diffuser or a damper. Dampers are at the supply plenum—not in the grille.*

characteristics—not according to an arbitrary assumption of single glazing at some guessed-at percentage of total wall area. The key characteristics of all the window assemblies will have been surveyed and recorded during the test-in visit.

Air Distribution Design *Really* Based on Best Practices

In most new houses, air distribution design is an afterthought. The installers are expected to shoehorn the ducts into the home somehow, without creating too much chaos for other trades, and without any respect for, or understanding of, the critical tasks of commissioning and maintenance. But with Performance Contracting, air distribution design can take center stage, because the goals are lowest energy and greatest comfort (as opposed to highest speed and lowest bid).

These goals free the HVAC designer to use the best practices that have been known for decades and well-documented by ASHRAE, SMACNA and ACCA, but seldom implemented in the past. Some best practices for air distribution design are described below.

Duct runs can (and should be mostly) short and straight

This is possible because the supply ducts can go from the air handler to the nearest corner of each space—not way out to the windows. With the improved enclosure, there's no need to send heating and cooling out to the windows. More important to comfort will be good air mixing in the space.

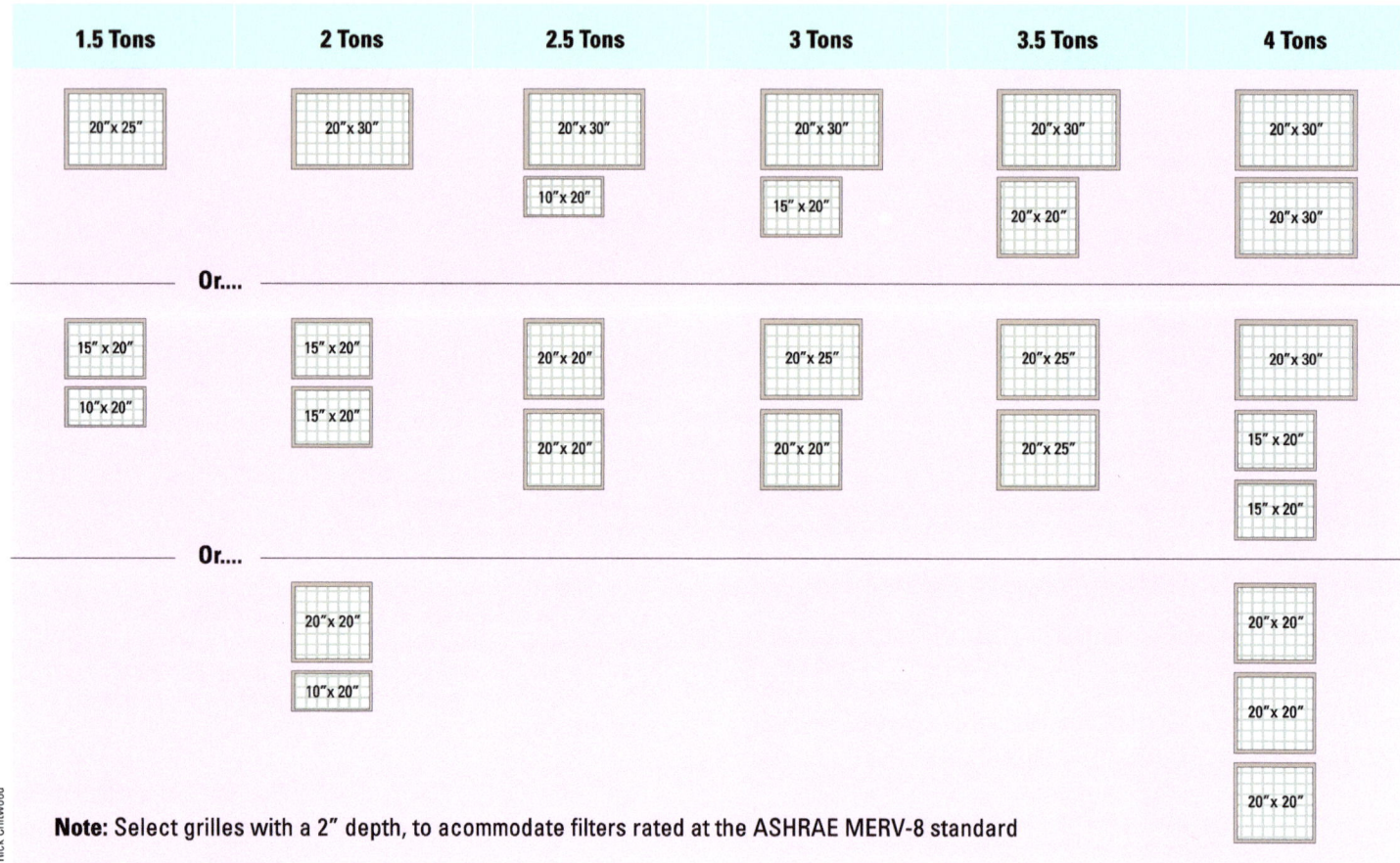

Note: Select grilles with a 2" depth, to acommodate filters rated at the ASHRAE MERV-8 standard

Rick Chitwood

Table 8.4 Check numbers for return air grilles
These selections are based on standard, commercally-available hardware which meets two basic design criteria: less than 250 fpm velocity through the return air filter, which in turn keeps the presure drop through the grille and filter to less than 0.07" w.c.

Supply ducts & grilles sized with the "Goldilocks principle"

In other words, supply air ducts and grilles must not be too big or too small, but juuust... right. The check numbers in table 8.3 will help you make sure your supply duct and grille sizes are in the right ballpark. Within that range of grille sizes, you'll get the delivery velocity you need for good air mixing and comfort. Any larger, and you'll have needless conductive losses from the extra duct surface area. Any smaller and the system will waste power overcoming duct friction.

Fast-and-straight air delivery - Supply air grilles without diffusers or dampers

Good air mixing in the conditioned space is absolutely critical to comfort. You want even, nearly-equal temperatures top to bottom and side to side throughout the space. That's achieved when the fast-moving supply air stream pulls in room air at its edges, and blends that air with the warm or cold supply air quickly and blows it throughout the room (preferably across the room above head level).

1.5 Tons	2 Tons	2.5 Tons	3 Tons	3.5 Tons	4 Tons
16"	18"	18"	18"	18"	18"
		10"	12"	14"	18"
Or....					
12"	14"	14"	16"	16"	14"
10"	12"	14"	14"	16"	14"
					14"
Or....					
	14"				16"
	14"				14"
					14"

Table 8.5 Check numbers for return air duct sizes

If the grille has diffusers, the smooth, fast flow of supply air is destroyed, and the supply air sort of stumbles out ineffectively, cooling or heating only the area in its immediate vicinity. And if the grille has a damper, setting the flow with that damper can disturb both smooth flow as well as its direction. You want the direction and speed to be constant and well-aimed, so that occupants don't get blasted with supply air.

Therefore, use supply grilles which keep the air moving straight and fast, without diffusers. And make sure that the necessary balancing dampers are installed at the supply plenum—not in the grille.

Placing the room's balancing damper deeper in the duct, away from the visually-obvious location of the grille, has the other advantage of discouraging the owner from fiddling with the flow after you have carefully balanced the system. (Uncomfortable owners sometimes try to get more air flow at the supply grille—they don't always realize that the usual problem is a dirty return air filter.)

Locate supply air grilles so they don't blow their high-velocity air onto room occupants.

Ideally we deliver supply air from the floor. Floor supply grilles provide excellent mixing in the heating season and very good room air

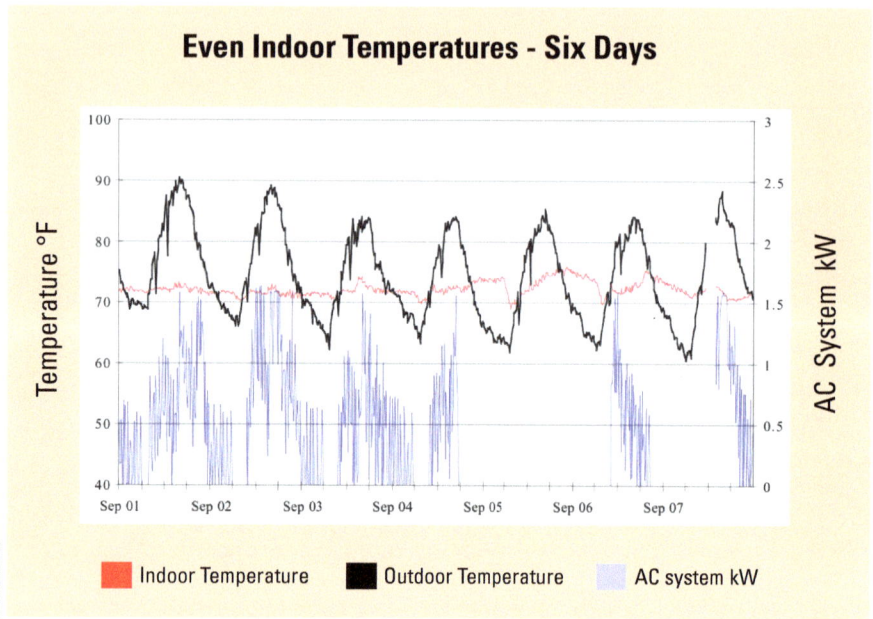

Fig. 8.3 Results from best practices
This house in Redding was designed and constructed using the best practices outline in this and other chapters. The homeowners didn't bother adjusting the thermostat... for six days. The system just works.

temperature mixing in the cooling mode. However, many California houses have slab-on-grade foundations, which means floor grilles aren't an option.

When supply ducts are in the attic (the most common situation) there are two supply grille options. The best option is a high-sidewall supply grille. These deliver a high velocity plume across the ceiling. However, high-sidewall grilles require a vaulted ceiling with side wall access from the attic, or a dropped ceiling so that the duct can be brought down from the attic and set into a side wall. These architectural features are not typical in most houses.

So the most typical supply air grille is a true curved-blade extruded aluminum supply grille mounted in the ceiling. This grille delivers a smooth, high velocity air plume across the ceiling (not straight downwards) for reasonable mixing and no drafts on the occupants.

Don't waste money running tiny ducts to small spaces

In small spaces like bathrooms, utility rooms and closets where load calculations call for less than about 75 cfm of supply air, don't bother running a separate supply duct. Just add the small space's load to the nearest large space, and upsize the airflow to the larger space accordingly. In a well-insulated and air tight home, there won't be any comfort impact. You'll save material, labor and fan power, while reducing conductive heat losses and gains from ducts.

For return grilles, bigger is better. But return ducts have to be "....juuust right"

The open area of return grilles and ducts must be large. Use the check numbers in tables 8.3 and 8.4 to ensure your design has enough open area at the return grill to allow smooth flow back to the air handler without excessive energy-consuming resistance at the grille.

Ducts, on the other hand, must not be too large, because they run through unconditioned spaces. When they are oversized, it's true that fan power is less. However, larger ducts also mean a larger surface area to lose and gain heat as the return ducts pass through unconditioned spaces. So for grilles, bigger is better. But for duct sizing follow the Goldilocks Principle and make them "...juuust right." ("Just right" sizing results in a combined total air flow resistance in the range of 0.35 to 0.45" WC for the supply and return duct systems, including all coils, filters, diffusers and grilles.)

The success of these best practices is quite remarkable. Indoor air temperatures are even and uniform, year-round. See figure 8.3 for one example, which shows a week of indoor vs. outdoor temperatures, along with the AC system's modest power consumption while achieving those results.

Design Calculations and Documentation Which Support Excellent Installation

The HVAC designer can help ensure excellent installation (and therefore excellent comfort) by the assumptions made during load calculations, and by the information on the load summary sheet.

Room-by-room load calculations

The heating and cooling loads must be calculated room-by-room, not by an arbitrary amount per ft2. From room-by-room load calculations, the air flow to each space can also be easily calculated by the HVAC designer. With that information, the technicians can quickly measure and set the air flows needed for each space.

Constant year-round supply air flow rate

For trouble-free comfort, air flow and air mixing must be excellent all year round. Supply air grilles and diffusers need a constant volume to ensure good air mixing. Therefore, the supply air flow rate must be the same for both heating and cooling seasons. (The flow rate will probably be set by the cooling load, in most of the State other than in snow country.)

Moderate supply air temperatures year-round

Extreme supply temperatures waste energy and create extreme comfort problems. Calculate the required year-round air flow rate based on a supply air temperature of no more than 100°F for heating and no less than 50°F for cooling. These are moderate temperatures which save energy. Lower temperature differences between the duct and the surrounding spaces mean lower duct losses and therefore less energy use, as well as less stratification, better air mixing and therefore better comfort.

Equipment Selection Which Provides Comfort Without Energy Waste

Equipment selection is a bit more complex than just picking a furnace with a high combustion efficiency rating and a cooling system with an impressive SEER. But it's not really difficult, as long as the designer keeps a few key points in mind.

Combined hydronic air handler is an excellent choice

For several reasons, combined hydronic air handlers (also sometimes called "hot water furnaces") are an excellent choice for well-insulated, tight houses in most of California.

These units allow the use of a hot water heating coil for winter heat, which can be sized to match the low heating load without overheating the supply air. Also, the air handler can be equipped with a DX cooling coil which has a larger-than-usual surface area. The larger surface area reduces air flow resistance, which in turn allows larger-than-

Fig. 8.4 Hydronic air handler, combined with a high-efficiency, sealed-combustion natural gas water heater

usual supply air flows and higher-than-usual supply air temperatures for cooling, which saves energy in the California climate for the reasons discussed in earlier paragraphs.

Finally, the "combined" part of the name comes from this equipment's ability to use hot water from the building's domestic hot water heater for HVAC heat. The hydronic air handler with its hot water heating coil and the domestic hot water heater are "combined" to form the HVAC system's heating equipment.

To understand why the combined hydronic air handler is such a good fit, it's important to understand the shortcomings of conventional furnaces and DX cooling equipment for the low loads that are typical of well-insulated, fairly air-tight homes in the relatively mild and dry California climate. There are problems in California for conventional furnaces even though that equipment is so economical and works so well in many other parts of the country:

a. Furnaces simply have far too much capacity. They will "short-cycle," switching on and off frequently, delivering too much and too little heat, rather than a smooth flow of just enough heat to keep up with the loads. In most of the State, you won't have heating loads of more than about 15,000 Btu/h per 1,000 ft2 of occupied space. The smallest available conventional central system furnace has about 40,000 Btu/h of capacity... more than twice the correct size for a well-built 1500 ft^2 home.

b. Conventional furnaces don't work properly unless they have a relatively high outlet temperature. If the supply temperature leaving the furnace is less than about 110°F, it means the temperature rise through the furnace is too low. That in turn means that too much heat remains in the furnace. So it shuts down, because you don't want to burn up your furnace. The problem is that for best comfort and energy efficiency we don't want a supply air temperature higher than about 90°F. Conventional furnaces can't provide such low supply air temperatures without damage to their heat exchangers.

c. If supply air temperatures are high, air in the room will stratify severely. Hot air rises. Very hot supply air rises quickly to the ceiling and stays there. It does not mix well with cooler air closer to the floor. So while your head is hot, your ankles are cold. Therefore, for better comfort and less energy waste we need moderate supply air temperatures during the heating season. These really can't be provided by conventional furnaces.

Combined hydronic air handlers are also a good fit for the customization of the cooling system which is so important in the California climate. Without the humidity loads that are typical in the rest of the country, in California we can maintain comfort using more air flow per ton and higher supply air temperatures for cooling than would be typical in other States.

d. In a humid climate, an air flow rate of 350 or even as low as 300 cfm/ton is a good choice, because the low flow allows deeper cooling and more dehumidification. But in California, we don't need or want that much dehumidification. It would waste energy and create uncomfortably dry conditions, because the system will be running for long periods. Instead, we need larger air flows and less-deep cooling. A supply air flow rate near 500 cfm/ton is a better selection for energy and comfort in our climate. And a supply air temperature of 60°F is better than 50 or 55°F.

e. But here's the potential problem. With such a high flow rate across the coil, what we save in cooling could be chewed up by resistance to air flow—unless the coil has a larger face area than would be typical in other parts of the country. See the check values in table 8.5 for ideal sizes of cooling coils compared to the total load on the system.

f. This important customization explains why the combined hydronic air handler is also a good choice on the cooling side of the system. The air handler allows better customization—larger cooling coils—rather than the smaller standard "A" coils. These have a smaller air flow capacity per ton, since they are designed to match the air flows through conventional furnaces.

Air-source heat pumps are another good choice

One of the traditional limitations of air-source heat pumps has been that they don't produce really high temperature supply air during winter operation. But for well-insulated and reasonably air tight homes, that's not a bug... it's a feature. We want 100°F or less (preferably 90°F).

Heat pumps make sense where there is no natural gas available for heating. Natural gas is generally the most economical fuel for hot water and for HVAC heat. But it's not available everywhere in California, and the alternative of propane-fired heat is very costly. So the all-electric, high-efficiency heat pump can be a useful alternative to the combined hydronic air handler in areas without natural gas service.

Another potential alternative would be ground-source heat pumps, which have received a great deal of attention nationwide. But these really don't have advantages in the mild California climate. Compared to air-source units, ground-source heat pumps are quite expensive to buy, install and maintain. And unlike other parts of the country, without long hours at extreme temperatures and humidities, in California there are no significant compensating advantages to the limitations of ground source heat pumps in single-family homes.

500 cfm/ton... OK, but how? Use a larger evaporator coil

As discussed earlier, the target range for air flow through the AC system is about 500 cfm/ton. That's difficult to achieve if one uses the manufacturer's usual recommendations for matching the evaporator coil to the condensing unit.

The more energy-efficient choice is to use "the next size up" evaporator coil for the load. The condensing unit and its compressor stay the same... but the evaporator coil is larger than usual. The larger evaporator coil allows air flows near 500 cfm per ton without excessive pressure drop.

The values in table 8.5 provides useful check numbers for pairing the right size evaporator with the load on the condenser.

COOLING COIL SIZE

System Size (Tons)	Evaporator Coil Size (Tons)
1.5	2 to 2.5
2	2.5 to 3
2.5	3.5 to 4
3	4 to 5
3.5	5
4	5

Table 8.5
Check numbers for A/C coil sizes

Limit high-efficiency filters to special situations

Excess filter pressure drop kills overall system efficiency. That resistance to air flow costs a lot in motor horsepower, especially since the well-designed HVAC system has very long run cycles.

It's helpful to educate the customer on this subject. Most consumers know they should have the oil and oil filter changed every so often in their car. They would also benefit by knowing that changing air filters monthly is an excellent way to ensure that comfort and energy savings continue after the system has been started up.

Typical modern HVAC systems are designed to accommodate very high-grade, MERV-8 pleated filters. Those filters remove more than 70% of particles between 3 and 10 microns in diameter—a huge reduction. These can be installed in the deep filter racks built into the return air grilles recommended in this chapter.

But if the client's home is located next to a highway or is in a dusty agricultural region, or if it has a particulate-sensitive occupant, the home may benefit from super-high-efficiency particulate removal at the MERV-11 level. In those cases, be sure to select a supply fan speed which provides full air flow at a pressure high enough to overcome the resistance of that high-efficiency filter.

For the more typical home (without sensitive occupants and without a nearby constant source of large amounts of fine particulate) the owner will save energy by avoiding super high-efficiency filters.

Chapter 9

Tips & Traps For Air Sealing The Enclosure

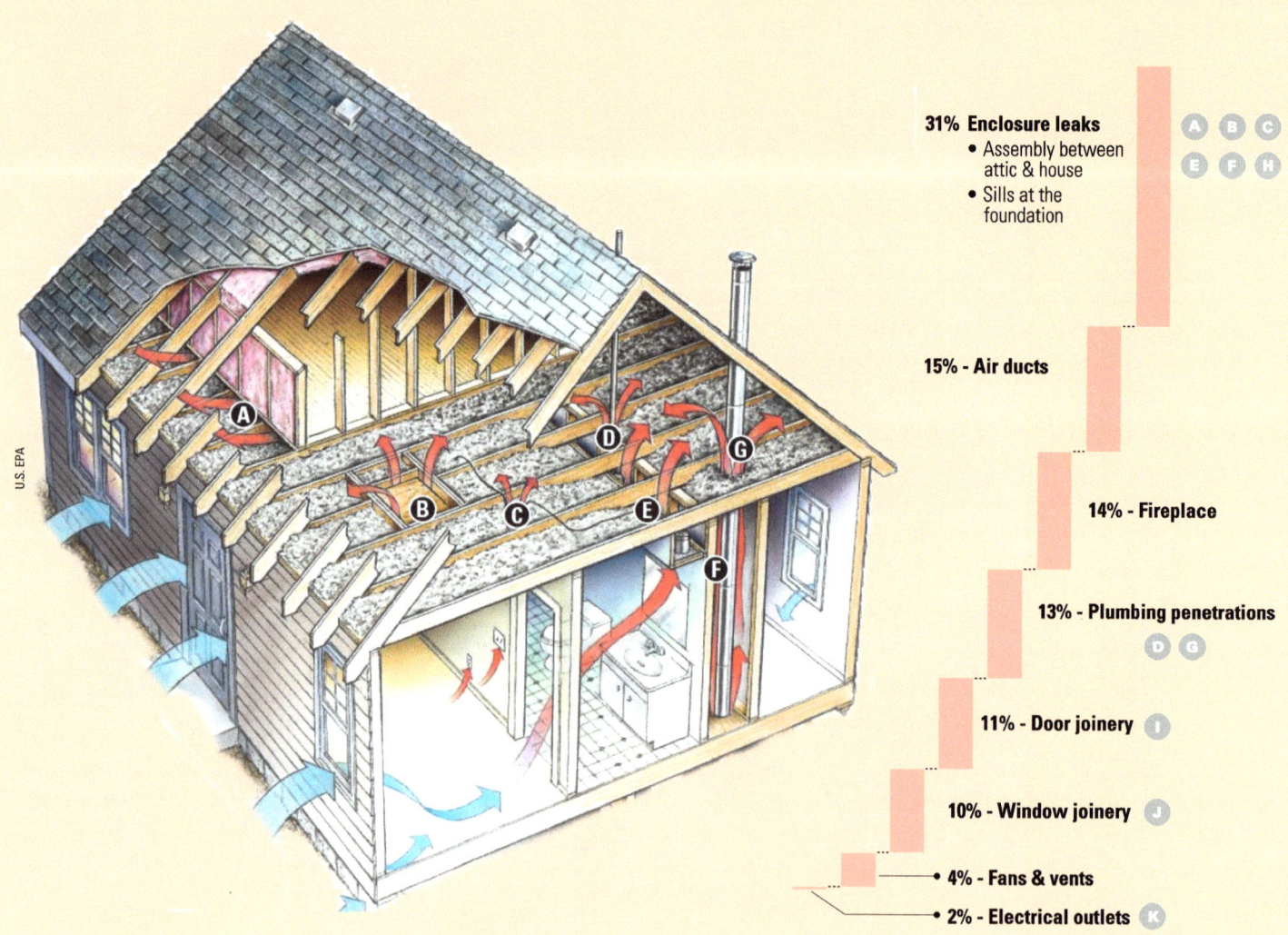

Fig. 9.1 Leak-hunters guide
The drawing show many of the typical locations of air leaks. The graph shows the probable percentage of annual air leakage in each location, based on computer modeling of a typical 1600 ft^2, single-story house assumed to be in Modesto.

Sealing the Enclosure

Sealing the enclosure is a very important part of the Performance Contracting project. It requires careful planning and in-process air tightness measurements. Careful planning is really critical, because if you're not careful a tight house can create serious life safety and moisture problems. And in-process air tightness measurements are also critical because if progress isn't being made, you might be sealing the wrong holes and wasting your effort. Here's a logical sequence for the air sealing part of your Performance Contracting project:

1. Don't proceed until you have:

   a. Removed any vermiculite insulation and/or rodent and pest infestation or droppings from the attic.

   b. Cleared and cleaned the attic (and crawl space, if there is one) for safe access to all potential leak locations.

   c. Reworked the exhaust ducts and properly terminated any fans or combustion appliances which may have originally exhausted to the attic.

   d. Fixed any roof leaks (or water accumulation in the crawl space, if there is one).

   e. Tested all natural draft combustion appliances for safety under normal and worst-case depressurization conditions and made any necessary repairs or replacements to ensure safe operation in an air-tight home.

2. Establish the target sealing rate.
3. Duplicate the test-in air tightness test to establish the baseline air tightness value.
4. Locate the leaks.
5. Seal big leaks before small leaks, and high and low leaks before middle-level leaks.
8. Run the blower door test about once an hour to measure progress towards the air tightness target.

Fig. 9.2 Before & after - Fix any moisture intrusion problems
Fix any moisture problems before air sealing begins. If you don't... you'll increase moisture problems by air sealing the building.

Pre-sealing Preparation & Safety Issues

Air-sealing the home should not be approached casually. If the home has moisture or indoor air quality problems, sealing the building can make these problems much worse. And in the case of combustion appliances, some problems can even become life-threatening.

Safely remove vermiculite insulation

Vermiculite is a naturally occurring mineral used in construction and gardening products. It looks like shiny, small pieces of popcorn, and is usually light-brown or gold in color. Vermiculite is still mined and distributed for a number of uses, including insulation.

This lightweight, granular mineral insulation is rare in California. But unless it's new it must be removed. Here's why. 70% of vermiculite produced before 1990 came from a single mine in Libby, Montana. That vermiculite was contaminated with a small amount of asbestos. Much of the Libby vermiculite was used as attic insulation. It was sold under the product name "Zonolite." The Environmental Protection Agency estimated in 1985 that 940,000 American homes contained Zonolite attic insulation.

Vermiculite mined today for use in insulation is from sources considered to be free of asbestos contamination. However, unless the vermiculite is known to be new and free of asbestos, it must be removed before you can safely work in the attic. Undisturbed older vermiculite is not believed to be a serious problem. But during your project, you will definitely be disturbing it, moving it and spreading dust. Older vermiculite dust from the Libby, MT mine may contain asbestos, which is a breathing hazard for both workers and occupants. If you need more detailed information about vermiculite, consult the U.S. EPA website: http://www.epa.gov/asbestos/pubs/verm.html

Clear and clean the workspace

Attics and crawl spaces are favorite homes for rodents and insects. So any infestation or droppings must be removed before you start creating airborne dust with your air-sealing activities.

Also, it's important to clear out any stored materials or belongings that get in the way of safe access to all the corners and edges of the spaces you'll be working in. You don't want to strain muscles or put a foot through a ceiling because you're trying to avoid disturbing clutter in an already confined and awkward space.

Make sure exhaust ducts and vent stacks don't vent inside the attic

Venting into the attic is never, ever appropriate or allowed by codes. But if "informal" workers or homeowners have inadvertently terminated exhaust ducts or vent stacks inside the attic, these must be extended out and terminated properly outdoors, before you begin your project.

If you wait until later, you'll just have to come back and seal up any new penetrations and re-do your final blower door test. So it's best to fix these problems before you begin air sealing, to ensure safe working conditions and to avoid costly rework.

Fix water leaks and moisture accumulation problems

See figure 9.2. Water intrusion problems like damp crawl spaces and roof leaks can sometimes go on for years without generating mold or odor problems. But after the home is tightened, the free flow of drying air that keeps moisture from accumulating will be gone. When the home leaks water, moisture problems can become more severe quite quickly, after the home is tightened up. So it's important to make sure that the roof does not leak, and that any leaks around windows or doors are fixed.

The same is true in the crawl space, if there is one. Make sure it's well-drained and has a vapor barrier installed over the ground before you tighten up the house. Also your crew will thank you for creating a more reasonable work environment in the crawl space. (Or they won't thank you—because it's still not much fun to work down there—but at least you'll know you've done the right thing!)

Test natural draft combustion appliances and fix them if necessary

Finally, and most important: if there are any problems with the combustion appliances, you must fix them or replace them before tightening the house. You can create a life-safety risk if you have a tight house with an appliance which is generating carbon monoxide.

Your test-in safety testing will alert you to any potential problems. That's one of the main purposes of the extensive test-in visit. So if there are combustion appliance problems, fix them before you tighten the home.

Establishing the Ending Sealing Rate Target

Establish your ending sealing rate target before you begin, so that you'll know when it's time to stop. In any project, you'll eventually reach a point where the sealing progress slows down so much that it is no longer cost-effective to try to find more leaks to seal.

Typical sealing rate targets are between 100 and 400 cfm50 per crew-hour. In other words, if after an hour of work a well-trained crew has not been able to reduce the air leakage rate by (a value that you've established between) 100 to 400 cfm50, then it's probably time to stop sealing and work on other parts of the overall project.

Ideally of course, we'd like to seal every home completely air-tight. But in the real world you'll need to stop after you've sealed everything which is accessible, or after the crew's progress falls below your sealing target rate. Otherwise the air sealing phase would be so expensive that nobody could afford it. Also keep in mind that if you are able to seal below a certain point (less than 0.35 ach50) you will need to either recommend or add ventilation to the HVAC part of your project.

Duplicating the Test-in Air Tightness

The first step in the actual air sealing project itself is to set up the blower door exactly as it was done during the test-in visit, and then run the test until you have duplicated the leakage rate measured during that test-in visit. That will be your baseline.

Leave the blower door test setup in place as you work, so that about each hour or so, you can re-test the air leakage, to measure your progress towards the target sealing rate.

Fig. 9.3 Blower door testing is repeated periodically during air sealing operations to provide feedback to the crew about their progress towards their air tightness target.

Locating & Fixing Typical Attic Air Leaks

Locating the leaks is relatively easy at the beginning, and then becomes progressively more difficult. You can begin by looking through the attic for the big holes and missing pieces of ceilings that are typically found there. Keep in mind the nearly obvious guidance that says: "find and fix big leaks before small leaks." Figure 9.1 showed some of the typical leak locations. Here is some additional discussion of each location.

Kitchen and bathroom cabinet soffits

In most houses, the tops of cabinets end at reachable hand-height, rather than going all the way up to the full ceiling height. Between the top of the cabinet and the ceiling level is often a "soffit." This is gypsum wall board formed into a wall between the top of the cabinet and the ceiling. But often, that soffit is open to the attic at the top, and sometimes also open to the room at its base, just above the top of the cabinet.

That air gap can be large, as shown in figure 9.4a. To fix it, you'll need to block it off with gypsum board or some form of insulation board which can support the weight of the additional insulation you'll be installing later. Then the edges of that board will need to be sealed with caulking, or with minimal-expansion foam.

Fig. 9.4a Open soffit, above bathroom closets

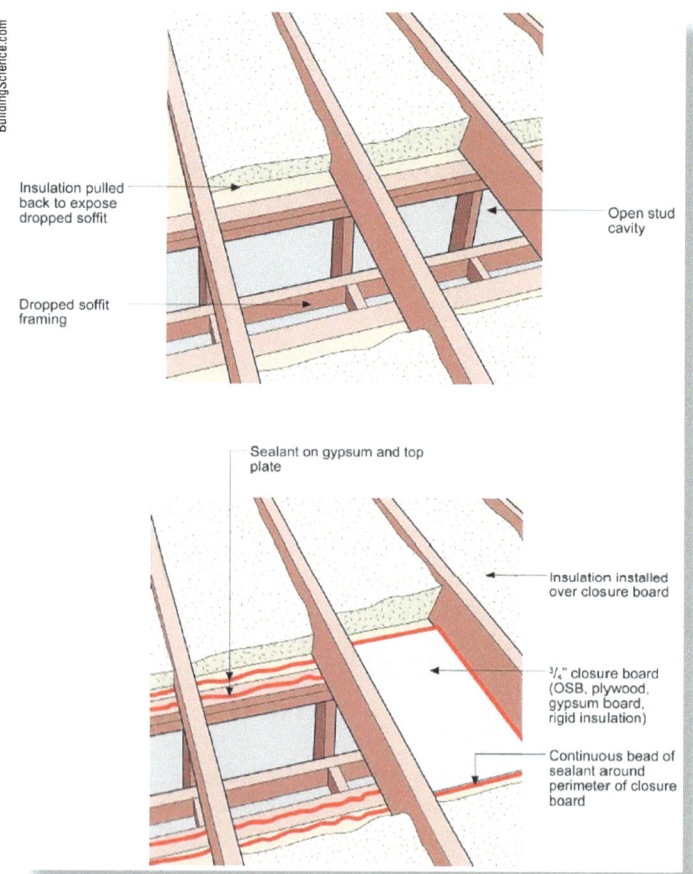

**Fig. 9.4b
Air sealing an open soffit**

Open stud bays

Sometimes, as shown in figure 9.5, the tops of interior stud bays project into the attic and are not capped. These can be stuffed with a folded batt of fiberglass insulation to act as backing, and then covered with a layer of spray foam to ensure a tight air seal.

Fig. 9.5
Plugging open stud bays with fiberglass.
The batts provide mechanical support for the spray foam that acts as the air seal.

Attic access hatches

Attic access hatches are seldom insulated (and sometimes missing). Every attic access gets three improvements:

1. Insulation, to at least R-19 with three (3) inches of foil-faced foam board (Polyisocyanurate).

2. Weather stripping, to limit air leakage, and..

3. A 10" to 15" dam on the attic side, to keep attic insulation from falling into the home when the access hatch is opened.

Fig. 9.6 Attic access hatchway

Duct penetrations, plumbing chases and shafts

Anywhere the supply and return ducts of the HVAC system penetrate the attic, the opening must be sealed up. In the case of small gaps, polyurethane foam-from-a-can is probably the preferred method. If there are larger gaps, then add a collar of gypsum board or sheet metal to narrow the gap before applying foam.

Fig. 9.7 Duct penetration

Chimney penetrations

A chimney will nearly always have a wide gap around it, to make sure that combustible material is not in contact with the hot flue. The wide gap is the easiest way to meet that code requirement.

When you seal this gap, keep in mind the need to prevent combustible material from contacting the flue. First fit a sheet metal collar to close the gap. Then use a fire-rated sealant to caulk the seam between the sheet metal collar and the masonry, as shown in figure 9.8. Be sure the joints are well-covered with sealant, because your next step will make those joints more difficult to fix later, if they leak air.

After the gap is air-sealed with the collar and caulking, build a vertical insulation dam out of gypsum board, taking care to keep a 2" air space around the masonry, as shown in figure 9.8 at left. The air space protects the insulation—which may be combustible—from coming in contact with the hot masonry.

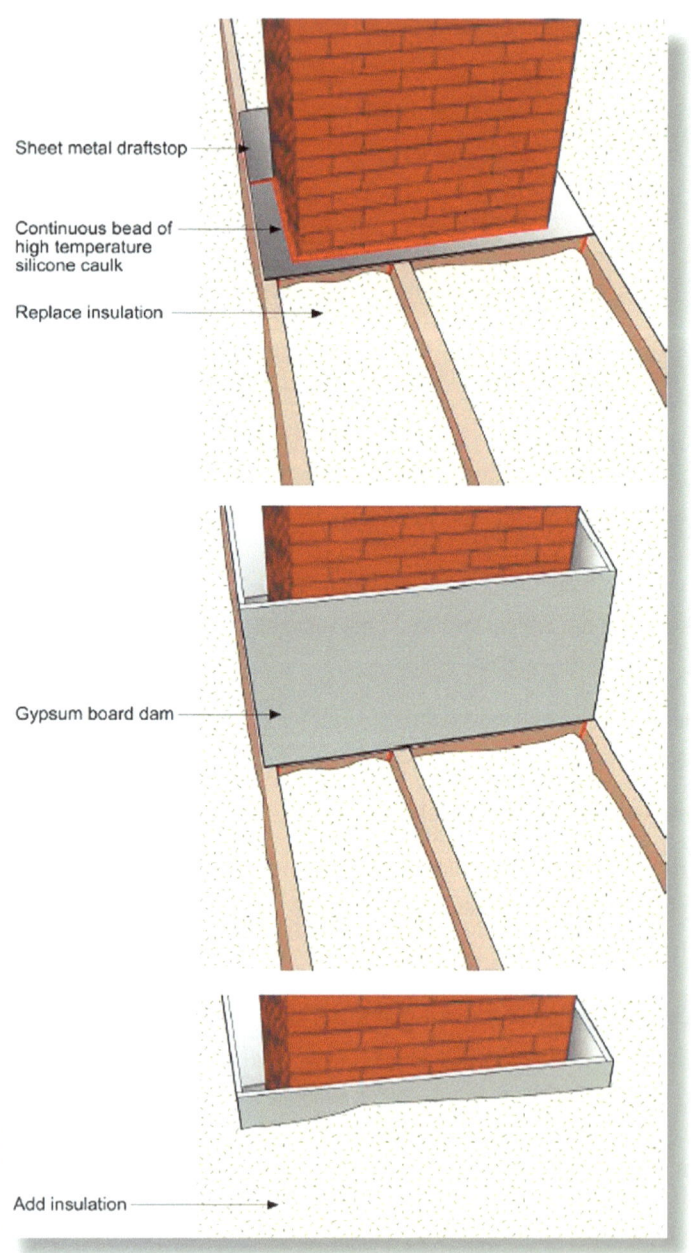

Fig. 9.8 Sealing a chimney penetration in the attic

Fig. 9.9 Sealing a furnace flue which penetrates the attic

Combustion exhaust stacks

Combustion exhaust stacks are like chimneys—except that they are made of metal and therefore conduct heat better than masonry. So it's important to keep the insulation away from their hot surface.

This is done in two steps, just like chimneys. First, fit a collar to the lower part of the stack, where it enters the attic. Seal the collar against air leakage, using fire-rated sealant or caulking. As with the chimney collar, be sure the joints are well-covered with sealant, because the next step will make those joints more difficult to fix later, if they leak air.

Next, make and install a metal insulation protection collar as shown in figure 9.9 above. Seal the bottom of the metal collar to the collar which seals the stack penetration, so that insulation can't accidentally leak under the metal collar into the air gap between the collar and the hot stack.

Fig. 9.10 Sealing plumbing and electrical penetrations

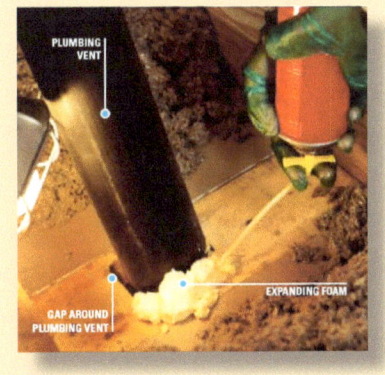 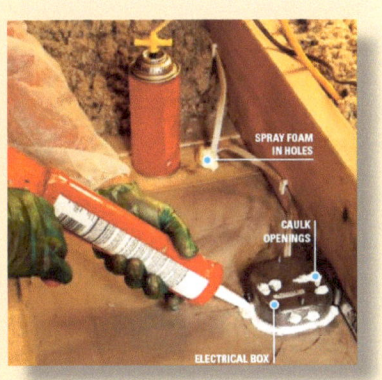

Plumbing & electrical penetrations

Plumbing penetrations are nearly a given in attics. Seal them with foam or caulk. There is no need to be concerned about stack temperature with plumbing or electrical boxes, so standard minimal-expansion foam is quite adequate for the task.

Fig. 9.11a
Insulated, air-tight cover for a can light which penetrates the attic

Can lights

Can lights which penetrate the ceiling need to be sealed up, air tight. Usually, replacing the fixture with a modern air-tight fixture rated for full insulation contact is the quickest and most economical way to ensure both air tightness and safety. But sometimes, circumstances dictate that you make combustion-safe covers for the can lights, and seal the covers to the ceiling with spray foam.

In those cases, keep in mind that older can lights were designed for air flowing upwards through the fixture to keep the wiring safely cool. So encapsulating such fixtures with an insulated, combustion-safe box is an uncertain solution. It may not provide adequate safety against overheated wiring if the owner keeps using high-wattage bulbs in the fixture. In those cases, equipping the fixture with a compact fluorescent bulb is at least a nod towards a safer fixture. But replacement is definitely the preferred option.

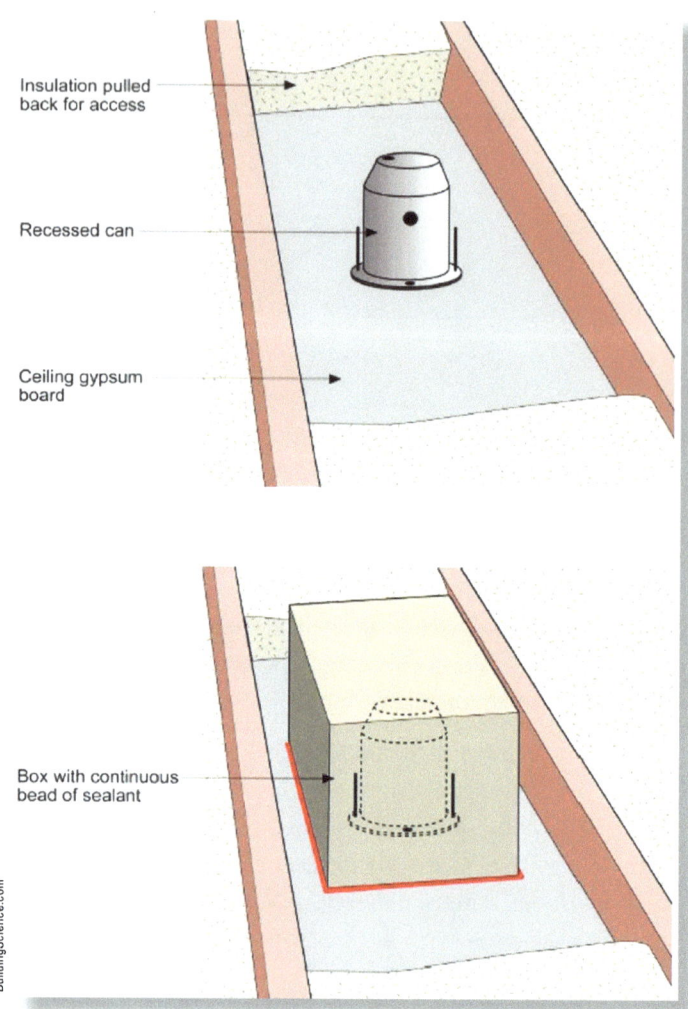

Fig. 9.11b
Diagram of an insulated, air-tight cover for a can light

Bathroom exhaust fans

Exhaust fans set into the ceiling of the upper floor often have sheet metal enclosures which leak a great deal of air into the attic. If these are not replaced with modern, more air-tight and more silent units, be sure to seal up the seams of the fan enclosure in addition to the gap around the fixture where it is set into the ceiling.

Ceiling gypsum board seams and wall top plates

The gypsum board which forms the walls and ceiling of the floor below the attic has seams which leak air at both the base of the wall, and at the top of the wall where it enters the attic. Seal up all of the top plates of the interior walls, plus the attic-side seams of the ceiling gypsum board, as seen in figure 9.13 below.

Fig. 9.13
Sealing the top plates of interior walls and the seams of ceiling gypsum board panels with spray foam
Also note the foam-covered, air-sealed electrical box

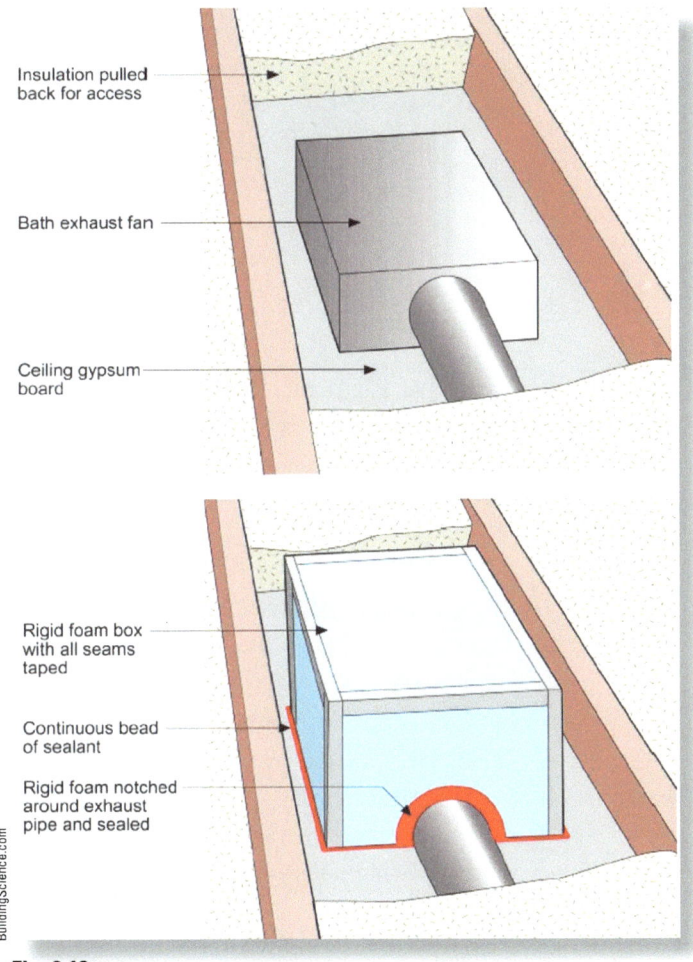

Fig. 9.12
Diagram of an insulated, air-tight cover for a leaky bathroom fan

PLUMBING PENETRATIONS... PLUS LEAKY TONGUE & GROOVE FLOORING

SPRAY FOAM, OVER THE ENTIRE MESS... NOW IT'S AIR-TIGHT

Fig. 9.14 Many plumbing penetrations from the crawl space
Also note the open joints of the tongue-and-groove subflooring.
The best plan may be to simply install spray foam over the entire surface

Air Leaks From The Crawl Space

Typical leaks from the crawl space to the 1st floor of the house are very much like the penetrations and air leaks in the attic. Seal up the joints around plumbing, electrical and duct penetrations.

Also in the crawl space, there are often openings where the floor joists connect to the exterior walls. To seal those big openings, there are two classic techniques. For many identical large openings, you can cut pieces of board insulation to fit, and then seal up all four edges with minimal-expansion foam. For smaller or more irregular openings, or opening which have pipes or wires running through them, you can stuff the openings with folded glass fiber batt insulation. Then cover the insulation with a layer of spray foam to ensure a tight seal.

Another classic leak problem in older California homes is tongue-and-groove subflooring, installed at a diagonal to the exterior walls. The joints between the boards open over time and leak a great deal of air upwards, into vertical wall cavities and other floor-to-ceiling paths like pipe chases, duct chases and chimney penetrations. Usually, there are so many penetrations and odd structural members supporting the floor that the most practical way to seal so many seams is simply to spray foam over the entire crawl-space side of the floor. That approach also allows for an excellent air seal around all plumbing, HVAC and electrical penetrations.

Progress Testing with the Blower Door

As you seal the home, for the first hour or two the major leaks will still be visually obvious to a trained crew. But after the obvious leaks are closed up, use the blower door every hour or so, to see how much work remains. The last blower door test, which shows that the target sealing rate has been reached, should be recorded as the test-out value. (Note: This will be an impressive improvement, and therefore worth mentioning and explaining to the owner.)

Finding Less-obvious Gaps, Cracks and Holes

In every home, there are gaps, cracks and holes which are simply very tough to locate, even for the most experienced of crews. That's why thermal cameras are such a useful tool when air sealing houses.

Fig. 9.15
Thermal cameras can help locate less-obvious air leakage points
*Be careful, however, to choose a camera with adequate thermal sensitivity (100 milliKevin or **less**, or **less** than 0.01°C).*

As shown in figure 9.15, a thermal camera can help you locate the areas where air is getting into the building. It shows surface temperature patterns. And often, those patterns indicate locations where cold or warm air from outdoors is leaking into the building.

Of course to be effective, a thermal camera needs two things: a significant temperature difference between indoors and outdoors, and a negative pressure high enough to pull outdoor air into the building. Without those, it's unlikely that the thermal camera will show you enough of a pattern to help you locate the problem areas.

Use the blower door to create the usual negative pressure inside the home, so that outdoor air will be pulled in through any leaks. Let the blower door run for about 10 to 15 minutes, so that the infiltrating air will have enough time to generate a visible temperature difference on the walls or ceiling near the leak location. And if the outdoor temperature is nearly the same as the indoor temperature, you may have to run the AC system or the heating system indoors for an hour or so to create a visually useful temperature difference.

The classic rule of thumb is that there should be a temperature difference of 18°F between indoors and outdoors for best results. But that old standard really misses the point. The useful temperature difference is simply one which generates a useful visual pattern. And that can be achieved at temperature differences as small as 5°F between indoors and outdoors, depending on your camera. The better your camera, the less temperature difference it will need to show you a useful pattern.

A word about thermal cameras for Performance Contracting

The camera needs to be sensitive enough, and must have enough pixels to show the thermal pattern of leakage. These days there is a wide range of thermal cameras available at lower and lower prices. But not all of the lowest-price cameras are useful for finding air leaks in buildings, even though they may be well-suited to inspections of electrical panels, where temperature differences are much greater.

If you're considering using a thermal camera to help with air leak detection, make sure the camera has a thermal sensitivity of less than 100 milliKelvin degrees. And ideally, the thermal sensitivity should really be 70 milliKelvin or below.

In specification sheets, this critical figure of merit is variously described as the "noise equivalent delta T (NEDT)", or the "thermal sensitivity." And the value is usually displayed as either thousandths of a degree C (0.01°C) or whole degrees milliKelvin (100 mK).

When the indoor and outdoor temperatures are close—as often happens in California— you'll need excellent thermal sensitivity to be able to see the subtle temperature patterns made by infiltrating outdoor air. When looking at thermal camera data sheets, keep in mind two principles: more pixels are better, and smaller thermal sensitivity is better. And don't bother with any camera that has a thermal sensitivity value larger than 0.01°C or 100 milliKelvin.

Note for the curious: Degrees Kelvin have the dimension as degree Celsius (1°K = 1°C), but the Kelvin scale begins at absolute zero (0°K = -273°C).

Chapter 10

Tips & Traps For Replacing Windows
By Steve Easley

Fig. 10.1 Window replacement
When accomplished as part a measured home performance retrofit, modern gas-filled windows with Low-E coatings will help downsize the cooling and heating equipment. To be sure, the cost of window replacement is high. But in addition to equipment and energy cost savings, the comfort benefits are significant—all year long.

Fig. 10.2 Extensive frame damage - Consider replacement
Single-pane glass stays cold during winter weather, which can lead to condensation and damage, in addition to high heating bills.

Fig. 10.3 Double-pane seal failure - Consider replacement
These older double-pane units have worn out, losing the seal that kept moisture out of the gap between the panes. Modern windows provide improved comfort, improved aesthetics and energy savings.

Tips & Traps for Replacing Windows & Sliders
By Steve Easley

Windows and sliding glass doors can be a significant source of heat gain and heat loss in a home as well as impact occupant comfort. While replacing windows and sliding glass doors won't reduce energy bills by enough money to offset the cost of their replacement, modern technologies do indeed save energy and increase comfort. Usually the homeowner is motivated by an intense desire to fix one or more of these annoying problems:

1. **Discomfort**. It's uncomfortable to sit or stay near the glass during sunny days or cold nights because the glass loses and gains so much heat.

2. **Leaks**. Rain or irrigation water leaks through or around the windows or sliding doors.

3. **Can't open**. Windows or sliding doors no longer open freely or close tightly. So the homeowner can't enjoy fresh air, and/or has to put up with hot air and cold air drafts near windows.

4. **Rot or rust**. Frames are rotted or corroded, leading to water leaks and drafts.

5. **Condensation**. The frames or the glass condenses and drips water, which in turn stains or warps the frames and sill, and stains the gypsum board under windows or stains the floor or carpet near the door. (Fig. 10.2)

6. **Window seal failure**. See fig. 10.3. The seal for the air gap between glass panes of an older-style double-pane window develops a leak. Moisture condenses in the gap between the panes, obscuring the view and ruining the unit's insulating value.

These aesthetic, durability and comfort problems are certainly worth fixing, and window replacement is an excellent way to solve them. When the windows need to be replaced anyway, the Performance Contractor can take advantage of modern glazing technology to reduce heating and cooling loads. When replaced as part of a comprehensive Measured Home Performance retrofit, modern glazing will improve comfort, allow further downsizing of cooling and heating equipment, and somewhat increase the overall project's utility savings.

Here's the Deal With Windows

Windows leak a lot more heat than insulated walls. A old-style single-glazed window has a thermal resistance of about R-1. Compare that to a code-compliant wall at R-13, and it's immediately obvious that old windows lose a lot of heat compared to the walls which surround them. Modern windows with high performance glass are a big improvement over old windows. In fact, they can be as much as 300% better than single pane aluminum windows at reducing heat loss.

But in most parts of sunny California, the window's R-value is not nearly as important as its ability to reduce the solar heat gain that gets through the glass. Old glazing allows a great deal of heat into the home, which increases the size of the AC unit needed to remove that heat. Windows are rated in this respect by their "Solar Heat Gain Coefficient" (SHGC). The SHGC is expressed as a decimal fraction of the total solar heat that they allow to pass. For example, the 0.85 SHGC of a single pane of conventional glass means that the glass is passing 85% of the sun's heat into the home.

In a retrofit situation, you don't want that extra heat in the house. Your client would much prefer a modern, gas-filled double-glazed window with a low emissivity coating on the glass and insulated frames, because that window has a SHGC of 0.27 rather than 0.85. Modern windows will reduce cooling loads related to older windows by about 70%. Since solar heat gain accounts for about 45% of the design cooling load, the 70% reduction of that 45% means the home will be more comfortable, and its AC system will be much smaller and will use less energy.

The much lower SHGC of modern windows, together with their 300% improvement in R-value, explains why it's useful to install high performance windows when old glazing is replaced.

Keep it real - Window replacement usually involves more than just the windows

Homeowners considering window replacement become enthusiastic when they see the relatively modest cost of the windows at their local home improvement store. These may or may not be of the quality necessary for improved comfort and thermal performance. Also, owners often forget or underestimate the cost of installation. And they are seldom even aware of the cost of fixing the occasional water leakage and air tightness problems ***around*** old window and door openings.

The Performance Contractor can only rarely pop out old windows and slide in new ones without disturbing the window casings, exterior siding and interior trim. New windows must be installed air-tight and flashed properly so they don't repeat or create water leakage problems. That means they must have structurally solid openings, durable siding and appropriate interior trim that can all be made air tight and water tight as the new windows are installed.

Usually, rough openings are sufficiently sturdy to support new windows. But sometimes, pulling out old windows exposes water leakage paths and rot around and under the rough opening, especially where the siding or stucco meets the window casing. In those cases, carpentry may be required to repair rotted structure, flash the window opening and the window itself, replace the exterior window casings, repair the siding where it connects to the new window assembly and replace interior trim to the owner's satisfaction.

The best time to discuss these facts of life with the homeowner is during the test-in visit, when the air leakage associated with windows is relatively easy to demonstrate to the owner with the blower door and thermal camera. If the costs of siding, new casings and structural repairs are not discussed early and tactfully, the homeowner will be in for major sticker shock, and consequently may suspect the contractor of highway robbery upon presentation of his proposal. Better to make a careful inspection and prepare the client for any high costs before the scope of the project becomes final in the customers mind.

Windows and Site Assessment

The test-in visit and evaluation will include an assessment of the existing windows' remaining useful life and their contribution to energy use. Without this information, the Performance Contractor would not be able to make a credible calculation of the home's heating and cooling loads. A useful assessment will include the:

1. General condition of the window: Does it operate smoothly and easily, and close tightly? Are the seals and weather stripping intact and resilient? Is the glass solidly set into the window frame so water won't leak in? Is there evidence of decay, water leakage or water stains on the windows inside, or around the window casings and siding on the outside?

2. Presence or absence of seal failure. If you see signs of condensation between the panes of glass of a multipane window, the seal is broken. Condensation occurs when warm, moist air infiltrates through an air leak in the seal that attaches the glass panes to the spacer. When infiltrating humid air contacts the cold glass, moisture condenses on its surface (inside the gap between the panes). Over time, repeated cycles of condensation and evaporation leaves a residue that discolors the glass permanently. There is no practical way to get rid of this residue and repair the insulating glass seal on a permanent basis. The unit should be replaced.

3. Square footage of each window and sliding glass door.

4. Percentage of glazing area compared to the total surface area for each exterior wall. (Pay close attention to measuring the square footage of west-facing glass, which has a greater effect on the cooling loads than does glass on the south or north sides.)

5. Depth of any overhangs, porches or similar shading devices, especially on the west and south sides of the home.

6. Amount of shading from nearby trees, tall bushes and buildings. (How much sun actually strikes the roof and windows?)

7. Frame material. (Aluminum, wood or vinyl)

8. Number of layers of glass in each window (Single or double)

9. Presence of low-E coatings (By using a low-E coating detector)

10. Net solar heat gain coefficient of the combined glazing layers, coatings and tints (By using a solar power meter)

11. Climate. If the heating season extends for several months instead of weeks, it may affect the choice of glazing.

Finally and perhaps most important; ask the homeowner if there are any plans to replace the windows because of problems with operation, comfort issues or for aesthetic reasons. If a home owner is going to replace their windows anyway, the additional cost of upgrading beyond a new double pane window to a high performance low-E, gas filled product is less than $1 per square foot.

Window Retrofit Options

There are three retrofit options. The best choice depends on the condition of the existing windows siding, window trim, sills and flashing.

Full window replacement

The existing frame is removed and the new window placed into the same position that was occupied by the old window. This is an opportunity to fix issues such as water or air leakage that may have occurred around the old frame.

Inserting windows in existing frame

The old sash, side jambs and trim are removed, but the original frame is left in place. The new window is inserted into this opening. Accommodate slightly out-of-square conditions of the existing frame if possible. Significant out-of-square conditions should be fixed with complete window replacement.

Sash replacement

Many manufacturers offer replacement sash kits, which include jamb liners to ensure good operability and fit. This option allows for relatively easy installation, but the existing frame must be in good shape so that air and water tightness are ensured.

Energy Savings From Window Replacement

The California Energy Commission reports that California has nearly 8.5 million single family homes. The average age of a California home is 37.2 years. On average California homes have windows that make up 15% - 20% of the wall surface area. This means that 15%- 20% of the walls of a typical home are insulated to R-1 or less. In addition the percentage of heat from the sun that gets through a single pane of glass is 85% which is a huge contributor to air conditioning loads.

High performance low-E windows did not become mainstream until the mid to late 1990's in California. There are millions of poorly performing single pane wood, aluminum and old-style double pane windows in the existing California housing stock. Most of the of windows installed in California from the early 1950's to the mid 1980's were single pane aluminum—the worst-performing windows from a thermal perspective.

Many existing windows in California are well beyond their service life. A 2007 study by the National Association of Home Builders of life expectancy of building materials and components reports that aluminum windows have a service life of 15-20 years. Measurements suggest that there is a tremendous amount of energy to be saved by improving window glazing in existing California homes. Today California energy codes require high performance window products.

Newer technologies provide a 300% increase in thermal performance as well as blocking over 70% of the sun's heat. In many homes, the largest component of the air conditioning load is the solar heat gain through glass.

Lowering AC loads keeps more kilowatts in the cheap zone

Not every kilowatt-hour has the same cost, even in the same house. Power companies have sliding electrical rates, depending on how much energy is used by the homeowner. The higher the consumption, the more each additional kilowatt-hour will cost.

The "base load tier" is cheap. But above a certain consumption level, the cost of an extra kilowatt-hour goes up dramatically. It's important to discuss with the homeowner that usage above their base load tier can triple their cost per kWh. That's why it's so important for the performance contractor to take the time to disaggregate the bill.

Homeowners use most of their base-tier power for lights, laundry, cooking and electronics. So their cheap kWh's are gone by the time it's hot enough to turn on the AC. In California, almost all air conditioning energy ends up being charged at the higher-tier rates. This real-world cost of air conditioning makes window retrofits more cost effective than one might expect, because modern windows make such large reductions in AC loads.

Incremental cost of excellent glazing is small

Based on a "first glance simple, payback analysis" retrofit windows are expensive. Given that fact, window retrofits make the most economic sense when the home owner is considering replacing their windows for reasons other than energy.

For example, modern windows improve comfort, reduce the potential for both window condensation and reduce UV fading of fabrics and furnishings. Modern windows also greatly reduce sound transmission—a significant benefit for those who have trouble sleeping.

When windows have to be replaced for reasons of durability or functionality, it does not take much more money to make them thermally excellent instead of just adequate (less than $1 per square foot of glass area).

Most studies show that the payback period for low-E glass rather than just conventional glass double-pane windows will be less than one year. This does not even take into account the cost savings of a downsized furnace and air-conditioner. Nor does it take into account the improved comfort of occupants, one of the greatest benefits of the revolution in glazing technology.

While the cost of replacing windows for energy reasons alone will be rather high, Home Performance Contractors would be remiss if they did not ask the homeowner if they already have plans to replace their windows, before deciding on the full scope of their home performance project.

Energy Losses and Gains Through Windows

Windows loose energy in the winter by conduction and re-radiation to the colder outdoors. In summer the windows add heat to the home via conduction and solar radiation. Windows lose and gain heat through the frame, the glass and the spacers that separate the glass in double pane products.

What's new about the new technologies

New window technologies for replacement windows have far better glass with low-emissivity coatings, gas filled spaces between two panes of that better glass, warm edge technology and thermally improved frames. Modern windows have net R-values of 3.3-3.8, (U .30-.26). This is a 300% improvement in R-value over single glazing. They also only let in 24% to 30% of the sun's heat. That's why upgrading windows reduces cooling loads dramatically.

High U-values bad, Low U-values good

A single pane aluminum window has a net R-value of 0.9. The R-value is used as a figure of merit by the insulation industry, and its range of values is familiar to contractors and homeowners. When you say that aluminum windows have an R-value of less than one... everybody more or less understands that aluminum windows transmit about 20 times more heat than an R-19 wall. The benefit of upgrading from an R-1 window to an R-4 window would be easily understood.

However, the window industry uses the U-value as a figure of merit instead of R-value. The U-value describes the *rate of transmission of heat*, rather than the degree of *resistance* to heat flow. The higher the U factor (transmission) the lower the R-value (resistance). So it gets confusing, because a high R-value is a good thing... but a high U-value is a bad thing. It's not good to have a high rate of heat transmission through walls or windows.

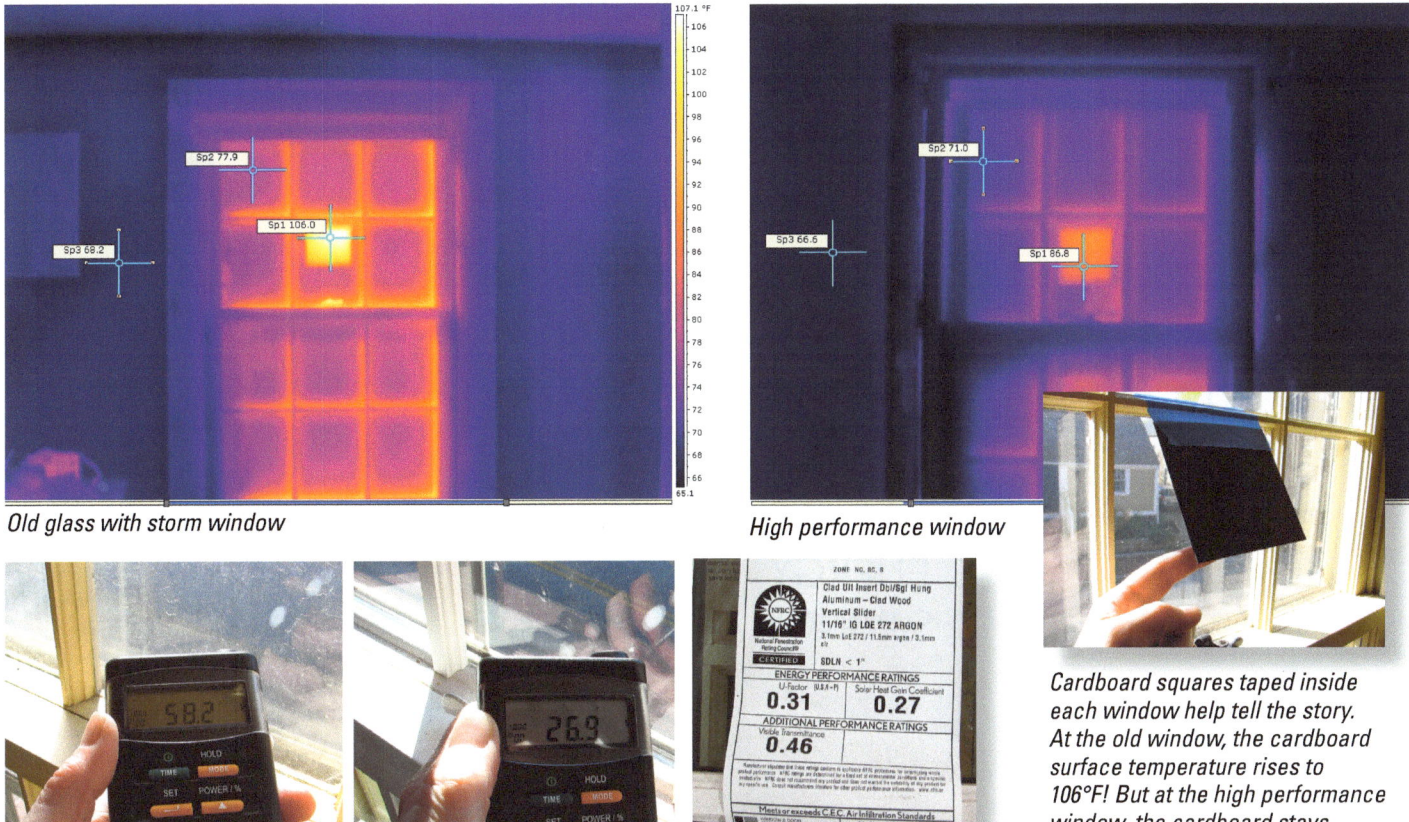

Old glass with storm window

High performance window

Cardboard squares taped inside each window help tell the story. At the old window, the cardboard surface temperature rises to 106°F! But at the high performance window, the cardboard stays below 87°F.

Fig. 10.4 High solar heat gain is not helpful
The old-style double-pane unit at left has a solar heat gain measured at 58.2. In other words, a little over 58% of the sun's heat comes though the window and into the house to increase cooling loads. In contrast, the measurement also shows the modern high performance gas-filled, Low-E window at right has a solar heat gain of only 26.9, indicating a satisfying match with the label that says the window's rated SHGC is 0.27.

But it's easy to convert between R and U-values. If you know the U-value, you can easily obtain the R-value of that assembly, because the R-value is the reciprocal of U-value, and vice-versa.

For example if a window has a U-value of 0.33, just divide 1 by that number to obtain its R-value: 1÷0.33 = 3.0. And the procedure works in the other direction as well. Divide 1 by the R-value to obtain the equivalent U-value: 1 ÷ 3 = 0.33. The bottom line is that when shopping for modern energy-efficient replacement windows, don't bother with anything that has a U-value above 0.33 (don't bother with a window R-value of less than 3).

On balance, low solar heat gain is the best choice

In California, solar heat gain through windows can account for up to 45% of design cooling loads. The solar energy load on every square foot of vertical surface is approximately 250 BTUs per hour. So the cooling required to offset the solar gain of two 5 ft. X 5 ft. east or west facing windows is about 12,000 Btu/h. That means you'll need one ton of air conditioning to remove the heat from those windows alone, unless you use modern windows, with modern glazing.

One might reasonably assume that such high solar gain would help reduce winter heating bills. But usually, the assumed benefits do not occur in real life, for three reasons:

1. Winter days are shorter, so there's less potential solar gain available than one might expect.

2. There is more cloud cover during cold months, so the actual solar heat gain never matches the theoretical potential.

3. The lower angle of the sun during the winter means its energy is more effectively blocked by nearby houses and trees.

The net result is that for the majority of houses in California, the best choice is low solar heat gain glazing. These windows keep cooling loads so low that for much of the year, houses in milder climate zones may need no air conditioning at all. And when air conditioning becomes a necessity, low solar gain glazing keeps the cost of that cooling to a minimum.

Modern Window Technologies

For pragmatic, cost-effective decisions, it's helpful for both the contractor and homeowner to understand exactly *why and how* modern window technologies provide comfort and energy benefits. This section provides a brief summary of key recent innovations.

Low-E coatings

Low–E coatings are standard in the industry today. Low-E stands for (low-emittance). Emittance is a term used to describe how well a material gives off its heat energy. Low–E coatings are also highly reflective to infrared energy. About half the heat from the sun is in the infrared spectrum (which is not visible to the human eye). These coatings are also designed to reduce heating costs in winter as well as reducing cooling costs in summer.

Of the many window technologies developed in recent years, none has had as great an effect on window energy performance as the

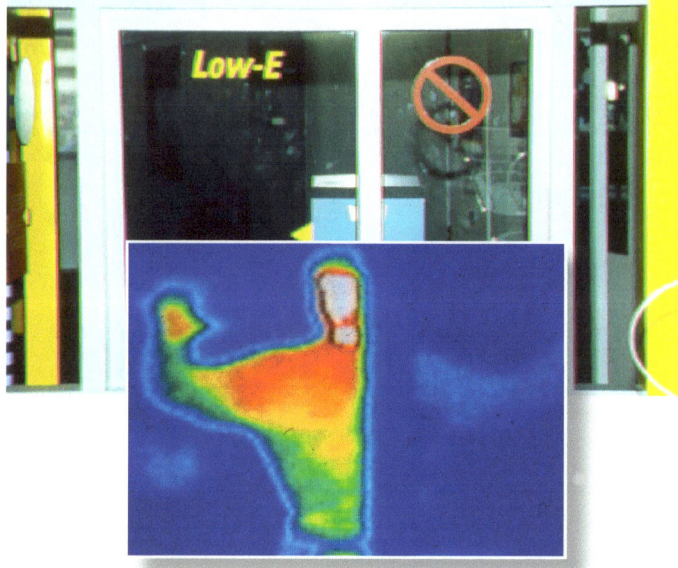

Fig. 10.5 Low-E coatings also keep heat in the house during winter
The thermal image shows how much more heat is reflected back into the house by the Low-E coating (the glass on the left) compared to the old-style uncoated glass on the right side of the same assembly.

low-E coating. A low-E coating is a microscopically thin, transparent metal layer applied to one of the glass surfaces in the sealed space of the insulating glass unit (IGU) that is heat reflective. In an ordinary IGU (no coating) about two-thirds of the heat transfer across the gap is via thermal radiation. Low-E coatings will block most of this heat transfer. The net effect is that double pane glass with low-E insulates as well as uncoated triple- or quad-pane glass.

Strategically-placed Low-E coatings also improve comfort in the winter. When the heat loss through the window is reduced, the room-side glass surface temperature is warmer during cold weather. The infrared photograph in Figure 10.5 shows two window units, one with low-e glass and the other without. The image on the left shows the heat from my body being reflected back to my camera from low-E glass. Compare that to the much lower amount of heat reflection from the window the unit on the right, which has ordinary double glass (no coating).

Low-E coatings increase comfort by making the inside surface of glass warmer, leading to less heat loss from the person to the window on a cold day. Also, people are more comfortable when a room's escaping heat is reflected back at them by low-E coatings. Another benefit is reduced condensation potential during he winter. A warmer surface on the inside of the glass means the outdoor temperature has to drop much lower than normal to chill the inside of the window low enough to produce condensation.

Spectrally selective Low-E coatings

Roughly half of the energy (heat) in sunlight is invisible to the human eye. Low-E coating manufacturers have learned how to design coatings that let most of the visible light pass through, with little tint or coloration, while blocking most of the solar heat. The different glass designs can be grouped into generic categories of high, medium, and low solar-heat gain.

Most homes in California have air conditioning. So a low solar gain product makes sense. Low solar gain low-E coatings also do a good job of preventing winter heat loss and reducing summer heat gain, while still allowing most of the visible light to enter the space.

Reduced fading with Low-E coatings

The spectral selectivity of low-E coatings also allows them to block significant amounts of ultraviolet (UV) light. Research into the fading of fabrics, artwork, finishes, and home furnishings, has shown that the radiant energy that affects fading includes portions of the visible light spectrum in addition to UV. The International Organization for Standardization (ISO) has proposed a damage-weighted scale called Tdw-ISO that accounts for the effects of both UV and visible light. The ratings for low-E glass suggest that low-solar-gain low-E glass would reduce the rate of fading by over 40% compared with clear glass.

Keep in mind, however, that for residential windows a claim that a glass type will "eliminate fading altogether" is highly suspect. Apart from spectrally selective, high-cost, low-visibility, museum-grade glass (not normally available in residential windows) there will always be a risk of some degree of fading. The rate of fading will vary with the type of material, the pigments used and the light exposure levels. Keeping sensitive fabrics, valuable documents and art work out of direct sunlight is always a good idea.

Warm edge insulating glass spacer systems

The aluminum spacer bars used to separate the two panes in old-style double glazing create a thermal bridge all around the edge of the glass. Consider the winter situation. Despite the warm center-of-glass temperatures achieved with low-E glass, the edges of the glass were cold because of thermal bridging. This can also lead to condensation (Figure 10.4) during cold periods.

The problem has been the spacer bars. Aluminum conducts heat 300 times faster than non-metallic materials. Today, more than 90% of the new or replacement residential windows use some form of "warm-edge" system. The designs vary from low-conductance metals (e.g., stainless steel) to foam or plastic replacements of the aluminum spacer. The thermal performance improvement from warm-edge technology is reflected in the improved (lower) window U-factors found on the National Fenestration Rating Council label (NFRC label - see figure 10.5). In addition to better thermal resistance, however, it's important to pay attention to window durability. Be sure to compare manufacturers' warranty provisions. Sometimes the best thermal performer will lack long-term warranty support due to concerns about the durability of new materials and technologies.

Gas fills

Adding an inert gas between the panes of glass to replace air improves the window's thermal performance. The gas, usually argon or krypton is heavier than air. Heavy is good. Heavier gas molecules slow down the energy-robbing convection loops (thermosiphoning) between the panes which allow heat to move from one pane to the other.

Argon and krypton also enhance the performance gains from low-E coatings. When used in conjunction with a Low-E coating argon or krypton will typically improve (reduce) the window U-factor by about 10%. People often ask if the gas leaks out over time. It does.. but not much. Leakage will be less than 10% over the life of the window unless there is a seal failure. But of course leakage can vary by manufacturer. It's important to read the manufacturer's warranty to understand their provisions regarding gas retention.

Triple and quad pane glazing

Double-pane glass is optimized by adding a low-E coating and gas fill. To provide even better insulating values, some new window designs are incorporating triple and quad-pane systems with multiple low-E coatings (one coating in each air space). Concerns with weight and thickness have some manufacturers replacing the internal layer(s) with plastic or suspended films

Tinted glass

All energy from the sun is transmitted through the glass or reflected or absorbed by the glass. Tinted glass is sometimes used to reduce heat gain in hot climates. However, tinted glass gets hot in sunlight (from absorption) and eventually re-radiates that heat into living spaces.

Tinted glass also suffers more loss of light transmission than low-E coatings. There are some spectral tinted glasses available today that have a high visible light transmittance... but their transmitted light is usually light blue or green. Most residential windows usually avoid tints, given the market preference for clear glazing. Also, these tints don't reduce the heat loss (U-factor), so they provide no benefit during the winter months.

Aftermarket applied films

Tint films are often retrofitted onto windows in rooms that overheat due to direct sunlight. While they can help address overheating, the films can be problematic because the low visible light transmission can excessively darken rooms. There can also be problems with film adhesion, and some window manufacturers will void their warranty if tint films have been applied. When buying new or replacement windows, look for products with a low SHGC, indicating that solar control is already built in to the window.

INTERIOR GLASS SURFACE TEMPERATURE

Double Pane Low-E coating	Summer day (89°F)	Winter night (0°F)
No coating	91° F	44° F
Low solar gain	82° F	56° F

Courtesy of Cardinal Glass

Table 10.1 Benefit of Low Solar Gain Low-E coatings
In nearly all cases, the low solar gain coating is the best choice. It reflects heat back to your body during the winter, so you feel warmer. And during the summer, the coated glass emits much less heat than uncoated glass, so your skin surface stays cooler, even when the indoor air temperature is relatively warm.

Comfort and High Performance Windows

Windows have a huge impact on comfort. A study commissioned by Pacific Gas & Electric several years ago discovered that the number one reason customers make energy-efficiency improvements to their homes is to increase their comfort. When it is 40°F outside, the inside surface temperature of a single-pane window can be 20°F colder than room temperature. Since our bodies radiate heat to colder surfaces at an exponential rate, a room full of poorly insulating windows can make us feel uncomfortable (by radiant cooling of our bodies) even if the home is well insulated. High-performance technologies can make windows feel warmer during cold weather by keeping the temperature of the interior glass surface higher.

Glass surface temperature strongly affects comfort

There's another subtle but very important comfort problem of poor glazing which increases cooling costs. Year round, and in all of California climates, windows can be the biggest source of thermal discomfort. (See table 10.1) During sunny days and clear nights, when you are sitting or sleeping close to windows, the inside surface temperature of the glass becomes just as important to your comfort as the indoor air temperature.

Consider the "open furnace" effect of poor glazing during hot sunny days. High solar heat gains, combined with the hot inside glass temperature make the occupant want to set the cooling thermostat about 4°F lower, to provide the same comfort as low solar-gain low-E glass. The lower the thermostat setting, the greater the cost of cooling.

We've already seen that the greater R-value of gas-filled double pane glass provides better insulation, which reduces the heating and cooling loads. But keep in mind that Low-E coatings add another energy benefit because occupants are not roasted by the glass surface temperature during summer or frozen during the winter. With less radiant heating and cooling from the glass, occupants are comfortable at more economical thermostat settings during both seasons.

Window Condensation, a Real Pain in the Glass

One common reason people replace their windows is because of inside surface condensation during cold weather. And if the home had window condensation *before* the Measured Home Performance Retrofit, the risk of condensation may go up afterwards, because the home will be so much more air-tight, keeping more humidity indoors (unless a ventilation system is part of the retrofit). But the good news is that adding window replacement with high performance glass to the project will significantly reduce the potential for condensation.

Home Performance and window replacement both reduce the risk of condensation

Many of the factors which led to past condensation will probably be eliminated by the Home Performance Retrofit.

Consider the ventilation improvement. When combustion safety and/or indoor air quality issues demand that the Home Performance Retrofit include a dedicated ventilation system, the risk of excessive humidity is reduced because humid air is exhausted and dry outdoor air is bought in to replace it.

Also, one reason for condensation is keeping curtains closed to avoid the body-chilling effect of large amounts of cold glass at night. The glass gets cooler, because the heat in the room does not get past the curtains. So even normal amounts of indoor humidity will condense on the windows, because they have become so cold. With better windows, there may be no need to close curtains for extended periods, because the glass surface won't pull so much heat out of the occupants.

Also, after a Home Performance Retrofit, there's little or no need to run a humidifier for comfort, because the indoor humidity is held in by the improved air tightness of the building. So there's less risk of over-saturating the air.

Predicting condensation

The chart in figure 10.6 shows the indoor relative humidity at which moisture will condense on the glass at given out door temperature, for different window configurations. The values come from the Building Scientists at the Department of Energy's Lawrence Berkeley Laboratory. As shown on the graphs, high performance windows with low U factors significantly reduce the potential for condensation.

The left side of the graph shows the indoor relative humidity (%) from 0-100%. The scale at the bottom of the graph represents outdoor temperature. So as an example, this chart shows us that if we have single pane windows and it's 30 degrees outside we will experience condensation on the surface of this glass at an indoor relative humidity of about 32%. If we look at the same conditions for a double pane, low-E window with argon gas the window is likely not to experience condensation on the glass surface unless the relative humidity is above 72%! (An indoor humidity level that would also lead to mold growth on cool surfaces.)

The frames also matter

To avoid condensation, the type of frame is just as important as the glass and the low-E coatings. This means paying attention to the type of frame, glass configuration, spacers etc. Selecting or specifying the wrong window technology for a cold climate can be a costly mistake.

Window frames can be fabricated from metal, wood, vinyl, fiberglass, and composite materials. It's important to understand that metal conducts energy several hundreds times faster that wood or plastic materials. You can have excellent thermal properties for the

Fig. 10.6 Condensation risk of glazing alternatives
The risk of condensation is much less with modern glazing. That's because the inside surface of modern insulating glass is much warmer than conventional glass during the winter.

glass but if you have a highly conductive metal frame you can easily experience condensation on the frame in cold weather.

In cold climates, condensation can still occur if indoor humidity is exceptionally high

Before you promise that new windows will solve all condensation problems, keep in mind that condensation can still happen in cold climates if the indoor humidity is exceptionally high. Windows neither generate nor eliminate the humidity that causes condensation—they only react to their environment. Indoor activities which sometimes lead to excessive indoor humidity include:

- Cooking or boiling water for hours rather than for minutes without operating an effective kitchen exhaust system.

- Deciding not to operate those annoying noisy bathroom exhaust fans as all sixteen members of the family (including the dogs) take baths and showers one after another.

- Implementing an interior decoration scheme based on the look of the Amazon rain forest, including dozens of plants which require daily watering.

- Drying clothes indoors during winter, or failing to connect the clothes dryer's vent hose to the outdoors.

- Operating a vaporizer for days rather than for a few hours.

If the home is in a cold climate zone and if any of those factors are at work and seem unlikely to change, the Performance Contractor will need to add a dedicated ventilation system to reduce indoor humidity, even if the replacement windows are superb.

The NFRC Label Is Your Friend

The National Fenestration Rating Council (NFRC) is a non-profit collaborative effort of manufacturers, the Dept. of Energy, utilities and other interested parties. The organization has been active in the public interest since the mid 1990's. It sets standards for rating energy

U-Factor

U-factor is a measure of how much heat escapes through the whole product. The lower the U-factor, the better the window is at reducing heat flow into or out of a home. U-factor is the inverse of R-value. 1/R= U and U =1/R. So a window with a U factor of .5 has an R-value of 2. The U factor is a helpful indicator of the window's winter performance. Look for U-Factors of 0.33 or less.

Visible Transmittance

This the percentage of visible light that comes through the entire window. The higher the number, the more visible light gets through the window. Basically this rating indicates how clear the glass is. Coatings or tints on glass increase energy performance — but also reduce the amount of light that gets through the window. You typically do not notice an appreciable reduction in light until the VLT gets below 0.5. It is important to remember that this is a total window rating so grids, larger frames etc. reduce the visible light transmission. For example two windows can have the same glass but if one has grids between the panes of glass it will have a lower VLT, even though the glass appears to be completely clear.

Solar Heat Gain Coefficient (SHGC)

Probably the most important number on the label for an air conditioned house. The SHGC is the percent of the sun's heat that gets through the window. In the cooling climates of California, 45% of the air conditioning loads are solar gain through windows. Look for an SHGC of 0.30 or less.

Air Leakage

This number indicates how many cubic feet of air leak through a square foot of window area, at a test pressure of 50 Pascals (Rougly the pressure created by a 20 mph wind). Less leakage is better. Typical air leakage ratings of modern windows are 0.1 to 0.3 cfm/ft2 @ 50 Pa.

Condensation Resistance

This rating indicates a window's ability to resist moisture condensation on the interior surface of the window. The values will be between 1 and 100. The higher the rating, the better the window is at resisting condensation. Windows with low U factors have good thermal performance and thus have a higher (better) condensation resistance factor.

Fig. 10.7 - The National Fenestration Rating Council (NFRC) Label

performance of windows and doors. The NFRC rating consists of a series of measurements that rate the performance of the entire window, including its frame and any grids or muntins as well as its glass. The values which define the each unit's performance are included on the NFRC label, a certificate which is attached to every window rated according to NFRC standards. In recent years, local energy codes have required the use of the NFRC label on windows and glass doors, to provide certainty about their energy performance.

An example of the NFRC label is shown in figure 10.5 above, along with an explanation of each variable which appears on that label. In general terms, the values indicate the window's winter performance, its summer performance, air leakage, the amount of light the window lets in and even its resistance to condensation. Comparing values on the NFRC label allows you to fairly compare the costs and value provided by different windows.

Because of their need for summer cooling, (or their desire to avoid mechanical cooling altogether) most homes in most of California are usually best-served by a window which has:

a. Argon-filled, double glazing

b. Low-solar-gain low-E glass

c. SHGC below 0.30

d. U-factor below 0.33

Energy Savings Comparisons

Energy savings from replacement windows are difficult to estimate accurately in a short (and economical) amount of time. In addition to energy costs, savings depend on the orientation, size and exact shading of each window, the design and operating characteristics of the HVAC system and of course the local climate in all its variations year-to-year.

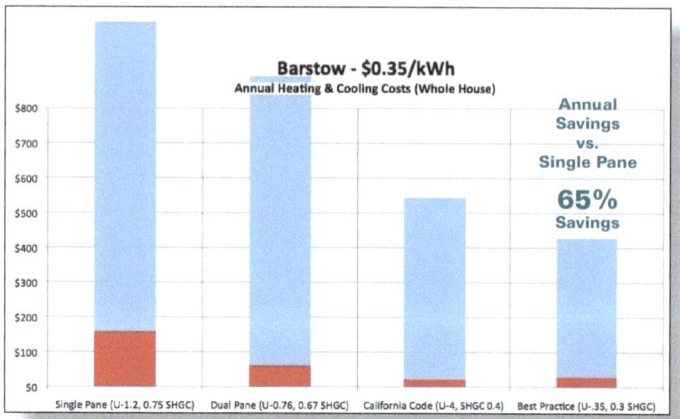

That said, it's possible to provide order-of-magnitude estimates which compare the effect of window choices on the whole house's annual heating & cooling costs in six California climates. These graphs show results for different costs of power—one which represents a current high-tier cost (24¢/kWh), and another (35¢/kWh) which may be common in the future. Other assumptions include:

1. Floor area: 2,000 ft^2

2. Total glazing: 15% of wall surface (300 ft^2 total), evenly distributed on all sides of the home, with no exterior shading.

3. Heat: Natural gas at $1.50/therm, 92% AFUE furnace

4. Cooling: DX with a COP of 4.0, with power costs as noted.

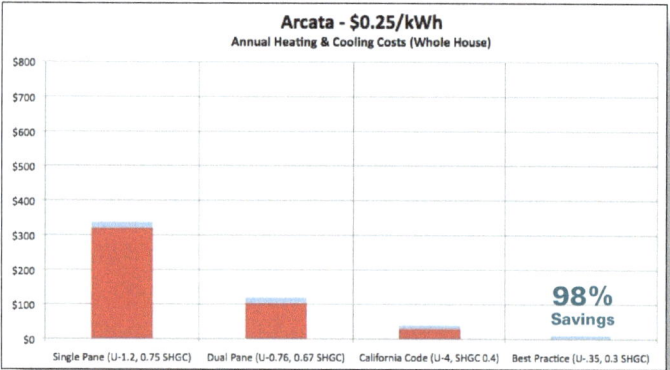

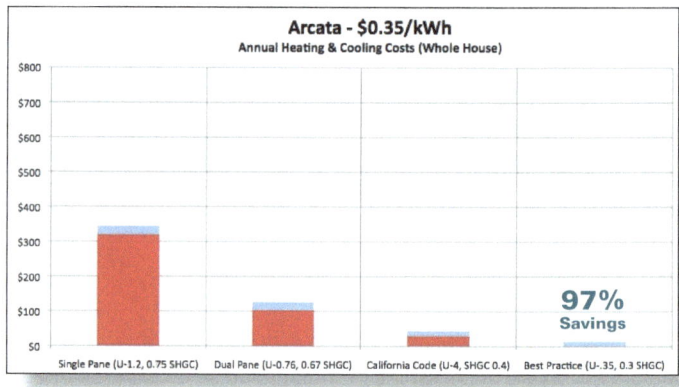

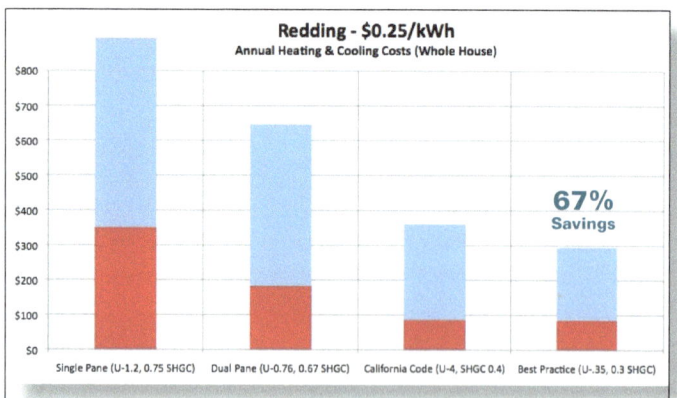

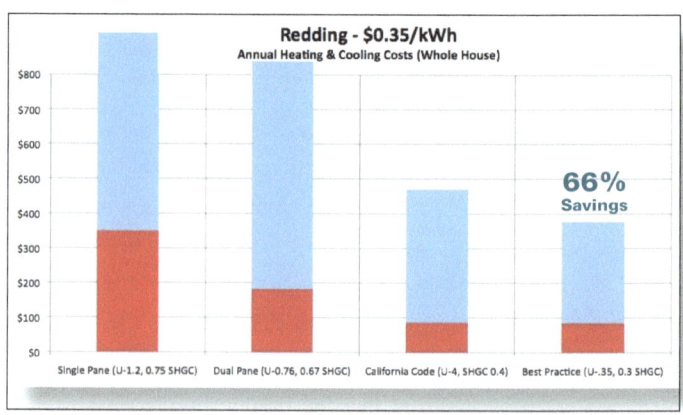

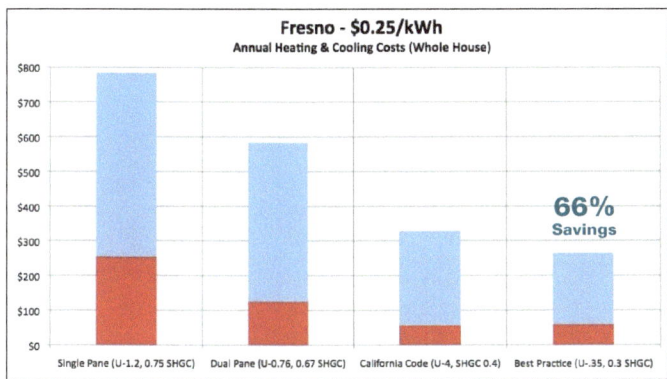
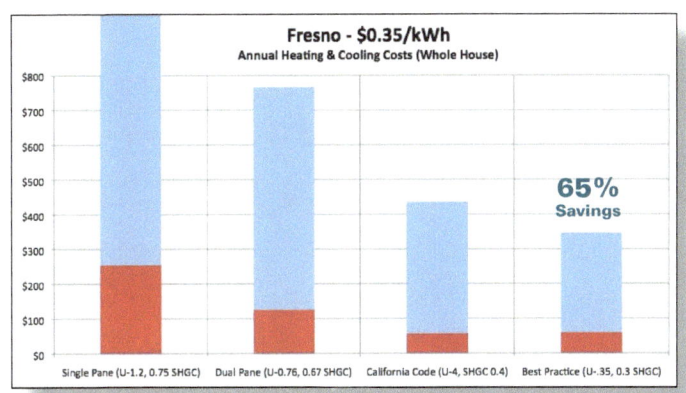
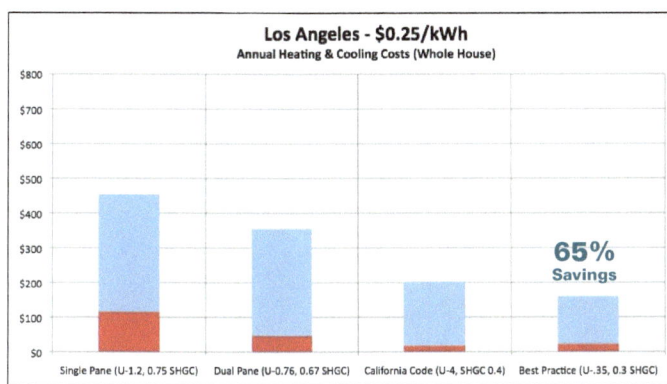
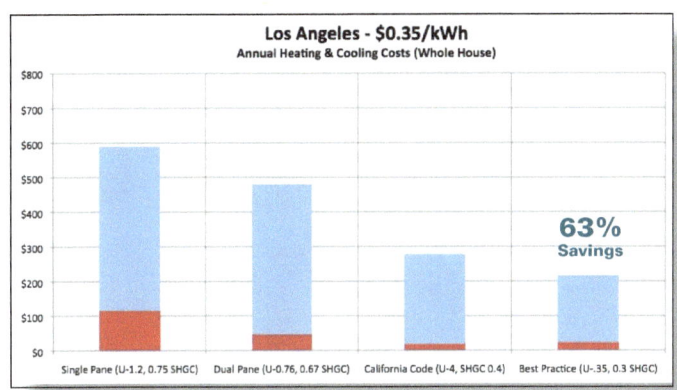
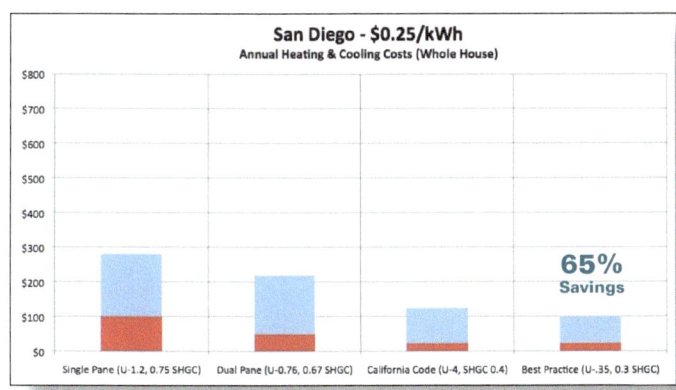
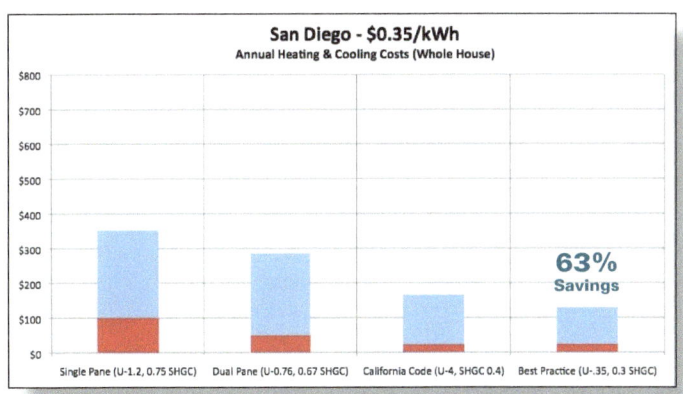

Chapter 11
Owner Education

Fig 11.1 Owner education
Because of their training and experience, Peformance contractors can often help homeowners understand what really saves energy and what does not. There are a lot of misimpressions out there!

Owner Education

Most homeowners who are interested in energy retrofits are also quite interested in learning what really saves energy and what does not. So they've been listening to many sales pitches, and doing a lot of research.

Energy-saving technology can be complex, and results depend often on exact circumstances. With respect to saving energy in California homes, here are a few of the simpler and more certain observations about what's been proven to work and what has not.

Suggestions which save energy

What really saves energy is simply to turn things off when you don't need them on. Most of these suggestions don't cost much money—but they do require a few seconds of time and attention.

In the summer, turn off fans when people aren't in the room

Fans don't cool buildings—they only cool people, cats and dogs. Actually, running a fan adds heat to a room, because all fans use electrical power, and that power is released as heat whenever the fan is operating.

When there are people in the room the fan creates a light breeze which improves comfort, even though it's adding a small amount of heat. But if there are no people in the room to enjoy that light breeze, a fan saves no energy—it's just consuming electrical power and heating up the room. To save energy, turn off fans if people leave the room.

Save energy by turning stuff off when nobody cares

Turn off any lamp, lighting fixture, electrical appliance or any electronic entertainment if nobody's using it.

This seems like a simplistic suggestion. But it's rather interesting to take a look around the house and realize how often the lights are left on when people leave the room, or how often the radio or TV is still on even though nobody's in the room to enjoy the show. More than 37% of all annual energy use is in the category of "other electrical."

So there's quite a rich mother load of energy savings to be mined by using the sophisticated, high-tech technique of simply "turning stuff off when nobody's using it."

Compact fluorescent bulbs save a great deal of energy

In recent years, compact fluorescent bulbs and have become widely available in every conceivable size and shape, and their light spectrum has improved radically from the cold, harsh light of industrial tubes to the warm, inviting light expected of domestic illumination.

The numbers really tell the story of the dramatic energy savings made possible by these bulbs. For example, the illumination formerly provided by a 75 Watt bulb is produced by a compact fluorescent bulb which uses only 20 Watts, or about 26% of what the old incandescent bulb required. Or consider the improvement in "flame-tipped" bulbs for decorative fixtures like candelabras or exterior door lanterns: 40 Watts of illumination for only 7 Watts of power consumption.

After turning stuff off, the greatest savings for the smallest investment is to replace all incandescent bulbs with compact fluorescents.

Energy costs?... Tiered rates make every Watt matter

When the home is served by an electrical utility company that provides "tiered rates," even very small additional electrical loads can cost big bucks if the home's base load stays high.

With tiered rates, the first few kilowatts of power used by the home are usually cheap—perhaps as little as a few cents per kilowatt-hour. But if the base load created in the home stays high, the consequences of even a little bit more power use can be surprisingly expensive. If additional power is needed when the base load is high, the next kilowatt-hour might cost as much as 35¢ instead of 9¢.

The rates are set that way to discourage the use of electricity at times when the system as a whole is heavily loaded, which is when the cost to generate that electricity skyrockets.

The implication for homeowners with tiered power rates is clear: keep your base load as low as possible by following the advice to turn stuff off when nobody cares, and by using fluorescent bulbs in all your fixtures. That way, when you have to use power at an "expensive time," you're less likely to exceed the consumption limit for your low-cost electrical rate.

Smart power strips can be great annual energy savers

For a small investment (less than $30.00) there's a way to make turning things off even easier. A "smart power strip" allows one switched appliance, such as a computer, to switch off all other appliances connected to the same power strip (such as a printer, scanner and display screen). That way, turning off five appliances only requires the attention and mind-space to turn off one.

Smart power strips don't make sense everywhere in the house. But they are an excellent way to reduce annual energy consumption of computers, electronic game consoles and audio equipment. All of those devices often have many peripherals which don't need to be switched on if nobody's using the primary appliance.

Replace HVAC filters every month

Replacing filters saves energy in several subtle ways. In the simplest example, clean filters present less resistance to air flow. More resistance means more energy consumption—less resistance means less energy consumption. That's a bit of an oversimplification, because different types of fans in different systems react to changing air pressure in different ways with respect to power consumption. But in general, it's true that clean filters save energy. In some systems they save more energy than in others.

The more subtle point is that when the air flow is correct, people will be comfortable, and when it's not, they won't. When filters load up, there's less air flowing through the system. Without enough air, occupants become uncomfortable, and change the thermostat setting more often, to regain comfort. Each change in thermostat setting costs extra energy.

That waste can be avoided by making sure the filters are changed once a month, so that the system air flow stays constant, and therefore occupants are comfortable without changing the thermostat setting.

There are also benefits within the heating and air conditioning equipment when the air flow is constant and set correctly. Constant and correct air flow saves energy, and helps the equipment last longer and require less maintenance. Again, the amount of energy and the length of life extension are quite system-dependent.

Taken as a whole (much like oil changes every 3,000 miles in a car) the modest costs of time, attention and 12 new filters each year will be repaid many times by better comfort, better indoor air quality and less energy, plus better system reliability and reduced maintenance. Monthly filter changes are simply a very good idea.

Items that don't save energy

There are many devices which can save energy in certain circumstances, but not in others. Here are a few items in that category—devices which under some circumstances might save energy, but which in typical homes in California either use extra energy, or which don't make much of an improvement.

With an efficient system, thermostat setback is a bad idea

Night setback and daytime setback makes sense if the home is leaky, poorly-insulated and has an oversized, poorly-installed HVAC system. Since sadly that's common, it's true that night and daytime setback can save energy in many homes in North America.

However, setback is nearly always counterproductive in air-tight homes which have good insulation and energy-efficient HVAC design and installation.

The reasons why setback doesn't save energy in excellent homes are not obvious. But here's why. A well-designed HVAC system has just enough capacity to keep up with the loads on a design day. Because it does not have wasteful extra capacity, it won't be able to heat up or cool down a house quickly. It's basically designed to be able to change the temperature in the home by about 3°F after it's been running for an hour. But if the setback has allowed the home to heat up to, say 85°F during the day, then it's going to need several hours to recover.

Since the occupants are not going to be comfortable during those hours of recovery, their natural reaction is to set the thermostat to more extreme temperatures. That won't work, because the system just does not have any wasteful extra capacity. Even so, the system eventually overshoots the target temperature, leading to more discomfort and more energy use to get the temperature back to where it really needed to be all along.

Here's the main point: because the home is so air tight and so well-insulated, the system does not use much energy to keep it at a constant temperature. It uses much less energy to keep it at a constant temperature than it would use when trying to recover quickly, after a setback period.

So unless the house is going to be unoccupied for more than a day or two (and unless you're going to allow several hours to recover temperature) don't use the setback feature of your thermostat. It won't save energy in your tight, well-insulated home with it's highly energy efficient HVAC system.

Whole-house fans and attic fans don't reduce AC costs

If the house does not have any air conditioning system, or if you choose not to run the AC equipment, then a whole-house fan can provide some comfort at relatively low electrical cost.

However, if the house is being air conditioned, then a whole-house fan (which pulls large amounts of outdoor air into the house) is counterproductive—it makes the air conditioning system use more energy, not less.

Further, when a house is being air conditioned, fans which ventilate the attic are net energy losers, because they pull air from inside the home. That expensive, conditioned air is replaced by unconditioned outdoor air. If you are running window air conditioners or a central AC system while the attic fan is operating, then the incoming replacement air is an extra load on the AC equipment. So now both the attic fan and the AC system are using energy. The AC system is using much more energy than it would if it didn't have to remove the extra load being pulled through the house by either an attic fan or a whole-house fan.

Higher SEER and AFUE ratings don't always save energy

The efficiency of HVAC equipment is rated, in accordance with Federal law, by measurements of seasonal energy efficiency ratio (SEER) for AC equipment, and by annual fuel utilization efficiency (AFUE) for heating equipment. And it's true that, if the home is well insulated and air tight, and if the HVAC equipment is designed and installed in accordance with best practices, then indeed, equipment with higher efficiency ratings uses less energy than equipment with lower ratings.

But that's a big, big pair of "ifs." In California, the average measured delivery of cooling and heating capacity is about 55% of the equipment's rated capacity. So there's really no point to investing in a more expensive piece of equipment to gain 10 or 15% of rated efficiency if the system's design and installation is going to throw away 45% of the equipment's capacity.

This reality is especially important to keep in mind when thinking about equipment replacement alone. If you only swap out old equipment for new, there may be some energy savings—or maybe there will be none—or maybe, if the system is typical of other California houses, the new equipment will now *use even more energy* than the old equipment did, because with its higher rated efficiency, it has more capacity to waste.

The key to reliable energy savings is lower loads and careful system design and installation. Those don't happen automatically by just removing old equipment and replacing it with equipment with higher lab-tested energy efficiency.

Chapter 12

Measured Results in Redding, California

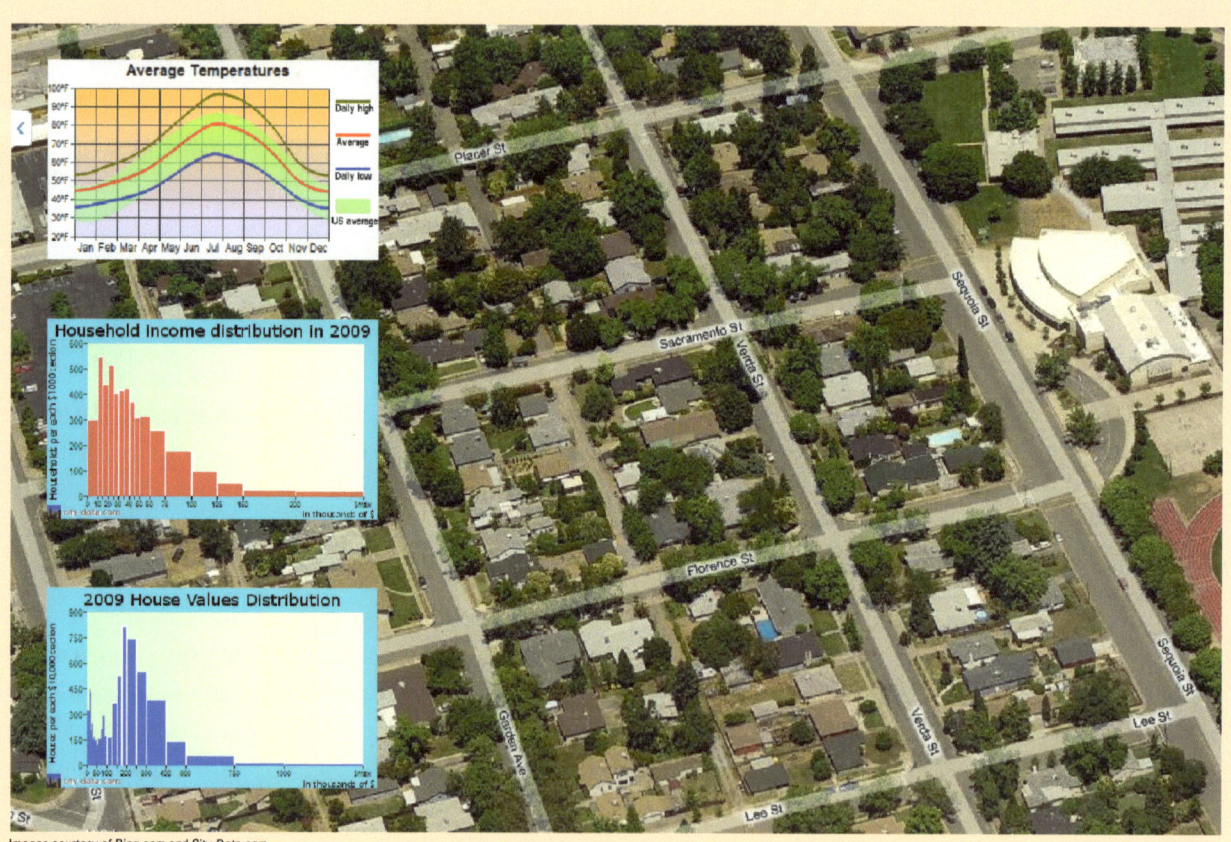

Fig 12.1 Redding, California
To reduce the cost of its peak electrical demand, in 2009 the municipally-owned Redding Electric implemented a home energy retrofit program based on the principles of Measured Home Performance.

The measured results of the program, presented here, show the value of this integrated, all-at-the-same-time approach to saving energy.

Laws Help, But Measured Results Are Better

Californians have a lot to be proud of. We use less energy per capita than residents of 46 other states in the U.S.[1] In part, that's because we build under Title 24, our California energy code. On the other hand, although the code is necessary—it does not ensure all the results we need.

For example, in 2009 and 2010, as part of the regular assessment of the effectiveness of Title 24 code provisions, 80 single-family homes were selected for on-site-measurement of the actual performance of their energy features. The homes were located in a representative sample of California's 16 distinct climate zones, and all were both occupied and new (completed after January 2007).[2] The results suggest that there is considerable room for improvement in the messy, real world of design and installation, even when the energy code is strong. Measurements showed that:

- The average maximum sensible cooling effect from the AC systems was 55% of the equipment's rated capacity.

- The delivered air volumes averaged less than 66% of what they should deliver in our climates.

- Fewer than 25% of supply air grilles provided the 500 to 700 fpm air velocities needed for good air mixing and thermal comfort.

- Air leakage (wasted air) from the HVAC systems averaged 10%.

- Of the 80 systems measured, *not even one* met the HVAC equipment manufacturers' requirement to limit system pressure drop to less than 0.5" WC to deliver the equipment's rated efficiency.

It remains a bit of a mystery that public outcry does not force our HVAC industry to improve. Surely, if cars were only delivering 55% of necessary highway speeds the public would complain.

On the other hand, there's a more positive side to this state of affairs—these houses—and hundreds of thousands of other houses throughout the State—represent golden opportunities for Measured Home Performance Contractors.

Measured Home Performance In Redding

In 2009, the municipally-owned Redding Electric Utility decided to implement a demand reduction program based on the principles of Measured Home Performance. But it was not an easy decision. The money allocated for reducing electrical demand was fixed. Utility managers could have decided to make small changes in many houses, rather than large improvements in fewer houses. Politically, helping a larger number of homeowners was an attractive option. But program managers decided to make big improvements in fewer houses for very good reasons:

- It was not clear that small improvements would make any measurable reduction in *peak* demand, even if the improvements made modest reductions in annual consumption.

- The target homes often had many problems other than high electrical consumption. Some of those problems had life safety implications. Those would not even be discovered, much less eliminated, by just replacing HVAC equipment or other minor improvements.

- Training local contractors in Measured Home Performance practices could help transition the local construction infrastructure from a culture of lowest dollar towards a culture of superior measured results. Any transition in that direction could reduce the local growth in electrical demand, which would in turn pay big cash benefits to the utility for decades to come.

The cost of electricity during periods of peak demand is a major problem for all electrical utility companies. For example, in many parts of California *their* cost to buy electricity at 2:00 am is often less than $2.00 per megawatt hour. ($0.002 per kWh) In contrast, electrical demand often peaks at 7:00 p.m. when everybody is home watching TV, playing video games, cooking dinner and turning on oversized air conditioners. By 6:00-7:00 p.m. the wholesale market cost of electricity skyrockets to more than $2,000 per megawatt hour. ($2.00 per kWh). Buying electricity at $2.00/kWh and selling it for less than $0.15/kWh is a really big problem for any utility company.

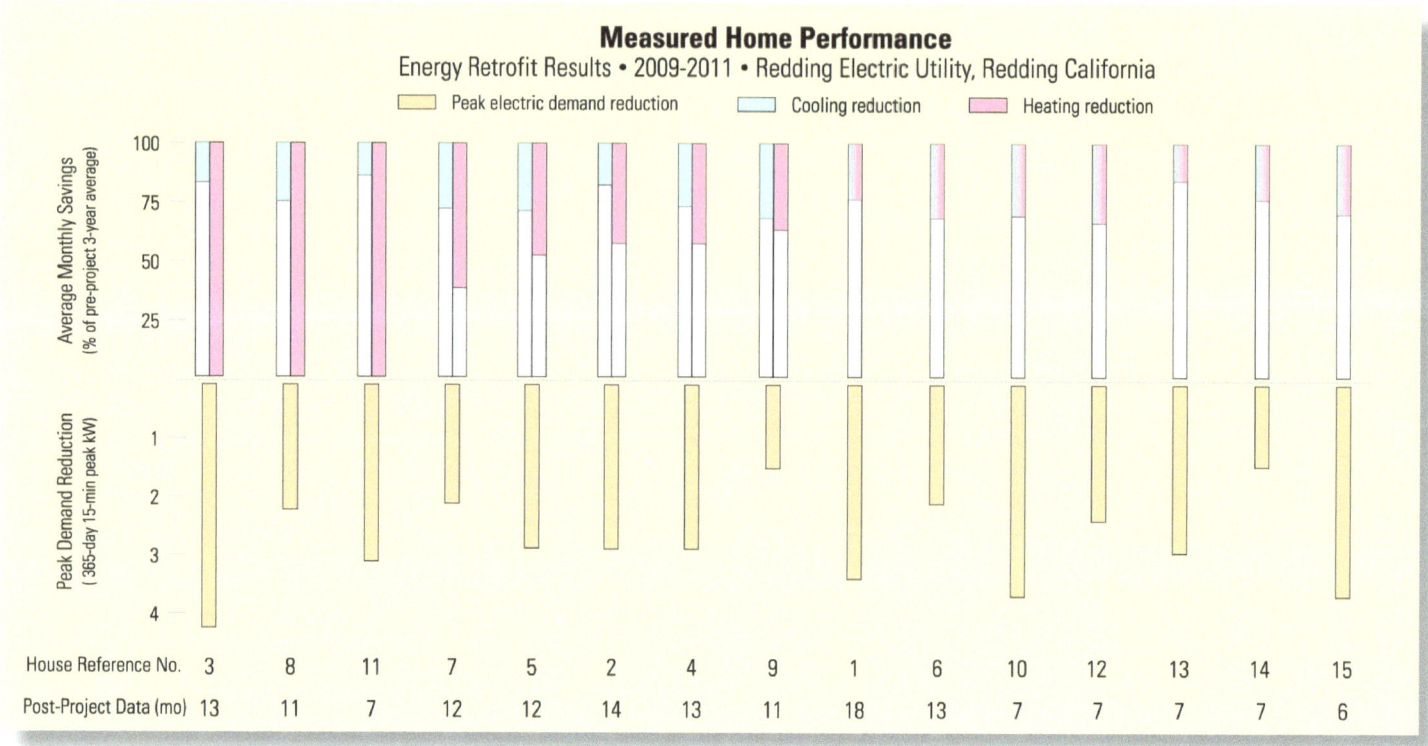

Fig. 12.2 Measured Home Performance results from Redding, California

Results in Redding

By any standard the Redding program has been very successful.[3] In the upgraded homes, the *measured* results to date include:

- Average 35% peak demand reduction
- 25% average monthly cooling energy reduction.
- 65% average monthly heating energy reduction.
- All safety issues fixed and documented.
- Trained 18 local general contractors, 18 HVAC contractors and 5 "HERS rater" consulting firms that provide 3rd-party verification of Measured Home Performance improvements.[Note1]

Figures 12.2 and 12.3 show more results from this program. Figure 12.2 shows the measured energy reductions based on at least six months of data compared to the three-year average of energy consumption in those same homes during previous years.

Figure 12.3 shows the improvements in two aspects of the building's HVAC systems that (in part) made those saving possible, namely the reduction of air leakage between indoors and outdoors, and the reduction in leakage of conditioned air out of the HVAC systems' duct connections.

Note 1: The acronym HERS stands for Home Energy Rating System. This score is based on a methodology that estimates, in advance of actual field measurements, the energy consumption of a residential building.

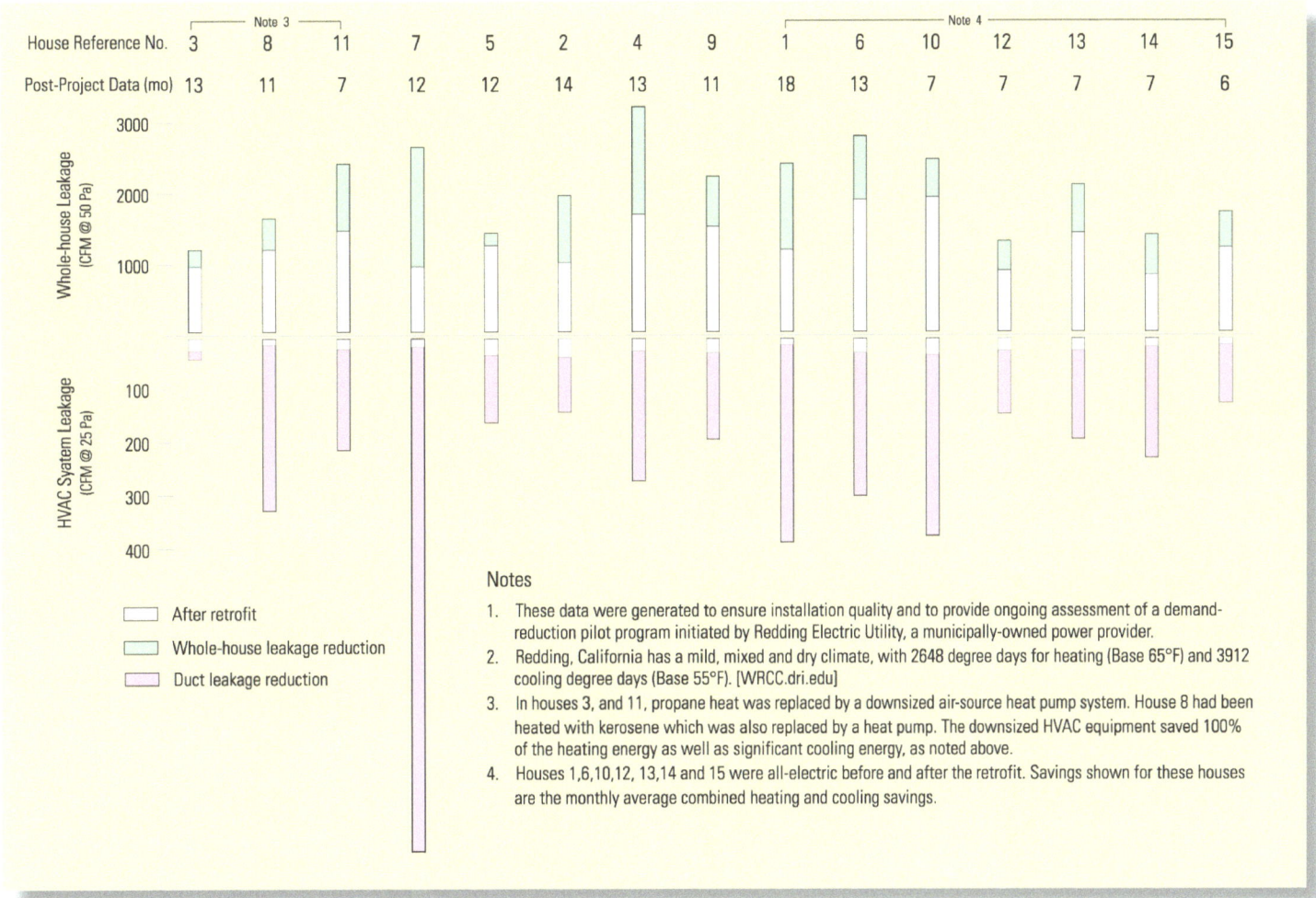

Fig. 12.3 Measured installation improvements that partly contributed to energy savings

Why peak demand reductions have persisted over time

The reductions in electrical demand have been persistent because the replacement HVAC equipment is in all cases, *much smaller*. It's not the rated energy efficiency of the equipment that matters—it's the maximum possible power draw. Smaller maximum amperage equals smaller peak electrical demand, period. There's no need to model this fact with computers. This characteristic of the retrofits in Redding may be the most important test for any contractor (or utility Program Manager) who believes they have accomplished retrofits that will reduce peak demand: is the HVAC equipment *smaller* than it was before the retrofit—or not?

If the equipment is smaller, then its peak demand will be smaller. If *not*... you're stuck in the uncertain world of hopeful speculation called computer energy modeling.

Why everything must be done at the same time

These projects cost quite a bit of money; typically between $15,000 and $40,000. That's usually between 7 and 10% of the cost of the houses that are involved, or roughly the cost to retrofit a kitchen. Given the cost, it's reasonable to question whether all these components need to be installed at the same time.

They do. Unless all of the energy features of the home are upgraded at the same time in a truly interdependent design with measured installation quality, either the big energy savings don't occur, or comfort is compromised, or the project creates problems that did not exist before, or the project is not large enough to provide a sustainable business for the multi-skilled contractors who are capable of doing the work. Experience of the last 10 years shows this fact, which has been confirmed (yet again) by the projects in Redding. In short, large-scale integrated design and installation succeeds, and small-scale, disintegrated design and installation does not. Here are some of the many reasons why:

- Air tightening the building without also measuring and ensuring combustion safety of natural draft combustion appliances can increase risks, as documented by the pioneering Canadian experiences of the 1980's.[4] When the structure is tight but the HVAC supply ducts are leaky, air pressures inside the tight enclosure can create negative pressure in the combustion appliance zone. Excessive negative pressure would pull products of combustion back into the home. Natural draft appliances must have adequate draft under worst-case depressurization conditions.

- Attic insulation seems like a good idea all by itself, but it's not. Before any insulation is installed, it's very important to air seal the penetrations and joints in the attic-to-upper floor assembly (the "attic plane"). If the attic plane leaks air during cooler months, moisture and later mold will accumulate in the attic as warm, humid indoor air drifts upward into that space.

- Changing older HVAC equipment for "higher efficiency" models does not save energy when the air distribution system is poor. There's not much point in installing "high efficiency" HVAC equipment if the rest of the system throws away 45% of that equipment's capacity (as documented by the 80-home field measurement project referenced earlier).[2]

So to get big results, one needs to do big projects, redesigning and reinstalling each energy feature of the home in an integrated way and in a logical sequence.

The importance of check numbers

The mantra of Measured Home Performance Contractors is to "measure before the project, measure during the project and measure at the end of the project." Figure 12.4 shows some of the check numbers which have been used in Measured Home Performance projects.

Those who work in commercial buildings may be startled by values shown in figure 12.4. It would be unusual (to say the least) to have a limit for air leakage of less than 20 cfm in an entire single-zone commercial HVAC system or a maximum cooling capacity of no more than 1 ton per 1,000 ft^2 of occupied space. But those are indeed the post-project values typical of the retrofitted houses described in figure 12.2.

For an example, consider house number 7. Before the project, its HVAC system leaked 895 cfm at test pressure. After the equipment was downsized and the air distribution redesigned and reinstalled, the total HVAC system air leakage was measured at 18 cfm.

The check numbers in figure 12.4 also help explain why the houses described by figure 12.2 were able to so greatly reduce their peak demand. Smaller HVAC equipment means lower peak electrical demand. From an energy perspective as in fashion, "extra capacity" is not better (see figure 12.5).

The importance of HVAC knowledge for 3rd-party verifiers

One of the lessons learned in the Redding project is the immense importance of training in HVAC equipment and systems for all consultants who check that the work has been done correctly.

CHECK NUMBERS FOR EVALUATING EXISTING HOMES

Number	Description
1 cfm$_{50\,Pa}$ • ft^2 (of conditioned space)	**Max whole-house air leakage.** Test values above this level call for better air-sealing of the building enclosure. (Values below this level call for installation of a dedicated ventilation system to ensure adequate indoor air quality.)
1 Ton per 450 to 600 ft^2 (Conditioned space)	**Max cooling capacity.** In existing homes in dry California, capacity of more than 1 ton per 450 ft^2 strongly suggests the system should be redesigned and downsized to save energy and improve comfort. If each ton of capacity serves 600 ft^2 or more, there is less benefit to replacing the system. (A new system in a well-sealed retrofitted home will be sized at about 1 ton for every 1,000 ft^2.)
0.35" to 0.45" W.C.	**Max external static pressure for the air handler's fan.** Maximum combined resistance of supply and return air distribution, including air handler cabinet, coils, filters, supply and return grilles (Target for Measured Home Performance retrofits is between 0.15 and 0.30")
40,000 to 60,000 Btu/h per 1,000 ft^2 (Conditioned space)	**Max heating capacity.** Capacity above 60,000 Btu/h per 1,000 ft^2 in the coldest regions of California strongly suggests the system is grossly oversized and can be redesigned and downsized to improve comfort. But if heating capacity is less than 40,000 Btu/h/1,000 ft^2 redesign would only be practical if equipment needed replacement. (A new system after Measured Home Performance will only need about 15,000 Btu/h per 1,000 ft^2 even in the mountain regions of California.)
20 cfm$_{25}$ or 2% of measured fan flow, whichever is less	**Max HVAC system air leakage.** The limit is for the combined leakage of supply side, return side and the air handler. Note: After a Measured Home Performance project, leakage less than 7cfm$_{25}$ (too low to measure with state-of-the-art equipment) is commonly achieved by well-trained crews.
- 2.0 Pa	**Max allowable depressurization,** when home is operating under worst-case depressurization conditions, for a combustion appliance zone (CAZ) which contains an independently-vented natural draft water heater.
- 0.5 Pa	**Min acceptable exhaust vent draft suction** under worst-case depressurization conditions and when the outdoor temperature is above 90°F.

Fig. 12.4 Check numbers that help contractors evaluate the as-built energy features of existing homes

The experts trained as "Energy Raters" are likely to be most knowledgeable about the big picture; the overall energy aspects of homes and their systems. They may have less detailed experience of operational characteristics of specific HVAC equipment and the critical details of its installation and commissioning. If the quality assurance inspector has authority—but does not actually understand equipment operational variations—that person can misguide the HVAC technician into illogical practices that damage equipment and eliminate savings.

For example, in the Redding project a common problem was 3rd-party verifiers (fully trained and certified to audit houses in California) who, armed with digital pressure guages, instructed HVAC technicians to add or remove refrigerant from AC systems to achieve target values. But the target numbers for subcooling and superheat change with load. Baseline numbers cannot be reached without adjusting for the actual running load conditions at time of test. Installer ignorance combined with verifier ignorance resulted in severely overcharged and undercharged equipment. In some cases they did not understand the behavior of AC equipment when operating at less than full load conditions. In other cases they did not understand that the test values obtained indicated faulty equipment rather than faulty installation. HVAC equipment has such a wide variety of configurations that it's really impractical for an energy auditor to be an expert in all types. So training on the specific models of HVAC equipment used in the program is critical, not only for installers, but also for verifiers.

Fig. 12.5 For tailors and HVAC designers, "extra capacity" is *not* evidence of excellence

In the case of the Redding projects, both the HERS Raters and the HVAC techs were guided and mentored as part of the program. They were trained (and monitored) by a knowledgeable HVAC and Measured Home performance consultant, to make sure they did not accidentally add problems during the installation process.

HVAC redesign is often the most difficult aspect of projects

Compared to other aspects of Measured Home Performance such as lighting replacement and air sealing, HVAC redesign and installation is pretty complicated for existing homes.

It's not that the principles are had to grasp—it's that existing buildings make it difficult to design and install systems the way we know they have to be done to save energy. And it's usually even more difficult to convince the owner that his system is so hopeless and horrible that it *must* be torn out entirely, redesigned, downsized and reinstalled in order to achieve comfort and save energy. But that's what has to happen.

The big difference from past practice is to simply design and install these systems the way we all know they should be done, rather than using equipment oversizing and energy waste to compensate for installation shortcomings. A few of the many design and installation imperatives include:

- Room-by-room load calculations. The "Manual J" procedures established by the Air Conditioning Contractors Association (ACCA) are the basis of the room-by-room calculations that provide the crew with the air flow numbers they will need to ensure correct flows and therefore comfort.[5]

- Air-tight systems. Air tightness is taken very seriously. The limit of 20 cfm leakage includes the entire system and the air handler cabinet, not just the duct joints. (Note: the actual goal is always "leakage too-low-to-measure.")

- Return air paths large enough to allow adequate air flow. The retrofit designer is both creative and ruthless about gaining adequate space for return air ducts that will bring all of the supply air back to the air handler.

- Short, straight duct runs. The longer and more twisted the path of the air, the more fan energy is needed to push and pull it through the house. This often means the air handler must be relocated from its distant location in the garage, to a central location in a closet inside the home, or to a central location in the attic. Then the duct runs can be shortened and straightened in a radial layout, as opposed to the all-too-common spaghetti configuration.

- Flow-setting dampers placed at the supply outlet plenum near the air handler, rather than at the supply grilles in the rooms. Keeping the air velocity high and the air flow straight as it leaves the supply grille is important for good air mixing. These projects use flow-setting dampers back at a supply air plenum box at the end of the air handler. Without dampers at the grille, the supply air flow is straight, fast and quiet as it enters the room. Excellent air mixing provides the constant comfort that keeps occupants content. Constant comfort eliminates the counterproductive and energy-wasting fiddling that desperate owners often are forced into when systems are poorly designed and installed.

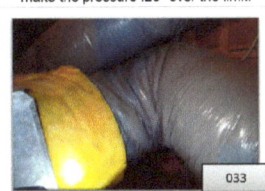

Fig. 12.6 Selling Comprehensive Measured Home Performance Retrofits
It takes a combination of relevant measurements and visual evidence to convince home owners that equipment-only retrofits are often neither effective nor safe.

- Air flows to each space measured and set with flow hoods. With a real, honest-to-goodness room-by-room load calculation, the air flows for each room can be established with certainty. This is accomplished by the installing crew, using their digital flow hood.

- High evaporator air flows. In warm and dry California, dehumidification is a *problem* rather than a virtue in the summer. So for these dry-climate systems, air flows of 500 to 550 cfm/ton are ideal. Using a flow plate to measure and set supply air flow to ensure those air flows is part of the installation crews' responsibilities.

- Insulated ducts, buried under attic insulation. Conductive losses from duct work become nearly negligible.

Summary

The results obtained in Redding are consistent with results obtained in other Measured Home Performance retrofits in California. These results all far exceed the hoped-for-but-never-measured energy savings of low-budget, equipment-only retrofits.

The fundamental principle of Measured Home Performance is consistent with the advice of a widely known 20th century statesman; Winston Churchill. He achieved success later in life after many disastrous early career mistakes. Churchill suggested: "However beautiful the strategy, one should occasionally look at the results." We always need to *measure our results rather than just hope* for them to be successful.

References

1. U.S. Energy Consumption by State. 2009. U.S. Energy Information Agency. www.eia.gov/state/seds/

2. "Efficiency Characteristics and Opportunities for New California Homes" Final Report of Project Number PIR-08-019 2011. Proctor, Chitwood & Wilcox, California Energy Commission

3. Home Performance Program Evaluation 2011, David Jackson & Kim Hein, P.E, Redding Electric Utility, Redding, CA

4. "Just right and air-tight." Joseph Lstiburek, ASHRAE Journal May 2011 pp. 58-66.

5. ANSI/ACCA Manual J - 2006 "Residential Load Calculations" (8th Edition), ACCA.org

Production Notes

This book was written, designed and illustrated by Lew Harriman of Mason-Grant Consulting, who also generated the print-ready files using Adobe InDesign CS3, running on a MacBook Pro (May 2011) with 8GB RAM. Photos, illustrations and diagrams were prepared using either Adobe PhotoShop CS3 or Freehand MX. The body type is Adobe Garamond Book Condensed. The heads are Adobe Univers Condensed. This book was specifically designed for distribution via the Amazon CreateSpace print-on-demand service.